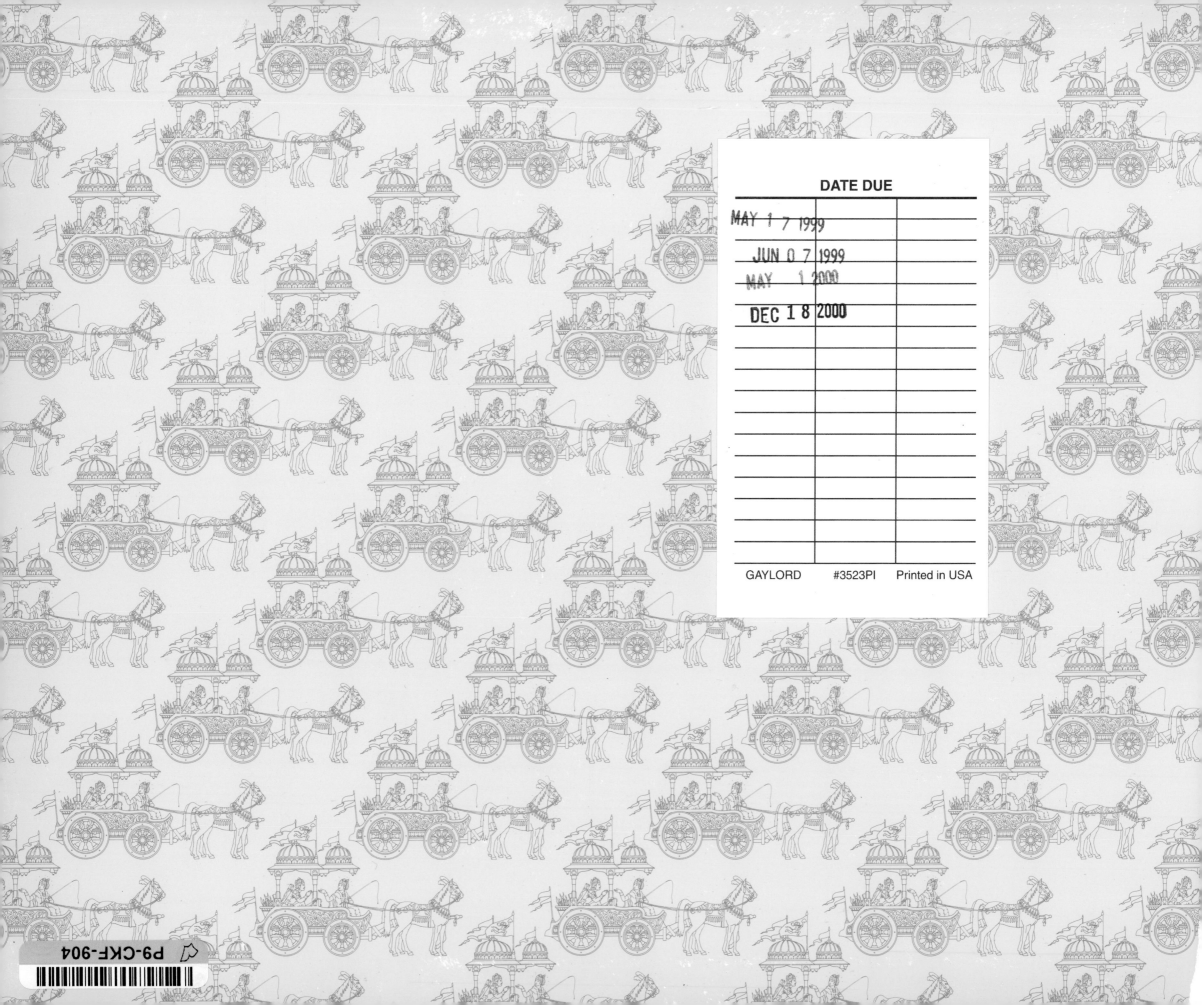

Vedic
Heritage
Foundation
Collection

Vaiṣṇava India

Author
GEARY J.C. SHERIDAN

Co-authors
Jack B. Hebner, Jr. and Daniel Maziarz

VEDIC HERITAGE FOUNDATION
Malibu Beach

The Vedic Heritage
Foundation Collection

Cover design: Christopher Sullivan

For information address:

Vedic Heritage Foundation
Geary J.C. Sheridan, President
P.O. Box 2712
Malibu Beach, California 90265-7712

Printed in the United States of America by Anderson Printing.

Suggested Catalog Card Data

Sheridan, Geary J.C., 1955-
Vaiṣṇava India/Geary J.C. Sheridan: foreword by Vishvambhar Goswami
800 pages 11″ x 14″ x 2″
Includes foreword, preface, introduction, map, map description, 15 chapters, 497 glossary words, 189 book sources, 1,082 notes and asides, 5,016 index entries, sanskrit pronunciation guide, 249 pages of color photographs, and author's recognition.
ISBN: 0-945421-00-1
1. Vaiṣṇavism - social science. 2. Vaiṣṇavism - philosophy.
3. Vaiṣṇava - major holy places of pilgrimage.
I. Sheridan, Geary J.C. II. Title.
88-50457

FIRST PRINTING, 1994 : 3,000 copies

In the memory of our ever well-wisher, His Divine Grace A.C. Bhaktivedanta Swami Prabhupada.

Dedication

This book is dedicated to

Shri Chaitanya Mahaprabhu

the incarnation of Shri Shri Radha Krishna,
in the role of the Lord's devotee.

Acknowledgements

I would like to first extend my gratitude to Steven Rosen for his early research work on *Vaiṣṇava India* and his collaboration with Jack Hebner, Jr., on articles which evolved into this present volume. I truly thank Barry Zuckerman, a pioneer photographer of Vaiṣṇava holy places in India, for providing me early and on-going inspiration for *Vaiṣṇava India*. I thank Mr. Zuckerman as well, for lending me his rare collection of books on Vaiṣṇava holy places and philosophy.

I want to thank furthermore, the many scholars, saints, and people of India who helped Jack Hebner, Jr. during his ten-year stay there. I especially acknowledge:

Bhaktinarayana Maharaja, for giving Mr. Hebner a tour of the holy places associated with Krishna's pastimes in Mathura and Vrindavan, while also revealing their confidential philosophical significance;

Rangaraja Bhattar, the head priest of the Shri Rangam temple, who arranged for a special tour of the temple complex and the house where Shri Chaitanya resided;

Vishvambhar Goswami, the head of the Radharamana temple in Vrindavan, who always provided warm hospitality in Vrindavan, giving his constant blessings and advice as well as penning the Foreward;

Dr. Asok Kumar Das, the Director of the Maharaja Sawai Man Singh II Museum in Jaipur, who gave a complete historical background on Jaipur, separating fact from myth, as well as arranging for the photography of some of the museum's most valuable artifacts;

Rajamata Gayatri Devi, for her life-long support and hospitality to visiting Vaiṣṇavas, particularly His Divine Grace A.C. Bhaktivedanta Swami Prabhupada and Jack Hebner, Jr. She also facilitated the tour of Jaipur museums;

Colonel Raja Singh, who started Mr. Hebner's collection of Indian artifacts by donating two swords that were family heirlooms;

the staff of the Archaeological Survey of India's office in New Delhi, Dwaraka, Mahabalipuram, and Madras, for their guidance and information;

P. Banerjee, the Director of the National Museum of New Delhi, whose life-long research into the art and antiquity of Krishna, as exemplified in his book, the *Life of Krishna in Indian Art,* provided factual and spiritual food for *Vaiṣṇava India's* chapters on art and and antiquity;

the staff of the Vrindavan Research Institute, for the use of their facilities;

the staff of the Maharaja Saroji Museum in Tanjore, for introducing Mr. Hebner to the wonders of Indian bronzes, palm leaf scrolls, and the evolution of Indian art;

Maharana Bhagwat Singh and his family, for their hospitality and tours of the museums of Udiapur;

and Munshiram Manoharlal Publishers, Pvt. Ltd., one of the most respected publishers of Vedic and Vaiṣṇava literature in India, for keeping the torch of authentic knowledge lighted.

In addition I thank Jack Hebner, Jr. and Bhavananda Roy Swami for accompanying me on my journey to India, equally sharing in the many hardships and rewards.

In the United States, I thank Robert Grant for giving me the right to use many rare photographs from The Bhaktivedanta Book Trust Archives, and William Stimpel for giving me the right to use quotes from The Bhaktivedanta Book Trust.

I likewise thank Daniel Maziarz for his extensive work compiling and editing *Vaiṣṇava India;*

Kurt Mausert for his detailed and highly comprehensive indexing;

and Robert Juergens for the transcription of the tapes containing the index entries.

I want to thank Thierry Bernard, David Osborn, The Smithsonian Institute and my mother, the late Elaine Naish Sheridan, for their photography work;

Tamara Greenstein for calligraphy on the map;

and Douglas Ball for his art work on the cover and within the pages of *Vaiṣṇava India.*

I wish to thank Christopher Sullivan for his art direction and services.

For their general support of this project, I acknowledge the efforts of John Gopee, Ragunatha dasa, and the late J. Rockwell, my brother.

I sincerely thank the staff of Computerized Publishing Services: Ramon Estrada, Bill Shoaff, R. Christopher Richard, Nick Sutton, Cliff Athey, Brad Daniel, Anne Kellogg, and particularly, Ricardo Garcia for his layout work above and beyond the call of duty in the production of *Vaiṣṇava India.*

Finally, I humbly beg the blessings of all incarnations of God, Vaiṣṇava saints, sages, teachers, and devotees who have made the production of this book possible by walking the path of divine, unconditional love, which is the essence of *Vaiṣṇava India.*

Geary J.C. Sheridan
Author

Table of Contents

Foreword

In spite of my advancing age and frail health, by Shri Govindaji's (God's) grace I have departed India for the first time to visit the United States twice in the past two years. My travels in America have been very pleasant, informative, and inspiring. One thing I know for certain—the American people are very much interested in religion. They are, as you say, "God-fearing." Also, they thirst to know more about the God. They love God and are inquisitive about God's nature. Everywhere I went, people requested to know something about God.

I also found a lot of religious confusion in America, because there are so many blends of the religions. India has a very ancient religious and philosophical history. We know of the different schools of thought and how to compare them. We can see how they work out in real life for millions of people over long periods of time. Since religion is the soul of a country's people, this knowledge can be very useful to Westerners during this time of ferment, when they struggle to know themselves better and the ultimate meaning of life. Old answers aren't as satisfying, and the people yearn for a deeper knowledge. They want to go beyond old formulas and sayings to reach direct experience of the God. This is a healthy trend that must be encouraged. To desire communion with the God is the supreme goal of life, and Vaiṣṇavism has so many ways to facilitate this relationship. I hope the scientific and cultural presentation contained in *Vaiṣṇava India* will advance this cause.

When I answered people's questions in America, I received a lot of agreement. A Vaiṣṇava uses logic, reason, and the protocol of debate; but most of all, answers which come directly from the heart touch people. By Shri Govindaji's grace, I was able to communicate; and, when I talked of Shri Krishna (God) and the teachings of Shri Chaitanya Mahaprabhu, my audience said it is very good and many of these same points are in Christianity or in such and such religion. To compare Christianity, Vaiṣṇavism, and other religions is a good thing from which we can all benefit. By accepting Vaiṣṇava principles as their own, Americans are proving they are open-minded. I am most hopeful that a fruitful exchange will continue on for some time.

Americans are also very fond of self-improvement and reform. Within the United States there is one group or another pushing for reform on almost every imagineable issue. Vaiṣṇavas feel very comfortable with this reforming spirit, since Vaiṣṇavas have been in the forefront of the reform movement in India from ancient times. Shri Krishna Himself was a great reformer and liberator some 5,000 years ago. That is why one of our names for Shri Krishna is "Mukunda," or the "Liberator." More recently, great Vaiṣṇava teachers like Ramanujacarya (1017-1137 AD) and Madhvacarya (1239-1319 AD) worked for spreading spiritual knowledge to all classes of people. But the greatest reformer in the medieval-modern period of Vaiṣṇavism is Shri Chaitanya Mahaprabhu (1486-1534 AD).

The existence of extreme forms of class prejudice and discrimination is a dark blot on the history of India. Especially under the heavy pressures inflicted on India by wave after wave of Islamic invaders and conquerors, Indian society petrified itself. The upper classes took advantage of the situation to become very powerful, and they used to control the whole of the community according to their wishes and whims. They discarded the lower classes, denying them the right to worship the God, perform religious and social rituals, and education in general. In this way, the original Vedic social system was utterly corrupted, and the people suffered.

The *Vedas* called for a society divided into groups based on a person's *guna*, or quality, and *karma*, or how they developed their qualities. A stratified society based on birth alone was never envisioned by the ancient sages, since the oldest scriptures have examples of people rising higher in society than the position of their family by dint of their hard work and extraordinary abilities. This upper movement was sanctioned by ancient Vedic society, not condemned. But, like many good things, the original Vedic society was misinterpreted and misused by greedy, selfish people.

Onto this oppressive scene stepped Shri Chaitanya Mahaprabhu, and there was a renovation in the social order. Shri Chaitanya Mahaprabhu said that the God isn't the exclusive property of a single community, nation, class, or stage of life. Every person who has taken birth on this planet has the right to worship the God. In this way, Shri Chaitanya Mahaprabhu revived Vaiṣṇavism.

Vishnu is a Sanskrit word for the God. Those devotees who worship the one, supreme Godhead—who is a transcendental person (*bhagavan*), intelligence (*paramatma*), and energy (*brahman*), complete with all spiritual potencies—are called Vaiṣṇavas. Indian scriptures record several different incarnations of God who have appeared on earth. However, Jiva Goswami and many other authoritative Vaiṣṇava teachers declare that Shri Krishna is the original fountainhead of all incarnations and manifestations of God and therefore is the supreme Godhead.

Shri Chaitanya Mahaprabhu declared that all peoples are entitled to worship and learn about Krishna, and, when they become sufficiently advanced in Krishna consciousness, they can be *gurus*, or teachers. Guru means someone who actually knows about Krishna—God. That is guru. Guru also means someone who is big, heavy, because they know everything about the God. This bold and true statement of Vaiṣṇavism really struck home to the upper classes, since it was by monopolizing the guru system that they kept control over the people. They vigorously opposed Shri Chaitanya Mahaprabhu, but all their efforts proved useless. Shri Chaitanya Mahaprabhu prevailed, and the pure definition of a Vaiṣṇava as a worshipper of Krishna without any distinction as to caste, creed, or social position was restored.

The story of Shri Chaitanya Mahaprabhu's life, teachings, philosophy, and activities are hardly known in the West, but He manifested the highest, most sublime truths of the God. Therefore, the strong emphasis on Shri Chaitanya Mahaprabhu in *Vaiṣṇava India* will fill a genuine and regrettable gap in most Western readers' appreciation of Vaiṣṇavism.

The true Vaiṣṇava sees himself or herself as the humble servant of the servants of the servants of the God. When Shri Krishna manifested His divine pastimes on earth 5,000 years ago, He also took a humble position. He was raised as a modest cowherd boy in an agricultural family. He went to the pastures, grazed cows, and played with His simple cowherd friends. Therefore, many people considered Him a common person.

Shri Krishna took part in many political upheavals in capital cities like Mathura, Hastinapura, and others, but He never craved a kingdom for Himself. Everywhere, He righted wrongs, restored legitimate and qualified men to the seats of power, and stood ready to serve the righteous. Even when He established a fortified city at Dwaraka to protect His family from inimical elements, Shri Krishna made His elder brother, Balarama, the city father. Shri Krishna's humility and serving attitude, His love of the common people and simple life inspires Vaiṣṇavas to approach the God as our brother, friend, master, or, if we can surrender everything at His feet, as our dearmost lover. Shri Krishna has multifarious faces and roles in His eternal life, and it gives Vaiṣṇavas great pleasure to relate to the God in these various ways.

I am most fortunate to be a Brijbasi, or a resident of Vrindavan, where Shri Krishna manifested the early portion of His Divine pastimes. These pastimes are the highest expressions of love. In Vrindavan the cowherd women, or *gopis*, demonstrated the purest love of Godhead. Their love is spontaneous. It is not forced; neither is it artificial or motivated by fear of the God or His punishment. In Vrindavan the gopis have spontaneous, unconditional love for their beautiful Krishna. Great authorities like Shri Chaitanya Mahaprabhu and the *Srimad Bhagavatam* glorify this spontaneous devotion over all other forms of religious worship. To come into contact with this kind of pure love is most fortunate for the soul and catches the innermost spirit of Vaiṣṇavism. It is not that other religions are ignorant of the necessity to love the God. However, the degree, intensity, and completeness of the love exchange between the gopis and Shri Krishna gives the Vaiṣṇava a distinct advantage.

The more we know about a great person, the easier it is to love that person. Similarly, the more we know about the God, His pastimes, associates, qualities, abode, and so forth, the easier it is to love the God and transcend the selfishness of the world. Therefore, *Vaiṣṇava India*'s journey through the holy places like Vrindavan from the point of view of a devotee gives the reader the chance of a lifetime to find the highest love possible anywhere in the universe—the love between Shri Krishna and the gopis.

There are two criticisms I have of the West, and I understand many sober Western thinkers have raised these objections, too. First, people in the West are too self-centered. They think the world is limited to them, and beyond that there is nothing. The spouse, children, and relatives are the family. For the most part, there is no wider conception.

In Vaiṣṇavism, we consider the whole world to be our family. We are not confined to ourselves. We have a very wide scope of thinking. Every creature, every living entity on this planet is a manifestation of Lord Krishna—and we love them. We don't want to trouble any living entity, because the God is in that living entity.

Next, I belong to a developing country, and we are progressing in material advancement and self-sufficiency. However, when I see the waste in America—the waste of paper, food, and many other things—my heart gets pained. I bought a carrying bag in America, and the bag was full of papers that were full of other papers. These papers were of fine quality, and I felt too much pain to throw them in the trash. I folded them, put them in a box, and carried them back to India. The average American wouldn't save these papers, because everything is in plenty in the United States. So why care for it? But in India we have shortages, so we know the value of things. When people have lots of money and material possessions, they usually don't find the time for spirituality—unless they get in trouble, or death approaches them or a loved one. There is danger in this mentality. America can lose its spiritual direction in an ocean of material things. That would be tragic, for your country has so much to offer the world if it can stay spiritually strong.

The Vaiṣṇava philosophy is "simple living and high thinking." Your great American author, Henry David Thoreau, championed this philosophy. We can't become lost in the luxuries of life. By limiting our consumption to the necessities of life, we give ourselves time for spiritual concentration. Vaiṣṇavism can help divert people's attention from materialistic desires, so they can advance their spiritual thinking and uplift themselves. There is no loss in following this path. The inner rewards are great. The mind is calm and happy. Our spirits soar, for the Vaiṣṇava finds genuine love in our relationship with the God and all living beings.

America has perfected material prosperity. Vaiṣṇavas have perfected spiritual prosperity. We are sitting on a storehouse of spiritual knowledge containing the highest revelations of the God's love, wisdom, and goodness. Let America and India exchange their abundance with each other, so a full life can be had by all. Good results await us if we can combine our prosperities. Then, we can feed the world's body and soul. I hope Vaiṣṇavism can make this contribution to America and the world.

I want to especially acknowledge the efforts of His Divine Grace A.C. Bhaktivedanta Swami Prabhupada in spreading the knowledge of Vaiṣṇavism to the United States and the Western world. I was fortunate to have Shrila Prabhupada's association in Vrindavan, India, before and after he went to America. He was totally absorbed in Krishna consciousness and only thought of how he could share this wisdom with the world. His passing to the spiritual abode in 1977 was a blow to all Vaiṣṇavas, but I am delighted to see that what he has started in the West carries on strongly today. He was a single person who commanded no army like Alexander the Great; yet, with his pure devotion, determination, and Krishna consciousness, he united so many peoples of the world under the banner of the God and Shri Chaitanya Mahaprabhu. I cannot conceive of the work he has done. Lord Krishna truly empowered him.

The Western disciples of Shrila Prabhupada often visit the temple and guest house I supervise in Vrindavan, often for as long as a month or more. They lead a simple life in Vrindavan and perform all of the traditional devotional practices with enthusiasm and love. Shri Chaitanya Mahaprabhu said this Vaiṣṇavism is for everyone—the entire world. These Western devotees in Vrindavan prove it.

I wish the Vedic Heritage Foundation every success on its first publication and pray that many more publications will follow. Books of this kind, which advocate the general betterment of the entire human society, need to be increased.

I pray Shri Radha Raman Ji Maharaj to bestow His blessings and success.

Jai Gour.

Acharya V. Goswami Maharaj.
October 10, 1985

Shanti Kutir
Shri Radha Raman Temple
Vrindavan, (U.P.) India.

Preface

India—in land area a subcontinent of unparalleled beauty and diversity.

India—a wide variety of peoples. All-India Radio broadcasts shows in 18 languages, 51 dialects, and 87 tribal languages.

India—a cradle of civilization, a storehouse of cultural wealth in every medium of human expression.

India—has produced the largest library of sacred scriptures and contains the most extensive body of spiritual experience in the world.

India is all of this and much more. Very few people outside of India appreciate the enormous debt world civilization owes to India. Although India in many respects has spawned world civilization, the vicissitudes of history have conspired to make India largely an unknown entity today, especially in the Western World.

But wherever there is the unknown, there are also special people who are drawn to investigate the unknown. They are the pathfinders of all cultures and societies, to whom we acknowledge our most respectful thanks. No matter what the age they have appeared in, their race, or their religion—these pathfinders have created a world heritage upon which we can build.

My dear friend, colleague, and senior spiritual seeker, Jagat Guru Swami (Jack Hebner, Jr.), is an American pathfinder. He is filled with the exploring spirit. A few hundred years ago, I could see him canoeing through the early American frontier as Davy Crockett. Go farther back in time, and I see him as Marco Polo traversing all of Asia. Whatever Jagat Guru Swami may or may not have done in a previous lifetime, one thing is certain—he has traveled the length and width of India's holy places for the last fifteen years in this lifetime, studying them scrutinizingly. During this time, Jagat Guru Swami served as an ambassador of a Gaudiya Vaiṣṇava School to India's foremost religious leaders. The faith and devotion of Jagat Guru Swami, along with his sound knowledge of Vedic and Vaiṣṇava cultures, have made him welcome into the top levels of Indian society. Nevertheless, he is one of the humblest and down to earth people I know.

Jagat Guru Swami's greatest joy is sharing transcendental stories from the endless annals of Vaiṣṇavism. As long as he has an attentive audience—be they royalty in Jaipur or children from a simple village or college students on the campuses of America—Jagat Guru Swami comes to life. Dressed in regal, authentic costumes, he reveals some of the most esoteric wisdom of life in the form of the most enchanting stories. One story after another rolls off his lips, increasing the audience's appetite for more with the telling of each tale. For truly, Jagat Guru Swami doesn't just tell stories. He becomes the stories he tells; and, because they are all related to the all-pervading Godhead, they take on a special power, grace, and significance. The hearts and minds of the hearers are opened to new spiritual realities. The soul vibrates, and you know you are alive in a fuller way than before. Reality becomes brighter, and you are automatically proud and full of love towards God. A sincere heart can experience this and more from hearing Jagat Guru Swami's stories of Vaiṣṇavism.

One story that particularly struck me was how the enormous elephant, Guruvayur Padmanabhan, exercised great personal self-control and restraint in order to avoid hurting a tiny child. Now, you may ask, what has an elephant to do with God and Vaiṣṇavism? A fair question and deserving of an answer. The elephant Padmanabhan was given in charity to the temple of Guruvayur in south India, which, uniquely enough, maintains the largest herd of elephants dedicated to God's service of any temple in India—and, even in India, a temple maintaining elephants is a rare thing.

The elephants definitely respond to the spiritual atmosphere in which they live. The temple of Guruvayur is in a tropical city paradise. Elephants and monkeys regularly roam the streets. The women of Guruvayur almost sparkle with a unique cleanliness of skin and aura, as well as always being brightly and attractively attired. But most famous of all earthly beings in Guruvayur are the devotional elephants of the temple, who are proud and dedicated to the role they play in the community's religious life and the worship of God.

Every night, 10,000 ghee (clarified butter) lamps are lit and placed on the walls and structures of the Guruvayur temple complex. Then, one to five elephants lead a procession in circumambulating the inner walls. The lead elephant is always special and carries the principal Deity of the temple on his head. Three priests also ride on top of the elephant. One priest holds the Deity, which has a solid gold backdrop shaped in the form of an aura. Another priest holds beautifully decorated fans, while the last priest is the most athletic of all and deftly whirls chamara whisks around in his hands in ancient and complex patterns in time with the accompanying religious music. The entire procession is playful and joyous, indicative of a warm and intimate bond between these people, their elephants, and God.

All of the people appreciate and applaud the noble elephants' role in these festivities. Many of the chief elephants of Guruvayur have become legendary because of their character and deeds. These elephants truly are exemplary devotees of God.

Guruvayur Padmanabhan was one of these legendary spiritual elephants. When Jagat Guru Swami spoke of him, a special power seemed to fill his body; you could feel the presence and strength of this extraordinary elephant, who gradually became the most important elephant in the entire Indian state of Kerala. Whenever Padmanabhan was present at a procession, he had to have the chief honors of carrying the Deity. According to the book, *Guruvayur*, as soon as the Deity "was placed on his head, he would stretch the whole of his body forward, and raise his head to the maximum so that he would appear to be the highest in the whole array of elephants." Padmanabhan maintained this posture for the whole procession and beyond, until the Deity was removed from his head.

While Padmanabhan was by far the strongest elephant in all of Kerala, he never hurt anyone—human or elephant—in his life. He was impervious to the everyday distractions around him. When other elephants challenged him, he simply displayed his prowess nonviolently by stomping on the ground; or, if they charged, he simply pushed them back in self-defense. The first of Padmanabhan's displays of strength were enough to settle the issue permanently. He commanded respect from elephants and people alike.

The best example of Padmanabhan's gentleness and nonviolence concerned his encounter with a two-year-old child, one of Jagat Guru Swami's favorite stories. One day Padmanabhan was chained near the quarters of the women who worked for the temple. His keepers left him alone, contently munching on palm leaves. A two-year-old child, whose mother was absorbed in cooking chores, wandered out and settled between Padmanabhan's front legs to play. At the time the elephant had a long and heavy piece of palm leaf stalk in his trunk which he was waving about. Suddenly, Padmanabhan sensed the presence of the child and froze motionless. Padmanahban could not see the child, therefore, in order to avoid injuring it, he knew he could not move a muscle. He did not even wave his tail. The child loved its position and did not budge for a long time, keeping Padmanabhan frozen in place.

Finally, the child's mother finished cooking and, while searching for her baby, screamed and almost fainted when she did. Quickly, however, she recovered and urged the child to come out. The baby refused, and Padmanabhan flapped his ears at the mother as if to say, "Please, hurry." The mother chanted God's name and begged the child to move—all to no avail. Exasperated, she cried for help, and Padmanabhan's keepers returned and easily rescued the child. Padmanabhan heaved an elephant-sized sigh of relief, put down the huge stalk, and calmly continued eating palm leaves as if nothing had happened.

On January 4, 1922, Padmanabhan was joined by a ten-year-old elephant, who would become Padmanabhan's successor after his demise in 1931. This new elephant was called Keshavan. At first he was erratic and uncooperative, earning him the nickname "lunatic Keshavan" for his antics. Special spiritual regimens and a diet were prescribed for him, including liberal and long visits to the temple to hear group worship and singing of sacred songs. These measures, along with the inspiring example of Padmanabhan, soon cured Keshavan's wildness. The new elephant imbibed all of Padmanabhan's good qualities and also mastered Padmanabhan's unique postures in carrying the Deity. When Padmanabhan died, Keshavan proudly carried on the devotional service of that great elephant and is even said to have exceeded Padmanabhan in nobility and devotion by the end of his illustrious career.

Maybe for the first time in history, an elephant had his golden jubilee celebrated in Guruvayur. By 1973, Keshavan had put in fifty years of faithful service to the temple and God. He was feted to a sumptuous feast, along with his twenty-one elephant companions. His golden jubilee present was a gold shield for him to wear on his forehead, engraved with the honorific title of "Gajarajan," or, "King of the Elephants."

Gajarajan Keshavan will always be most remembered for the incredible way he passed from this world in 1976. At the start of a major procession, Gajarajan Keshavan looked as majestic and inspiring as ever. But suddenly, he began shivering uncontrollably, and the Deity was transferred to the elephant standing next to Keshavan, who was now slowly led out of the temple. Outside, Gajarajan Keshavan turned and faced the temple, looking intently at the golden flagmast. He was perfectly still and appeared to be meditating on God.

Doctors arrived and started treatment, but Keshavan did not want to be disturbed. He refused food and drink. Night fell and morning came. The people were anxious for his welfare and milled about, but Keshavan kept meditating, oblivious to all the hubbub around him. Ceremonies continued in the temple, and the intensity of the prayers and songs caught Keshavan's attention. The particular prayers being sung made Keshavan realize that his meditation had begun twenty-four hours earlier, and the final apotheosis of his life had come. He moved forward and filled his trunk with water. He did not drink, but bathed himself and stood still, ready. A sacred conchshell's sound filled the air. The Deity was now open to view in the temple. Gajarajan Keshavan stretched down on the ground, his trunk facing the temple of God whom he had so devoutly served. In this posture of obeisance to God, Gajarajan Keshavan departed his material body.

When Jagat Guru Swami finishes this true and amazing story, the audience knows they have been transported to a magical realm where God, humanity, and nature all intertwine harmoniously to form one universal family of life. God is omnipresent, present in all things. Vaiṣṇavism makes me more aware of the omnipresence of God than any other culture I have ever encountered. In the Western World it seems we have to take a "leap of faith" to believe in God. But the Vaiṣṇavas see no need to leap, since they clearly and dearly perceive the omnipresent Godhead appearing in an infinite diversity of ways all around and within them. It is this deep, experiential quality of Vaiṣṇavism that most impresses me. There is no need to leap when you know, and I feel we could use more of the spiritual "knowingness" of the Vaiṣṇavas.

I became enthused by Jagat Guru Swami's enthusiasm and skill in communicating this vision of the earth (the plants, animals, and humans) and the spiritual world living together in intimate union. That is the Vedic and Vaiṣṇava heritage which the world needs to know if we are to live together in peace and solve the enormous political, environmental, and economic problems confronting us today. Based on this inspiration, I assembled a skilled team to start the Vedic Heritage Foundation.

Our goal is to communicate to the Western World the experiential nature and techniques of Vedic and Vaiṣṇava culture, which results in direct perception of the pure, individual self and the omnipresent Godhead.

The first step we are taking in this direction is the publication of *Vaiṣṇava India*. Because Vaiṣṇavism is so experiential and relies on so many forms of communication other than linear writing, which is all any book can be, we have included numerous full color photographs. The Vaiṣṇavas believe in using all the senses to appreciate and worship God. Therefore, any serious study of Vaiṣṇavism must include using as many forms of Vaiṣṇava communication as possible. At least, the visual portion of this experience will be liberally represented here.

Because Jagat Guru Swami had so well prepared me by his stories, my first actual visit to Guruvayur was very profound and sweet. In a new and real way, I saw how it was God's plan for plants, animals, and humans to co-exist in peace and genuine love. The harmonious and cosmic dance of God was plainly visible in Guruvayur. I believed in and loved my God, the One God of us all, in a deeper way than ever before. Who can ask for a more priceless gift?

Just as Jagat Guru Swami paved the way for me to have my own personal experiences of the spiritual potency of Vaiṣṇavism, I and my co-authors hope this book can be a bridge to link the Western World to the real contributions Vaiṣṇavism has made—and can continue to make—to the West. We cannot hope to catch all of Vaiṣṇavism within the narrow confines of these pages. However, we can give a sketch, an outline, impressions, facts, tidbits to whet your appetite for more. Vaiṣṇavism is like an ocean of nectar. Wherever you dive in, the water tastes sweet. Unless you dive in, though, you will never be able to judge the taste of the water. If *Vaiṣṇava India* sufficiently impresses our readers to investigate the subject matter more closely and to read some of the original literatures in authentic translations, then we shall have accomplished our primary goal.

Fate seems to be smiling on our endeavor. For decades, relations between India and the United States were chilly and distant because of geopolitical vagaries. Then, during the late Prime Minister Indira Gandhi's visit to President Reagan in 1982, a historic cultural exchange program was agreed upon as a means of thawing this relationship. The cultural exchange concept has caught on and grown by leaps and bounds, so much so as to make the 1985 to 1987 "Festival of India" the largest cultural exchange program in the history of the United States. It seems to be that many people are seeing the obvious—the United States and India have far more mutual interests and things to exchange than a first glance may suggest. And *Vaiṣṇava India*, by God's grace, is being published during the "Festival of India" to substantiate the need and value of this exchange.

The United States is undoubtedly the grandfather of all democracies in the world, but India with over 740 million people is the largest. India is still experiencing great stresses and strains in unifying her diverse peoples under one national banner. The United States success in this area—although we also had our conflicts along the way—is largely due to the efficacy of the American melting pot and economic opportunity. Overall, the American social system was designed to be impartial and equal to all peoples, regardless of race, religion, or color. And to a large extent, we have succeeded. Most of the people's energies went into constructive channels without ancient taboos or social barriers to obstruct them. Everyone could dream. Everyone could work. Everyone could advance themselves. The world sees the result—the most prosperous nation in the world. Socially, politically, and economically, India could learn a lot from the United States.

Democracy, however, is not foreign to India. For most of India's history, the democratically elected village council was the most important and influential level of government for the vast majority of the people. Decentralization prevailed and prospered in government for most of India's long history. Let's say this was an Indian version of "states' rights." It worked so well that India can proudly claim to have governed more people democratically over the last 3,000 years than any other country in the world. Democracy was born, bred, and brought to maturity in India over a period of thousands of years, while the peoples of the West suffered from brutal political oppression and economic exploitation.

The democratic social machinery of India was disrupted and corrupted by foreign invasions and internal weaknesses, leaving India with enormous challenges today. However, the civilizing effect of thousands of years of democracy in a God-conscious and rich culture could not be eroded from the people's hearts.

In the recent bestseller, *The City of Joy*, by Dominique Lapierre, life in the wretchedest Calcutta slums is described very vividly. It is a heart-wrenching story. But amid the mind-boggling poverty, suffering, disease, corruption, and oppression, one thing shines out brightly above all else—the people of Calcutta never lose their inner peace and dignity and always manifest as much civilization and humanity as their precarious situation allows them. The people of India are extremely civilized, cultured, refined, and spiritual. Their political and social machinery needs overhauling, but the people of India have a lot to teach us about the refinements and grace of living in a wide array of areas. The people of India are sound and loving, as *The City of Joy* so touchingly presents.

Nor is social utopia foreign to India, either. In fact, the grandest and most successful social utopian reformer in world history was Emperor Ashoka, who ruled India from 273 BC to 232 BC. Ashoka's India was immense, nearly the size of India today. He started his reign like previous monarchs—by engaging in wars of conquest. However, after subduing the state of Kalinga in 261 BC, Ashoka had a change of heart. He underwent a spiritual transformation and dedicated the full resources of the government to the physical and spiritual well-being of his people. And *people* extended beyond humans in Ashoka's kingdom. Ashoka included all animate beings and "existing creatures" under the protection of his government's law.

Also, government officials did not simply wait for social unrest or problems to arise before springing into action. Ashoka believed in prevention, and highly-trained government officials were deputed throughout the country to act as "peacemakers." Their mission was to actively promote good relations between all segments of society.

The evidence shows that Ashoka's experiment—all the more remarkable because of the size of the country and population involved—succeeded in every respect. From 261 BC to Ashoka's death in 232 BC, peace reigned within and without all of India. This peace was sustained for 30 to 40 years after Ashoka's death, making this period the most peaceful in world history for a major country.

The success of Ashoka's peace-oriented government demands our attention. His experiment worked, not in an isolated community but in an entire country. Can we adapt his methods to the world today and achieve similar results? I feel we can, and the Vedic Heritage Foundation is dedicated to supporting this thesis.

The concept of inalienable, self-evident human rights has been evolving and expanding since the beginning of America. At first, black people were denied the equal protection of the law and lived in servitude and bondage. Only 125 years ago, this country plunged itself into our bloodiest war over this issue, and it was only by the force of arms that black people regained their inalienable rights. My great-grandfather, General Philip Henry Sheridan, was a leader of the Union Forces in that struggle. I thank him for fighting to give us a country where all people are free and equal in the eyes of God and the law. And, as my great-grandfather grappled with the issues of his day and made the choice to extend the protection of law, I feel I have to make my contribution to this evolutionary process of bringing our society into greater and greater harmony and justice.

Vaiṣṇavism teaches that, where animals are protected and extended the same rights under law as humans, peace and prosperity reign. Ashoka certainly proved the feasibility of this proposition. Today, leading social thinkers and experts in America are also recognizing the potentially incredible liberating powers vegetarianism holds for national and world transformation. Alvin Toffler in his book, *Ecospasm*, contends that, if a religious movement advocating vegetarianism becomes popular in the West, many of our seemingly intractable environmental and human problems could be resolved. Using natural resources to support the raising of animals for food is the most inefficient and harmful method of producing food. If America became vegetarian today, we would have enough surplus food to feed almost all the world's hungry and impoverished people. And government studies show we would be healthier to boot and would live longer.

If we want peace, we must create peace. Since war and conflict are so pervasive in our world, obviously some of our most cherished habits and patterns must be supporting strife. We must be courageous enough to engage in serious self-analysis as individuals and as nations to discover the root causes of these hostile tendencies. Then, we must take the appropriate corrective measures.

Animals, especially higher forms of animals, are integral members of the same family of life to which we belong. Vedic culture teaches that, by killing higher animals to eat them, we slowly and surely become acclimated to and implicated in a relatively high level of violence in our everyday lives. This process desensitizes us. Considering the overwhelming scientific evidence in favor of eating less meat and the ecological inefficiency and problems caused by raising animals for food, it is time for us to face the possible negative psychological and social consequences as well.

Progress and evolution sometimes require us to reconsider long-standing practices. Slavery was once the norm all over the world. Today, in its grossest and most abusive forms, it has almost disappeared. Now, let us reexamine our relationship with the animal realm and at least protect higher animals against unnecessary death and pain.

Ending world hunger, increasing our health, creating a supportive environment for peace—these are all startling and possibly revolutionary consequences that we can actualize by applying the principles of Vaiṣṇavism to our present situation.

One motto of America is, "E Pluribus Unum," or, "Out of many, one." For many Vaiṣṇavas, this proposition not only makes political sense but is also the highest metaphysical truth. The Sanskrit equivalent of this Latin saying is, *acintya-bhedabheda tattva,* or, "the truth of inconceivable and simultaneous individuality and oneness." Simply put, this means that a soul always has individuality, as well as oneness with God.

Christianity proclaims the same truth under the name of the Mystical Body of Christ. A part of a body is in the body, but it is not the whole body. It is and it isn't. According to Vaiṣṇavas, in the experience of unconditional love of Godhead this difficult and apparently contradictory truth is realized.

The spiritual philosophy of Vaiṣṇavism, then, perfectly complements America's political principles and even lends it a strong, metaphysical foundation. Americans believe in the sanctity of the individual and protecting his or her rights. For the Vaiṣṇavas, this is the way of the universe and God.

America is also based on competition. Vaiṣṇavas feel that, when people compete with each other within an overall context of spiritual unity, most people will be stimulated to do their best; and, prosperity will result. In this approach, people are competing not to beat each other, but to do the best of which they are capable; the entire society will benefit, and God will be pleased. As the successes in the world market of more cooperatively and democratically organized Japanese corporations are proving, the days of "rugged individualism" are numbered. If our modern world is to survive, the cooperative forces in it must be strengthened enormously. However, we do not want to lose the tremendous motivating power of competition either. Vaiṣṇavism teaches us how to bring competition to a higher level where it is constructive, rather than destructive; where it is based on expressing one's fullness, rather than trying to hide one's deficiencies. We need to make competition and cooperation work better together, and Vaiṣṇavism may hold a key to achieving this end.

For thousands of years and until very recently, the popular culture of India was dominated by works which presented spiritually and morally uplifting themes. Audiences loved them, and the culture reinforced the positive and constructive message of religion. Since popular culture is based on the actual collective experiences of people who live in society, we can safely say the people of India are highly spiritual.

American popular culture today, however, gives us a radically different picture. Writing in 1941—and it has certainly become worse since then, not better—Dr. Pitirim A. Sorokin tells us:

> To sum up, contemporary art is primarily a museum of social and cultural pathology. It centers in the police morgue, the criminal's hide-out, and the sex organs, operating mainly on the level of the social sewers.

Rather than acquainting us with positive role models, "God, saints, and real heroes are, as a rule, conspicuous by their absence . . ." in modern culture according to Sorokin. The overwhelming majority of critics, social thinkers, and audiences feel Western culture needs a dramatic transfusion of positivity and basic humanity, what to speak of spirituality. There is a consensus that our culture is selling us short and selling us out; that in many ways, it is weakening the basic moral fiber of society.

India's experience is that when God is alive and well in the people's hearts, the culture reflects that awareness. Vedic and Vaiṣṇava cultures present us with the largest body of humanly uplifting cultural material in the world today. The lifeblood of this culture just might be the transfusion we need. Certainly, throwing more of Vedic and Vaiṣṇava cultures into the American melting pot will strengthen our country's moral fiber and give us good examples of how we can laugh, cry, and be entertained without having to bathe in the sludge of our social sewers.

Lastly, I want to add a special note of thanks to my father, Jack R. Sheridan. Without his love, encouragement, and support, *Vaiṣṇava India* and the Vedic Heritage Foundation would not have been actualized. In many ways, I feel my father was an ideal parent. He helped to give me the tools of life, and then allowed me the freedom to explore my own path. With the self-confidence he instilled in me, I could transcend cultural barriers to find the good in all peoples. Because he freed my mind, rather than trying to mold it, I have found a most satisfying vocation—learning the Vedic and Vaiṣṇava cultures and sharing them with the public. Again, father, thank you. You've helped me hit the cultural jackpot.

Geary J.C. Sheridan, President
Vedic Heritage Foundation
March 25, 1986

Introduction

The purpose of this book is unique—to present in English, along with profuse illustrations, as comprehensive a picture as possible, considering the enormity of the subject matter, of Vaiṣṇavism in its birthplace on earth, India. In many respects, Vaiṣṇavism is the root and trunk of the entire Indian civilization.

Unfortunately, the United States and the Western World in general know little about Vaiṣṇavism, whether it be its religion and philosophy, culture, or history. Most of the Indian holy people who have visited the West have belonged to an offshoot branch of Vedic religion that started only in the 9th century AD. Therefore, the West is still in its infancy in understanding the original Vaiṣṇava culture.

The importance of India and Vaiṣṇavism to world civilization is elaborately described by Will Durant in his monumental 10 volume, *Story of Civilization*. In his *The Case for India,* Durant sums up his findings:

> India was the mother-land of our race, and Sanskrit the mother of Europe's languages; that she was the mother of our philosophy . . . of our mathematics . . . of the ideals embodied in Christianity, mother, through the village community, of self-government and democracy. Mother India is in many ways the mother of us all.

The Vedic Heritage Foundation and the authors of *Vaiṣṇava India* feel it is time for us to start knowing our mother better.

The qualities of Vedic civilization listed by Will Durant are the same qualities cherished by most Americans. For this reason, Ernest Wood wrote in 1929: ". . . America owes a debt to India in connection with those very qualities of character which America values most and for which the rest of the world admires America."

Historically, it is easy to prove by a preponderance of evidence that Vedic civilization has existed for well over 5,000 years. The incredibly advanced stage of civilization, knowledge, and technology contained in India 5,000 years ago presupposes a long stage of development and maturation beforehand. If this perspective is accepted, then Vedic civilization is the oldest on-going culture in the world today.

From scriptures, artifacts, and other evidence, we have access to at least 5,000 years of historical Vedic culture. On the whole this culture has served its people abundantly well. The test of time has proven it. Concerning this point, the late President of India, Dr. Radhakrishnan, who also was a renowned philosopher and teacher, wrote in *The Hindu View of Life*:

> [Vedic civilization] has stood the stress and strain of more than four or five millenniums of spiritual thought and experience. Though peoples of different races and cultures have been pouring into India from the dawn of history, it has been able to maintain its supremacy and even the proselytizing creeds, backed by political power, have not been able to coerce a large majority of Indians to their views. The Hindu culture possesses some vitality which seems to be denied to other more forceful currents.

What explains the strength and longevity of Vedic civilization? The tradition itself attributes its success to God—that some time in the distant past of earth, Vedic culture was revealed to humanity directly through divine agency. Actually, as *A Handbook of Hindu Religion* reports, the religion of this culture "is not a historical religion, but it is a religion without any historic founders. . . ." Whereas we know the founders of all other major religions in the world, no human person has ever been credited with founding or revealing Vedic knowledge. As far as the Indian people are concerned, this way of life has always existed, although their understanding and practice of it have undergone evolution and development.

We shall begin our journey into timeless Vaiṣṇava India by visiting its most holy places, starting with the Himalayas. The reader faces a most difficult task. The West is filled with misinformation and distortions about Vedic India, much of which has been spread with premeditation and ignoble motives. The reader must see through this smokescreen and the cultural differences that exist between the West and India. Then and only then can true understanding begin. To help clear our minds and broaden our perspectives, the authors feel a visit to the earth's grandest vistas in the Himalayas would be the most appropriate place to start.

The Badrinath Range.

CHAPTER 1: HIMALAYAS

A bathing ghat on the Ganges at Hardwar.

The Vaiṣṇavas, however, have no desire to conquer nature. They want to integrate and harmonize themselves with the natural order. In the frantic rush of modern development in the West, the "conquering nature" spirit has reigned supreme and the West's technology has grown by leaps and bounds. "Harmonizing with nature" was thought of as a quaint, archaic attitude at best and superstitious primitivism at worst. Now, the pendulum is swinging back the other way. Unbridled technological development has ravaged land, air, and sea. The modern science of ecology has proven beyond a shadow of a doubt that unless Western technology is harmonized with nature—and soon—we face living on a fatally poisoned planet. Therefore, understanding the Vaiṣṇava's reverence for nature and sense of harmony can provide a philosophical and inspirational basis for the hard scientific demands for an ecologically sound human society. And the sweet taste of the natural purity of the Himalayas can whet a person's appetite for this harmony.

The Vaiṣṇavas never saw the Himalayas as a challenge. To them, the Himalayas nourish their country and provide a refuge for those people who seek to understand the deepest mysteries of life.

To the residents of the lower hills of the Himalayas, who have labored mightily to terrace the steep slopes for farming, the mountains provide everything they need for life. They have succeeded in creating a hardy, healthy race of people, whose difficulties have brought them closer to nature and God.

The physical importance of the Himalayas to the rest of India is immense. By separating India from the Asiatic mainland, the Himalayas bar entry to the freezing winds from Tibet, serve as a screen within which the life-giving monsoon rains operate, and provide a steady source for India's three great river systems—the Indus, the Ganges, and the Brahmaputra—that water the alluvial plains below. As a result of erosion, the rivers also carry a vast quantity of silt, which constantly enriches the plains. In fact, the alluvial plains of India may be the deepest in the world, going down to perhaps 10,000 feet.

Ashrams lining the bank of the Ganges in Hrishikesh.

Terraced field in a Himalayan valley.

Every corner of India has its holy places, shrines, temples, and pilgrimage sites. All of these can be found abundantly in and around Hardwar and the Himalayas. Hardwar is known especially for its ashrams, or schools of spiritual study and practice. Unlike theology schools in the West, these ashrams, which line the banks of the Ganges, emphasize more the practical application of religion through meditation and devotional practices, which result in direct communion with spiritual realities. Nevertheless, philosophy and intellectual studies are not neglected. The wise saints and sages of Hardwar and the Himalayas are legendary.

It is customary for pilgrims from all over India and other parts of the world to start their Himalayan journey with a sacred bath in the holy Ganges River at Hardwar. The story of why the Ganges is holy catches the very essence of the Himalayan experience. In these mountains it is easy to see heaven touch the earth. You feel as if you are at a place where various dimensions of reality meet and intermingle with each other. And, according to ancient Sanskrit sources, the Ganges River *is* a penetration of the spiritual dimension into the physical, earthly plane.

In the timeless past, an incarnation of God called Vamanadeva pierced a hole in the material universe. According to the *Srimad Bhagavatam,* or *Bhagavat Purana,* "Through the hole, the pure water of the Causal Ocean entered this universe as the Ganges River." Eventually, this spiritual river reached earth.

The Ganges River flowing toward Hrishikesh.

A hiking trail along the cliffs of the Gangotri Valley.

The benefits of bathing in the Ganges are described in the *Srimad Bhagavatam* as follows: "Every living being can immediately purify his mind of material contamination by touching the transcendental water of the Ganges, yet its waters remain ever pure." In commenting on this verse, the most successful popularizer of Vaiṣṇavism in the West, His Divine Grace A.C. Bhaktivedanta Swami Prabhupada, writes:

> The water of the Ganges is called *patita-pāvanī,* the deliverer of all sinful living beings. It is a proven fact that a person who regularly bathes in the Ganges is purified both externally and internally. Externally his body becomes immune to all kinds of disease, and internally he gradually develops a devotional attitude toward the Supreme Personality of Godhead.

As early as 1896, Western scientists proved, to their utter amazement, that the Yamuna (a tributary of the Ganges also originating in the Himalayas) and Ganges rivers were physically purifying. In an article entitled *L'Action Bactericide des Eaux de la Jumna et du Gange sur le Microbe de la Cholera* published in the *Annales de L'Institut Pasteur,* M. E. Hankin of the Laboratory of the British colonial government at Agra writes:

> It appears then that all the impurities produced by a large town . . . are without influence upon the power which the water of the Jumna [Yamuna] possesses of destroying the cholera microbe.

A Himalayan valley near Badrinath.

When studying the Ganges, M. E. Hankin found

> that unboiled Ganges water kills the cholera microbe in less than three hours. The same water boiled has not the same effect. The water of wells is, on the contrary, a good environment for this microbe, even though it be boiled or filtered.

This scientist concludes that Yamuna and Ganges water "contain an antiseptic exerting a powerful bactericidial action upon the cholera microbe."

In his book, *Slowly Down the Ganges*, Eric Newby sums up what scientists have observed about the Ganges water:

> European scientists discovered . . . that its water has remarkable properties. Bottled, it will keep for at least a year. At its confluence with the River Jumna which particularly at the time of the great fair . . . contains dangerous number of *coli*, the Ganges itself is said to be free of them. At Banaras thousands drink the water every day at bathing places which are close to the outfalls of appalling open drains. They appear to survive. The presence of large numbers of decomposing corpses seems to have no effect on it . . . . Even cholera, one of the great killers, does not go down the river.

In spite of the Ganges purifying powers, undoubtedly pollution of it by modern industries and sewers ought to be stopped. While modern science has verified the above mentioned extraordinary phenomena about the Ganges, scientists have only been able to *theorize* as to the cause of them. So far, no purely natural explanation suffices.

The findings of science, then, lend credence to the Vaiṣṇava scripture's revelation that the Ganges and Yamuna are no ordinary rivers but bring to earth special potencies from other dimensions. However, the purifying effects of these rivers are not to be abused. To sin again after being purified can nullify the good effects, and to sin while thinking, "I shall purify myself of this sin by bathing in the Ganges," is considered to be a most abominable mentality. Purification is not simply mechanical or automatic but also relies on sincerity.

A waterfall on the Ganges at Gangotri.

One power in the mystic yoga system is the ability to prolong life. Some of the most advanced mystic yogis in the Rishikesh district are reputed to be at least one thousand years old and totally disinterested in publicity. Whether this claim can be proven empirically or not, the yogis of Rishikesh radiate such great energy, power, and light that their visitors leave convinced that something very extraordinary and miraculous is happening here.

From Rishikesh the pilgrims journey further up into the high mountains. Until perhaps forty years ago, a Himalayan pilgrimage was made traditionally by foot. Today, trains, buses, and cars go to most pilgrimage sites. However, the more remote places of pilgrimage are still reached by foot. Many pilgrims prefer the traditional footpaths over modern transportation, even when it is available. They can see more on foot, they say. Besides, considering the treacherous roads and conditions, it is a lot safer.

The Ganges River flowing out of its earthly source at Gomukh with the Bhagiratha snow caps in the background.

When pilgrims reach Gangotri, they stare spellbound for a long time, watching the waters of the Ganges rushing forth from a glacier valley with a deafening roar and falling into a deep ravine below. The only way to arrive at Gangotri is to hike almost seven miles from the village of Lanka. By walking another 11.8 miles along the twisting path of the Ganges, the pilgrim comes, at the 12,770 feet mark above sea level, to a massive ice glacier known as Gomukh near Mt. Bhagirath. When the glacier is first approached, it appears to be a gigantic mountain cliff, but as the pilgrim gets closer and closer, he or she can see it is solid ice. In a cave in this ice, the pilgrim discovers the source of the sacred Ganges River—water flowing from the melting section of the glacier. Outside the cave overlooking you is the snow-capped peak of Mt. Bhagirath (23,555). Silhouetted against a brilliant blue sky accompanied by lingering clouds, the peak of Bhagirath appears to be a temple spire crowning the glory of the sacred Ganges. And beyond this view is only heaven.

Pinnacles of ice reaching skyward at Gomukh.

The ice cave at Gomukh where the Ganges originates.

Most of the Himalayan holy places are only accessible from spring to early fall. For the rest of the year, the Himalayas are buffeted by fierce storms, blinding blizzards, and forceful winds. Right before this season, there is a general migration south to the lower elevations and safety. During this time, the local residents say that only the devas, or angelic beings from higher dimensions, come to the high country to maintain the temples. However, some renounced yogis stay in the high mountains even during the depths of winter. They remain deep in meditation, hidden away in their mountain caves.

While the natural wonder and beauty of the Himalayas are very impressive, they are not the only or chief reason the Himalayas are considered holy. To a Vaiṣṇava, a place is holy if God has appeared there personally to reveal the divine nature or give instructions valuable to humanity. In the Judeo-Christian tradition, Mt. Sinai is revered for the same reason. At Mt. Sinai, God revealed Himself to Moses as blinding fire and light. God spoke to Moses and gave him the Ten Commandments, which have guided Western civilization ever since. For the Vaiṣṇavas, the presence of a great saint, who is in direct communion with God, also makes a place holy. And, as noted before, the Himalayas have hosted many such saints.

According to Vaiṣṇava scriptures, an incarnation of God appeared in the Himalayas at Badrinath millions of years ago. This incarnation is called Nara-narayana and is famous for having taught the ancient sages how to control their senses and meditate on the Supreme. Befittingly, the temple at Badrinath celebrating Nara-narayana's appearance is the most famous of all Himalayan pilgrimage sites. This temple houses a Deity form of God that is said to have been given to the sages directly by divine agency.

A billboard welcomes pilgrims to Kurukshetra.

CHAPTER 2: KURUKSHETRA

Sunset at Vishnu Temple on the banks of the Kurukshetra Tank.

Indians have revered the sacred area of Kurukshetra for all of known history. In this district, which is north of New Delhi and east of Hardwar and Rishikesh, it is said that Vedic society took on definite form and shape. The sacred river Saraswati, named after the Goddess of Learning, flows through Kurukshetra. On the banks of the Saraswati, the immortal compiler of the ancient Vedic scriptures, Vyasa, wrote down the great epic *Mahabharata,* or "Great India." In fact, most of the ancient Vedic scriptures—the *Vedas, Upanishads,* and *Puranas*—were authored here.

Kurukshetra is considered so holy that to die within its environs guarantees a soul entry into a higher state. It is for this reason that the forces of the Pandava and Kuru families fought perhaps the most devastating war of ancient times at Kurukshetra approximately 5,000 years ago. The Pandavas, who were heavily outnumbered by the Kurus, chose Kurukshetra as the battle site for its spiritually inspiring qualities. Also, they felt the fallen soldiers on both sides could at least attain a better next life.

The story of the rivalry between the Pandavas and the Kurus makes up the subject matter of the *Mahabharata,* which is one of the most important literary productions of ancient India. The *Mahabharata* consists of 100,000 stanzas, qualifying it as the longest poem in literary history—about eight times as long as the *Iliad* and the *Odyssey* combined.

Briefly told, the five Pandava brothers were the legitimate heirs to the throne. However, when their father dies untimely with his sons too young to rule, the head of the Kuru family becomes the regent, doing everything in his power, including attempted assassinations, to eliminate the Pandavas so his family could rule exclusively. After many trials, tribulations, and hair-raising close calls, including fourteen excruciating years of exile, the Pandavas are ready to claim their inheritance. The Kurus refuse to recognize the Pandava claim. In humility the Pandavas then ask for only five villages, so each brother could at least have one village to rule. At this point, the Kurus reveal their total greed and selfishness. Their chief, Duryodhana, answers that he will not give the Pandavas enough ground to stick a pin in.

Therefore, after having exhausted every avenue of peacefully and diplomatically resolving this conflict, the Pandavas reluctantly decided to fight. Each side amassed huge armies, recruited from all over the Indian subcontinent and beyond. However, the Kuru army had a pronounced numerical superiority, as well as having more great warriors in their ranks. The Pandavas' assets lay in their great spiritual faith and honesty, which greatly endeared them to all the people of the kingdom. The honesty of the chief Pandava, Yudhisthira, made him a legend in his own lifetime. Truth and the name Yudhisthira became synonymous.

The spiritual and moral excellence of the Pandavas gained them the unswerving friendship and support of the most powerful and influential personality in all of Indian history—Shri Krishna.

The answers to the questions "Who is Shri Krishna and what is our relationship to Him?" make up the whole of Vaiṣṇava religion and culture. The way in which Vaiṣṇavas regard Shri Krishna will unfold gradually in this book. For now, let us say that Vaiṣṇavas consider Shri Krishna to be a complete manifestation of the original Godhead, or Supreme Being. In Christian theology, Jesus is considered to be the "Son of God." In Vaiṣṇava theology, Shri Krishna is held to be "God the Father Incarnate." To the Vaiṣṇava, when Shri Krishna speaks, God the Father is speaking. The teachings of Shri Krishna are taken as the highest authority on spiritual matters.

Historically speaking, Shri Krishna lived on the earth planet for 125 years during the Mahabharata period. As a youth, He overthrew the tyrannical and oppressive regime of King Kamsa. For the rest of Shri Krishna's stay on earth, He fought against the warlords who overburdened India at that time. One of Shri Krishna's most intimate friends was Arjuna, one of the five Pandava brothers. Shri Krishna did everything in His power to mediate the Pandava-Kuru conflict, but to no avail. When war became inevitable, Shri Krishna made a startling proposal: one side could have his powerful army, and the other side could have Him personally. However, Shri Krishna would not fight but only advise and assist in other ways. The Kurus, who always calculated their own advantage according to materialistic considerations, chose Shri Krishna's army. The Pandavas were more than happy just to get Shri Krishna on their side.

When the armies finally faced off against each other, millions of soldiers, accompanied by military elephants, chariots, and horses were ready to fight. For Vedic civilization the Battle of Kurukshetra would prove to be on a World War scale with crippling consequences.

During the battle, Shri Krishna would serve as Arjuna's chariot driver. Before hostilities broke out, Arjuna asked Shri Krishna to drive his chariot in front of the Pandava and Kuru lines so he could see all the combatants. While there, Arjuna is overwhelmed by what he sees. Arjuna says:

> My dear Kṛṣṇa, seeing my friends and relatives present before me in such a fighting spirit, I feel the limbs of my body quivering and my mouth drying up. My whole body is trembling, my hair is standing on end, my bow Gāṇḍīva is slipping from my hand, and my skin is burning. I am now unable to stand any longer. I am forgetting myself, and my mind is reeling. I see only causes of misfortune, O Kṛṣṇa, killer of the Keśī demon.

At the end of this passionate outpouring of sorrow at having to fight in this fratricidal war, Arjuna "cast aside his bow and arrows and sat down on the chariot, his mind overwhelmed with grief."

An old Chinese proverb says, "A calamity is a time of great opportunity." Shri Krishna seized upon this calamitous moment as the perfect time to speak to Arjuna the *Bhagavad-gita,* or "Song of God." The *Bhagavad-gita* covers an enormous scope of material in its pithy 720 verses, including the nature of God, the self, the material universe, time, and activities. This amazing work is as fresh, inspiring, and enlightening now as it was the day it was spoken.

Aldous Huxley, one of the twentieth century's greatest writers and thinkers, called the *Bhagavad-gita* "one of the clearest and most comprehensive statements of the perennial philosophy ever to have been made. Hence, its enduring value is not only for India, but for all mankind." By perennial philosophy, Huxley meant a timeless kind of wisdom that appears here and there in the works of all great thinkers in all times and places. Huxley is not alone in giving this status to the *Bhagavad-gita*. Many learned people from around the world have heaped praise upon praise on this masterpiece.

Mammoth lake and bathing ghat in Kurukshetra.

The Kurukshetra Tank. In the background stands the shrine commemorating the Battle of Kurukshetra.

Besides supporting the existence of a true self, the *Bhagavad-gita* also reveals an entire system of practical, applied psychology for happy, fully-actualized living. In the Encyclopaedia Britannica's *Macropaedia,* the *Mahabharata* is credited for recording the world's first system of psychology. The psychology section of the *Mahabharata* is the *Bhagavad-gita,* which, while a small part of the *Mahabharata,* has proven to outshine the larger work in its powers to inspire and transform lives. The *Macropaedia* reports that the *Bhagavad-Gita* "disclosed five senses, and an intermediary faculty (*manas*) for receiving sense impressions that were transmitted to *buddhi* (intuitive discernment, intellect) before reaching 'soul' or self (*atman*)."

The progressive branches of modern psychology are recognizing more and more the importance of nourishing and developing a healthy sense of self, while the behavioral school of psychology bucks this trend by denying altogether the self's existence. Many experts in the mental health field see this stand of behavioral psychology as part of our contemporary mental health problem rather than a source of its solution. Dr. Karen Horney, who is certainly one of the most influential psychiatrists of the twentieth century, used to cite the following excerpt from an anonymous letter as a fitting explanation of psychological difficulties: "In a word, I saw that we *become* neurotic seeking or defending a pseudo-self, a self-system, and we *are* neurotic to the extent that we are self-less." *Bhagavad-gita* certainly concurs with this diagnosis.

Emphasis on a healthy sense of self is not the only parallel between the *Bhagavad-gita* and contemporary psychology. Much of Dr. Abraham Maslow's work (Dr. Maslow is considered the "father" of psychology's "Third Force" or "Humanistic Psychology" and was a leading figure in the development of Transpersonal Psychology) can also be found first in the *Bhagavad-gita*. Maslow's description of the "self-actualized" person nearly duplicates Shri Krishna's description of the self-realized person. Both Shri Krishna and Dr. Maslow urge people to identify and associate with the healthiest people they can find. And both say that destructive habits and patterns can only be released permanently by giving a person a direct experience of a better pattern. In the *Bhagavad-gita,* Shri Krishna says, "The embodied soul may be restricted from sense enjoyment, though the taste for sense objects remains. But, ceasing such engagements by experiencing a higher taste, he is fixed in consciousness."

Progressive psychology and the *Bhagavad-gita* both recognize the futility of punishment and repression as a means of transforming people. Only by giving a person a "higher taste," a more natural and nourishing way of life, can negative habits be terminated and a person "fixed in consciousness."

After the most exhaustive assessment of health in the United States of America, the federal government also came to the same conclusion as taught by Shri Krishna. In *Healthy People: The Surgeon General's Report on Health Promotion and Disease Prevention,* Joseph A. Califano, Jr., the Secretary of the Department of Health, Education, and Welfare, states:

> We are killing ourselves by our own careless habits.
>
> We are killing ourselves by carelessly polluting the environment.
>
> We are killing ourselves by permitting harmful social conditions to persist—conditions like poverty, hunger, and ignorance—which destroy health, especially for infants and children.

Secretary Califano and the Surgeon General's Report emphasize that only by improving people's life-style habits, can further health improvements be made in the United States. To the Vaiṣṇava, the teachings of the *Bhagavad-gita* hold the key for improving life style, and contemporary psychology is having great successes in applying some of these principles. This cross-fertilization of Vaiṣṇava thought and modern psychology is bearing fruit, but we are only in the infancy stage of this hybrid. As the West becomes even more familiar with the intricacies of Vaiṣṇava psychology and its applications, it will be interesting to observe future developments.

To those readers who are acquainted with Eastern thought but new to Vaiṣṇavism, this chapter's emphasis on the eternality of an individual self may come as a surprise. It is true that most Eastern systems do not posit a true, individual self—or else remain uncommitted on the subject. For most Eastern systems, enlightenment involves the more or less total loss of self. Because of this tendency, many Westerners shun Eastern disciplines as being too nihilistic and negative in their ultimate goals. Daniel Cohen in his book *The Far Side of Consciousness* rightly asks:

> Do we really want to attain these higher states of meditation at all? Though, like all spiritual or mystic experiences, the highest states of meditation defy description, they appear to involve a total loss of self, and a sort of "blank mind" state.

On the Battlefield of Kurukshetra, Sri Krishna speaks the Bhagavad-gita *to Arjuna.*

So, we can trace the journey of Shri Krishna's teachings to Arjuna 5,000 years ago on the Battlefield of Kurukshetra to the Mediterranean Sea area and Pythagoras some 2,500 years ago. These teachings then became one of the influences on Jesus and the founding of Christianity 2,000 years ago. And today, progressive psychologists and thinkers are applying the principles of the *Bhagavad-gita* to improve contemporary life. In all of these times and places, Shri Krishna's message was and is embraced warmly and proves to be a positive force in the forward march of humanity.

Five thousand years ago, Kurukshetra was already considered an ancient holy land. Five thousand years ago, Kurukshetra provided the earthly environment for yet another divine miracle—the speaking by Shri Krishna of the *Bhagavad-gita*.

Ashrams, temples, and bathing ghats line the eastern bank of the Ganges in Banaras.

CHAPTER 3: BANARAS

Another skyline view of Banaras.

If you travel by boat down the Ganges River about one-half of its 1,560-mile length, you'll come to the ancient and venerable city of Banaras. After reaching the city limits, continue by boat for three miles. On the left riverbank you'll see temples of many kinds and shapes and other fascinating buildings. Also, elaborate structures with many stone steps, called bathing *ghats,* grace the bank. Usually they are crowded with pilgrims and local residents taking a religious bath in the Ganges. Finally, you will see several funeral pyres burning. Taken together, these sights of Banaras create one of the most unique and intriguing skylines to be found anywhere in the world. Pictures of these scenes appear in most books on India. They almost have become an official symbol of Vedic culture.

When Mark Twain visited Banaras, he caught the city's essence in his pithy, penetrating style. He said, "Banaras is older than history." Reverend M. A. Sherring, a Christian missionary stationed in Banaras during the mid-nineteenth century, was also impressed by the sheer weight of Banaras' antiquity. According to Reverend Sherring's research:

> Twenty-five centuries ago, at least, it [Banaras] was famous. When Babylon was struggling with Nineveh for supremacy, when Tyre was planting her colonies, when Athens was growing in strength, before Rome had become known, or Greece had contended with Persia, or Cyrus had added lustre to the Persian monarchy, or Nebuchadnezzar had captured Jerusalem, and the inhabitants of Judea had been carried into captivity, she had already risen to greatness, if not glory.

Many experts feel that Banaras just might be the oldest living city in the world, which is not surprising, since Vedic culture is the oldest living culture in the world.

Brahmin waits to receive pilgrims on the bank of the Ganges.

Banaras suffered a great blow in AD 1194 when Muslim armies conquered her, destroyed all the ancient temples, and massacred the inhabitants. Under the rule of Emperor Akbar, however, religious tolerance, long a staple of the Indian people, was restored, and Banaras again became a flourishing center of Vedic culture.

Nowhere are the realities of life and death for the human body more evident than in Banaras. And nowhere are they more obvious in Banaras than at Manikarnika Ghat—the most famous and busy cremation site in the world. Many Westerners were at first appalled by the Vedic custom of burning the bodies of the dearly departed. Today, however, cremation is recognized as an excellent, respectful, and hygienic way of caring for corpses, especially in the tropics. When futurists gaze into their crystal balls, they see cremation becoming increasingly popular and practical for much of the world's population.

While the Vedic custom of cremation is scientifically sound, it is not the most important lesson Banaras has to teach us about life and death. It is just the tip of the iceberg. Western industrialized society has been criticized severely for not preparing her people to face the death of the physical body. The West is a "death denying" culture. Death is swept under the rug, isolated, and hidden from common view. Therefore, when the specter of death begins to hang over a family, neither the dying nor their relatives or friends know what to do. When that which is denied inevitably happens, a heartache and sorrow beyond a healthy sense of grief and loss is often experienced. Or, the reaction to the death is suppressed and repressed completely, often causing psychological troubles for many years. In Vedic culture, as symbolized by Banaras, death is a fact of life that is consciously and openly faced for all people to see and benefit from.

Still, when a person stays in Banaras, they can see that the spiritual standard of living has never fallen. In Banaras the aging are not psychologically regressing while waiting for the grim reaper. Instead, they feel that their lives are reaching a glorious climax. Now, they are totally free and supported to contemplate the loving face of God and all spiritual truths. To them, they are not so much preparing for death as preparing for the next stage of life. This spirit is a gift that money cannot buy and we of the West can definitely learn from.

Pilgrims worship at the Dasasva-medha Ghat.

Daily life on the steps of a bathing ghat.

Reincarnation

While people dip into the sacred waters of the Ganges at Banaras' bathing ghats and experience spiritual renewal and rebirth, at a neighboring ghat corpses are cremated to the sounds of timeless Sanskrit prayers. Life appears compacted, intensified, and accelerated in Banaras. Death and rebirth are constantly visible. It is as though the lifetimes of thousands of people are always on view for inspection. Banaras makes you wonder where you came from before you were born and what will happen to you after your death. Banaras is the perfect place to discuss the Vedic doctrine of reincarnation, or transmigration of the soul.

Reincarnation is an essential complement to the Vedic conception of an individual, eternal self. In orthodox Christianity it is believed that God made souls at some point in time and that these souls will live forever into the future. For followers of the Vedic way, this analysis presents only one-half of eternity. In the Vedic conception, the soul as an intimate part and parcel of God shares the exact same nature as God, but only in minute quantity. Therefore, the soul is like God in that both have always been, are now, and always will be.

However, the soul is always free to choose a form of spiritual amnesia. The soul can forget its relationship with God to pursue self-centered, egoistic goals. This choice is said to be the root cause of all of a person's negativity and trouble in life—the decision to be narcissistic and selfish. To facilitate the desire of the individual souls, God, through the agency of cosmic laws, puts the soul into a material body in the physical world. The soul then

> takes the phenomenal world for reality and involves itself in it. Consequently, it becomes subject to the process of Time, which is manifested in unceasing cycles of creation and destruction. For the atman or self this means *samsara* or rebirth, which is likewise a ceaseless process of dying and being reborn. . . .

Reincarnation, then, is the study of the soul's journey through various material bodies in the physical universe.

Residents of Banaras wash and dry their clothes.

The above mentioned verse of the *Bhagavad-gita* regarding reincarnation is well-grounded in modern medical knowledge. Actually, even within the span of time between the birth and death of a person's outer frame, the self transmigrates through several physical bodies. According to medical science, all of the molecules composing a human body are replaced completely within a seven-year period. Therefore, a person who is seven years old has nothing in his body he was born with. At a person's twenty-first birthday, he is officially entering his fourth body. When we approach the half-century mark or forty-nine years old, we gain our *eighth* body. In spite of shedding and entering so many different bodies within one lifetime, the self experiences a continuity of identity and consciousness. By meditating on and thinking about this continuity of consciousness, we can experience it directly along with our eternity. The prospect of shedding the present physical body entirely and receiving a brand new body becomes at least reasonable, and with mature meditation, it becomes a realized fact. The logical soundness of reincarnation allows the mind to enter deeper and deeper into the spiritual realm, until the core of us, which is spiritual itself, realizes its own nature and the cosmic laws governing its travels in this universe.

A little further on in the *Bhagavad-gita,* Shri Krishna continues this theme by saying, "As a person puts on new garments, giving up old ones, the soul similarly accepts new material bodies, giving up the old and useless ones." Besides reaffirming reincarnation, this verse also gives us insight into how a follower of the Vedic way views approaching death. If a person has lived basically a good, moral life, they know either they will achieve full spiritual fulfillment or their worn-out bodies will be replaced by a new one, so the person can continue his or her evolution. While death means leaving one situation, it also means a renewal—and to a person with a clear conscience, that realization brings a peace and joy that overrides the sorrow of death.

Grace is God's ever-present love for all souls. Vaiṣṇavas know that only by accepting this love and grace into their lives can they gain the spiritual power to transcend the materialistic tendencies of this world. While this principle is usually couched in religious terminology, it is also very scientific. In a deep sense, "We are what we identify with." If I identify with God through love and devotion, I now have the power of God to propel me along on my path. Shri Krishna makes this point in Chapter 7 of the *Bhagavad-gita.* "This divine energy of Mine [the world] . . . is difficult to overcome. But those who have surrendered unto Me [God] can easily cross beyond it."

In commenting on the *Bhagavad-gita,* Dr. Long elaborates that God "has the power to cancel out the effects of all human actions and thereby to liberate the eternal and undying soul of man from bondage to rebirth and redeath." In this respect, both Christianity and Vaiṣṇavism see the necessity for people to actively open up to and accept God's love or grace in order to evolve to a higher dimension of being. However, Vaiṣṇavas point out that detailed knowledge and experience of the laws of karma and reincarnation make the process a lot easier. Dr. MacGregor agrees: "Knowledge of cosmic laws, which in the last resort are psychic and moral principles, is a tremendous time-saver and an infinitely valuable saver of energy." As in our present society, ignorance of a law is no excuse for violating a law. So, ignorance of karma and reincarnation will not help us to avoid their consequences if these principles truly guide the movements of all souls. Dr. MacGregor points out such ignorance can get us sidetracked into years and lifetimes "of wearisome work" we could "happily and profitably avoid."

The Cremation Ghat.

An elephant guards the gateway to a local temple.

In his book *Reincarnation*, Irving S. Cooper enumerates seven reasons supportive of reincarnation. They are:

Reincarnation makes possible the attainment of perfection.

Reincarnation illuminates the problem of evil.

Reincarnation is in conformity with the economy of Nature.

Reincarnation and a divine moral order are inseparable.

The results of all that we do in one life cannot be worked out immediately.

Reincarnation explains the enigmas of heredity.

Reincarnation explains the mental and moral differences between people.

In keeping with its gentle temperament, Vaiṣṇavism does not ask its followers to believe in reincarnation on faith alone. Usually, in the normal course of Vaiṣṇava spiritual life, a devotee will have one or more personal experiences of the validity of reincarnation. While much empirical evidence exists to support the theory of reincarnation, it is hard to prove scientifically the existence of inner or spiritual realities. Just as there is no scientific test to determine if one person really loves another person, yet people continue to believe in love, so there is no perfect scientific test to prove or disprove reincarnation. Still, for at least one-and-one-half billion people on earth today, it better explains the mystery of life than any other system.

The Vaiṣṇavas say the door is open for anyone, East or West, to have one's own experiences. You simply have to desire truth more strongly than anything else and be willing to follow truth wherever it may lead.

Village women sell flowers in the market.

The Nature of God

A famous Vedic parable illustrates how difficult it is for people to understand the nature of God. Once there were ten blind men. They were brought to an elephant and asked to identify the thing before them by only touching it. The person holding a leg said it was a tree. Another person grabbed the tail and said it was a snake. One person felt the massive body and concluded it was a wall. This story demonstrates two fundamental Vedic principles. One: a human being's physical sensory apparatus is so limited in range of capabilities that it can never give us an accurate picture of reality or God. For instance, the human eyes can only see a tiny slit of the electromagnetic spectrum of energy that we know to exist by means of our also imperfect and limited scientific instruments. Quite frankly, while the senses are very useful for operating in the world, our senses have definite limitations and cannot give us a view of the big picture.

From this fact comes the second point: since we cannot grasp God by our senses alone, we need to receive inspiration, revelation, and education from sources with a larger perspective. Vaiṣṇavism recognizes three such sources—*sadhu, guru,* and *shastra*. *Sadhu* means the community of holy people—those who have realized the philosophy of Vaiṣṇavism and who practice it in their daily lives. *Guru* means spiritual teacher. Vaiṣṇavism places a great importance on aspirants' finding a highly qualified, honest, and realized teacher, or guru. *Shastra* means the written body of sacred knowledge. In these three sources of Vaiṣṇavism, a spiritual student can find the most extensive information and revelation about the nature of God existing in the world today.

The wealth of Vaiṣṇava insights into the nature of God is relatively unknown in the West, except to some scholars specializing in the field of Vedic or Vaiṣṇava studies. Until His Divine Grace A.C. Bhaktivedanta Swami Prabhupada came to the United States of America in 1965 and successfully started to teach Vaiṣṇavism throughout the Western world, no Vaiṣṇava gurus had ventured out of India. Therefore, the Western world really only knew about the "monist" conception of God developed by Shankara and mistakenly took it to be representative of Vedic thought in general. This mistake was quite natural and almost unavoidable.

There is no doubt that Shankara was an incredibly powerful and brilliant personality. In his short life of thirty-two years, Shankara (AD 686-719) developed his system of absolute monism, which, as the *Encyclopedia of World Religions* points out, "dominated Indian philosophy from . . . the 9th century, up to the present time. . . ." For instance, in the *Area Handbook for India,* published by the Superintendent of Documents, U.S. Government Printing Office, in 1975, and intended to be a comprehensive briefing to government personnel who are assigned to India, the much more ancient philosophy and religion of Vaiṣṇavism is hardly explained at all, while Shankara's philosophy is presented as if it comprises all of Hinduism. Because of this recurring error, many Westerners have a fundamentally incorrect impression of Hinduism.

Monism derives its name from the word *mono,* which means "one." For Shankara, as described by Dr. Basham,

> the whole phenomenal universe . . . was unreal—the world was *Māyā*, illusion, a dream, a mirage, a figment of the imagination. Ultimately the only reality was *Brahman,* the impersonal World Soul . . . , with which the individual soul was identical."

The *Area Handbook for India* describes Shankara's philosophy as follows:

> There is only one reality—the transcendent, impersonal, attributeless, universal soul, Brahman—that is all and causes all. Appearances to the contrary are caused by maya, which obscures the soul's true nature in the illusory flux of being and becoming. When the veil of maya is rent, the individual soul realizes its union with the universal soul and ceases to be."

Banaras fruit vendor.

Brahmin stands in front of the shrine commemorating Shri Chaitanya's visit to Banaras.

When Shri Chaitanya began to exhibit His spiritual ecstacies in Banaras, the local monists, headed by Prakasananda, criticized Him and were sorely disappointed by His behavior, especially since Shri Chaitanya had been initiated previously into a Shankarite order. The monists felt Shri Chaitanya was embarrassing their tradition by carrying on with great emotion and fervor. The students of Shri Chaitanya were disheartened by this criticism and implored Shri Chaitanya to do something about it. At that moment a respected brahmin priest arrived and invited Shri Chaitanya to join him and all the leading spiritual personalities of Banaras—including Prakasananda and all the monists—at his home for lunch the following day. Shri Chaitanya smiled and accepted the invitation.

When Shri Chaitanya arrived the next day, His personal beauty and brilliance at once charmed everyone there. He was asked to sit in an honored place and began discussing *Vedanta* with Prakasananda. *Veda* means knowledge and *anta* means the conclusion or end purpose of something. Therefore, *Vedanta* means the conclusion or end of knowledge. All religions teach basic morality, but *Vedanta* deals with the ultimate goal of religion.

By indirect interpretation of *Vedānta*, Shankara had stated that God was impersonal. Shri Chaitanya now presented *Vedanta* on its own terms. "According to *Vedānta* philosophy, the Absolute Truth is a person . . . who has all spiritual opulences. No one can be equal to or greater than Him." Now, to a Vaiṣṇava, God being a person does not mean God is a human person. Vaiṣṇavas do not believe in an anthropomorphic God—or God made in the image and likeness of humanity. For the Vaiṣṇava, "The Absolute Truth (God) is that from which everything is emanating." If consciousness, intelligence, personhood, and personality emanate out of the Absolute Truth, then the Absolute Truth must contain these qualities in fullness. Something cannot come out of a source unless that source contains that "something" in its nature. People exist, therefore their source must be the reservoir of all personhood. People are made in the image and likeness of this source, not the other way around. Also, this personhood of God is called by the Vaiṣṇavas *Vasudeva,* which means all-pervading. Certainly, an all-pervading personality of God cannot be equated with any anthropomorphic concept. An all-pervading person simply doesn't exist on the human level.

Massive ashram built by the royal patrons of Banaras.

Shri Chaitanya's statements to Prakasananda and the assembled monists were well-received. By using logic, scriptures, and the overwhelming charisma of his personality, Shri Chaitanya opened the minds and hearts of the monists, and they had to agree to the soundness of His propositions. As a skilled teacher, Shri Chaitanya did not ask the monists to have faith or believe in the personal feature of God. Instead, He continued to give them logical and spiritual evidence until they could make their own decision. His next reason was, "The word *brahman* means 'the greatest.' This means that the Supreme Personality of Godhead is full in all six opulences. However, if we take the one-sided impersonalist view, His fullness is diminished."

To the monists, this argument really struck home. Monists like to say that if God has personhood, God must be limited. As just stated previously, Vaiṣṇavas worship God as an all-pervading or unlimited person. God-as-person is only limiting to the concept of God if God is held to be anthropomorphic. However, by saying God is impersonal, the monist actually limits the concept of God. The monist is saying that the entire realm of personhood, personality, and personal expression is off limits to God. To a Vaiṣṇava, this viewpoint is absurd because it denies that God has inconceivable powers and abilities, which can and are expressed on all dimensions of being. For a Vaiṣṇava, God only makes sense when you accept God as having inconceivable and unlimited potencies.

During the 1972 Chaitanya festival, His Divine Grace A.C. Bhaktivedanta Swami Prabhupada was the special guest of honor because of his tremendous success in spreading the doctrines of Vaiṣṇavism and Shri Chaitanya to the West. His Divine Grace rode through the streets of Banaras in a gilded carriage drawn by four white horses. With him were his students from North and South America, Europe, Australia, and other places. These students chanted and danced ecstatically, proving to the local population that Shri Chaitanya's message is universal and has true international appeal. The explosion of love that was and is Shri Chaitanya and that is based on the soul's interpersonal love relationship with God-as-person remains alive and strong in the world today.

Let us review the pitfalls of monism and elaborate a little more on this crucial subject. First of all, as Dr. Jung states, monism provides an unhealthy basis for development of full human potential. On the spiritual level Christians feel that monism deprives a soul of the most important thing in life—a loving interpersonal relationship with God. Vaiṣṇavas certainly agree with this critique, although some Christians mistakenly assume that Vaiṣṇavas share the impersonalist views of many other Eastern religions and philosophies. In actuality, Vaiṣṇavism has developed the strongest and most sophisticated exegesis of God as a transcendental person. Because Christian theology did not create as developed a presentation of God-as-person, many Westerners rejected the idea of a personal God altogether, accusing Christianity of being anthropomorphic. Serious Christians could acquire real benefit by deeply studying Vaiṣṇava theology regarding God-as-person and assimilating it into contemporary Christianity. Such a move could only deepen and strengthen Christian faith in the common Divine Father of us all.

Pilgrims worship together.

Shri Mandir, the central temple of Jagannath Puri.

CHAPTER 4: JAGANNATH PURI

The British visited Jagannath Puri very early in their stay in India, and they received some of their first impressions of the sacred Vedic culture here. Without the benefit of any preliminary briefing or education in Vedic culture, the British were at a decided disadvantage in understanding what was going on. Quite frankly, they probably experienced a severe culture shock. India can be very overwhelming to newcomers. The *Area Handbook for India* explains that even today, these difficulties exist:

> The result of the spiritual and intellectual efforts of hundreds of millions of people over a period of millennia, this religious tradition is undoubtedly more subtle, complex, and various than that of the West. Attempts by foreigners to perceive it across the chasm of their differing assumptions are generally doomed to superficiality at best, for Indian religious thought has explored in detail areas of experience that most Western religions bypass.

When you add a large dose of racial and cultural prejudice, along with potent feelings of superiority, to the above-mentioned cultural gap, it is inevitable that the British would bring back to the Western world a highly distorted view of Vedic religion and culture. Many of the misconceptions brought to the West by the first Europeans to visit and colonize India still cloud Westerners' comprehension of Vedic religion.

A panoramic sweep of the Ratha Yatra Festival.

Devotees ready themselves for the Ratha Yatra Festival.

Many other open-minded experts have come to the same understanding. Edwyn Bevan observes:

> It is hardly possible that anyone thought of the deity worshipped as simply the image he saw and nothing more. The personality of the deity was not confined to the image in the sense in which my personality is confined to my body. The deity was certainly conceived of as a person active in the world apart from the image.

In 1929 Ernest Wood wrote an excellent book, *An Englishman Defends Mother India,* which tried to clarify misconceptions created by his fellow people. On the issue of idolatry, he said:

> Surely the very term "idols" is now out of date! We do not speak of people of other religions in these days as "idolators." We know quite well that they do not worship graven images, that the statuettes and pictures which they use are but instruments and materials of worship, representations of invisible beings and intelligences or of great religious ideas.

Sad to say, fifty-six years after this enlightened book was written, a well-respected fundamental Christian television evangelist, who is very sensible and sophisticated on many other issues, made a public show of destroying a significant quantity of non-Christian religious objects on the grounds they were "graven images."

Underlying this ethnocentric mentality is the belief that God and nature are almost somehow unrelated. Jesus said, "The Kingdom of God is within you." He praised the lilies in the fields and the birds in the air, pointing out how God loved and provided for them effortlessly. But, as the *Encyclopedia of World Religions* reports:

> This is an aspect of Christianity which since the Reformation has been by and large allowed to lapse. More and more emphasis has been put upon the god 'out there' or 'up there,' the God of judgement and justice. Protestant Christianity (apart from the Quakers and similar dissident sects) has tended to separate God from man, and so in the long run it has made God irrelevant to man.

A leading Protestant theologian of the twentieth century, Paul Tillich, decries this tendency too, going so far as to say, "Protestant protest has . . . brought to the verge of disappearance the sacramental foundation of Christianity and with it the religious foundation of the protest itself." Roszak and others feel that Western people's ravaging of the environment is partially explained by this banishment of God from nature. Lynn White observes that this belief has allowed Westerners "to exploit nature in a mood of indifference to the feelings of natural objects." Roszak adds:

> But what becomes of a world purged of its sacramental capacities? It dies the death of the spirit. . . . For most, the desacralized world is doomed to become an obstacle inviting conquest, a mere object. Like the animal or the slave who is understood to have no soul, it becomes a thing of subhuman status to be worked, used up, exploited.

From this analysis, it is easy to see that putting God away in an intangible realm can have serious consequences for the well-being of the physical world. As Roszak rightly points out, this attitude reduces a people's sensitivity to nature. On the individual level, this deadened sensitivity can lead to the adoption of unnatural life-style habits, including poor diet, overly sedentary patterns, and a pessimistic mental outlook. These individual deficiencies inevitably lead to social problems, including the health-care crisis, crime, and polluting industrial practices.

We have physical bodies that need to be nurtured by the pure energies of Mother Nature. Any plan for the advancement of humanity must give a prominent place to the science of ecology and a harmonious interaction between humanity and nature. Religious or philosophical attitudes that label the world as unsacred, illusory, or separate from the divine are counterproductive to this vital effort.

Lord Jagannath, the "King of the Universe," is carried by His servitors onto His huge chariot.

Even today, this feeling of God-centeredness is powerfully alive. There is a paved highway stretching the thirty-five miles from the capital of Orissa, Bhubaneswar, to Jagannath Puri. When Bart McDowell rode down this highway in 1970, researching an article on Orissa for *National Geographic* magazine, he noticed an elderly farmer praying in his rice field. McDowell's guide told him that the people of the area were devoutly religious, and "Many country people, when they approach this highway, fall down and kiss the pavement—simply because it leads to the Temple of the Lord Jagannath."

As the *Area Handbook for India* reports, "Religion is the ground for Indian life and culture as it has not been in the West since the great age of faith in the Middle Ages." Long before the great cathedrals of Europe were built to serve a similar purpose as the temple of Jagannath, India had a flourishing spiritual culture. And that humble farmer praying in his rice field, as well as many savants of India, know, "Touch him on spirituality, on religion, on God, on the Soul, on the infinite, on spiritual freedom, and I assure you, the humblest villagers in India are better informed on these subjects than many a so-called philosopher in other lands." Spiritual devotion permeates the life of Jagannath Puri and India like nowhere else in the world.

Surrounded by His devotees and seated on His chariot, Lord Jagannath smiles upon the universe.

An artisan carves a Deity of Lord Jagannath.

Jagannath is also described as being a Deity who is easily approachable. Many people fear God or divine retribution or are awestruck by the infinite magnitude and multidimensionality of God. The Jagannath Deity is purposefully simple and childlike to invite the soul to discard fear and awe in the face of God. God is a very intimate and loving being. The science of exchanging love between the individual soul and God is the essence of Vaiṣṇavism and is called *bhakti-yoga*—or yoking (*yoga*) the individual soul to God—Krishna—Jagannath—through unconditional love and devotion (*bhakti*).

While class discrimination has raised its ugly head at some temples in India, Jagannath has always been very merciful. All classes were allowed to serve Him during the cart festivals. Therefore, the spiritual power of Jagannath is said to be especially potent. In a phrase, Jagannath charms the heart. His simplicity, joy, and friendliness beckon the soul on to a more intimate relationship with God.

Jagannath has inspired beautiful, devotional poetry. The following traditional verses in praise of Jagannath show the esteem and love the Vaiṣṇavas have for Him:

1) Sometimes in great happiness Lord Jagannāth, with His flute, makes a loud concert in the groves on the banks of the Yamunā. He is like a bumblebee who tastes the beautiful lotuslike faces of the cowherd damsels of Vraja, and His lotus feet are worshiped by great personalities such as Lakṣmī, Śiva, Brahmā, Indra, and Ganesh. May that Jagannāth Swāmī be the object of my vision.

2) In His left hand Lord Jagannāth holds a flute. On His head He wears the feathers of peacocks and on His hips He wears fine yellow silken cloth. Out of the corners of His eyes He bestows sidelong glances upon His loving devotees and He always reveals Himself through His pastimes in His divine abode of Vrindāvan. May that Jagannāth Swāmī be the object of my vision.

3) Lord Jagannāth is an ocean of mercy and He is beautiful like a row of blackish rain clouds. He is the storehouse of bliss for Lakṣmī and Saraswatī and His face is like a spotless full-blown lotus. He is worshipped by the best of demigods and sages, and His glories are sung by the *Upaniṣads*. May that Jagannāth Swāmī be the object of my vision.

4) When Lord Jagannath is on His Ratha-yātra cart and is moving along the road, at every step there is a loud presentation of prayers and songs chanted by large assemblies of *brāhmaṇas*. Hearing their hymns, Lord Jagannāth is very favorably disposed towards them. He is the ocean of mercy and the true friend of all the worlds. May that Jagannāth Swāmī be the object of my vision.

Artisans paint Deities of Lord Jagannath to sell to pilgrims.

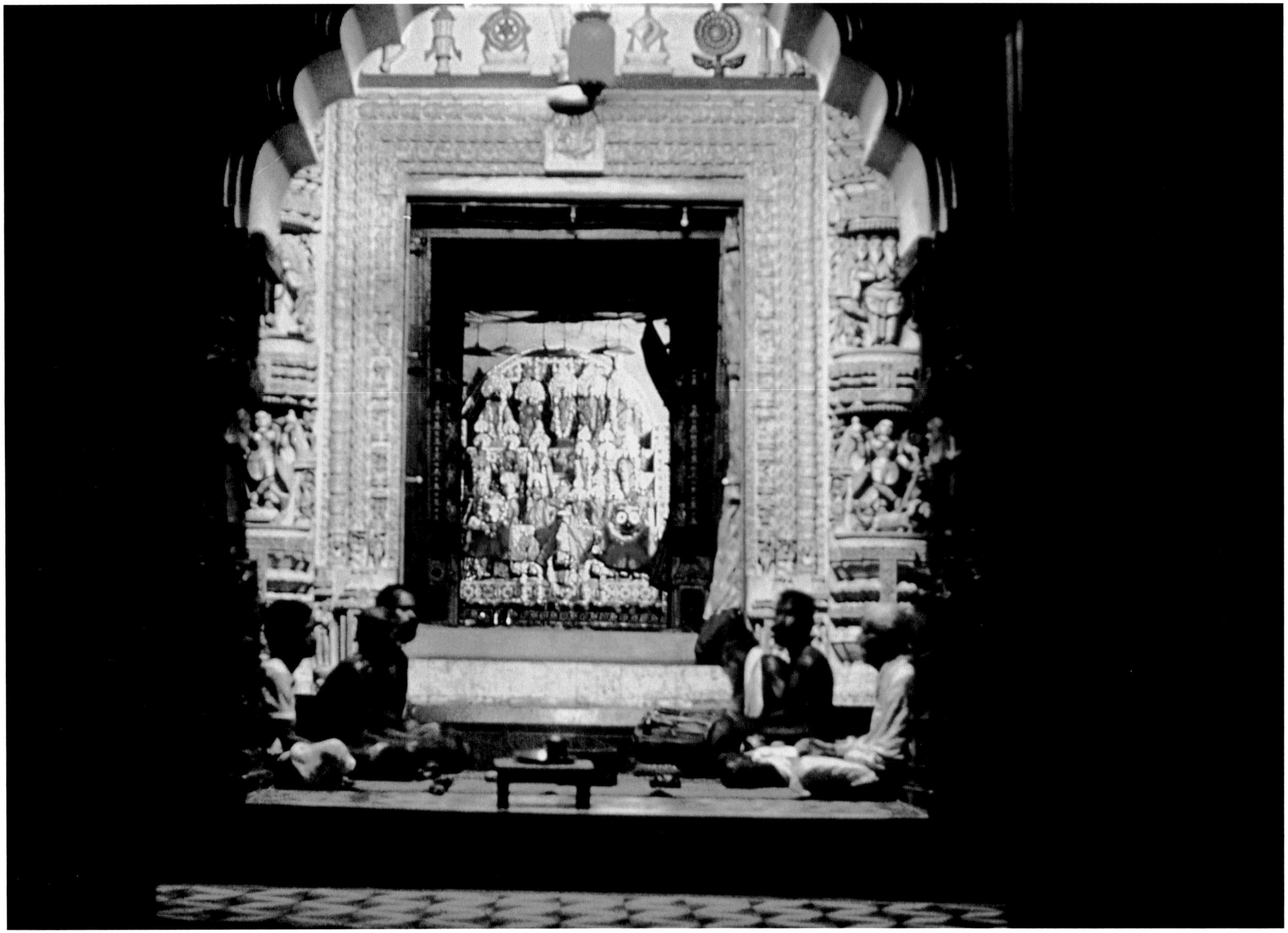

One street away from Shri Mandir, devotees publicly chant (kirtan) in front of an exquisite, little Jagannath shrine, a kind of vest-pocket temple popular all over India.

If a person believes or experiences God to be real, then it must be accepted that God is fully present everywhere. This is the unmistakable conclusion of Vedic religion, which Thomas Troward has ably translated into more contemporary language and terms. Therefore, God is fully present in a Deity as God is fully present in everything else. What the physical eye can see in a Deity is only its surface reality. Modern science tells us that one atom of stone or metal contains a vast universe of particles in it, which our unaided eyes could never hope to see or comprehend. The Vaiṣṇava tells us that besides a material universe being present in each atom, a spiritual dimension exists as well. Therefore, a Deity is not just a "symbol" or "reminder" of God. When authentically perceived with spiritual vision, the Deity gives the worshiper a direct experience of the omnipresent Godhead. To see the Deity as a symbol would actually weaken the chances of spiritual success and in a way denies God's omnipresence.

Psychologists, who use and teach the science of visualization to aid people in integrating their lives and achieving their goals, use the same principle. Whatever is visualized must be perceived as a living, concrete reality for the visualization to have the greatest effect. However, the Vaiṣṇava does not mentally project a divine life into the Deity. The Vaiṣṇava perceives the divine life that already exists in the Deity and everything else. Ordinarily, because of our conditioned state of awareness, we are not seeing God everywhere. Our spiritual awareness is weak, and the power of material nature often distracts us and makes us forget. Therefore, we must start somewhere in time and space to regain this inherent consciousness of God, which is beyond time and space. Vaiṣṇavas use Deity worship as one of their principal starting points for regaining, reinforcing, and evolving their consciousness of God.

Theodore Roszak describes Deity worship as "a window, both seen and seen through . . . where perception and revelation mingle and are married." His Divine Grace A. C. Bhaktivedanta Swami Prabhupada also describes Deities and spiritual pictures as "windows" to spiritual awareness. Actually, when Deities are worshiped according to the instructions of Vedic literature, the devotees on a daily basis often have the most profound, enjoyable, and enlightening experiences, which they then strive to integrate into their daily lives. To them, Deity worship is an indispensable spiritual food that nourishes their soul. That is why Vaiṣṇava teachers recommend starting each day with Deity worship and other spiritual exercises. Then, the devotees' chances of seeing God in the rest of the day's activities are greatly enhanced.

Deity worship has passed the test of time. For thousands and thousands of years it has been used effectively to produce the highest states of spiritual realization and ecstasy. In 1975 the president of the American Psychological Association, Dr. Donald Campbell, shocked his colleagues by defending the scientific validity of many of traditional religions' practices and attitudes. In an earlier address entitled "Scientific Reasons for Not Trusting Psychology When It Conflicts with Religious Tradition," Dr. Campbell said, "Products of tradition deserve a kind of quasi-scientific respect as the product of the test of long standing usage." Appealing to the scientific method of trial and error, Dr. Campbell went on to say:

> There are aspects of our religious tradition which guide the lives of individuals and families and which have thus been tested out in application for generations. These ways may be regarded as the winnowed-out wheat from a large chaff of other ways of living life. The resultant recipes for life might well be regarded on scientific grounds as better tested, better confirmed, than are those speculations of psychologists which have not been tried out either in true experimentation or in even two generations of practical living.

Boys play the roles of Shri Chaitanya and His associates, who ecstatically chanted and danced through several decades of Ratha Yatra Festivals five hundred years ago.

Time magazine was sufficiently impressed by Dr. Campbell's arguments to report them under the headline "Morals Make a Comeback," while in the same month, *Psychology Today* ran an in-depth interview with Dr. Campbell. Along these same lines, one purpose of Deity worship is to help human beings transcend their selfish, self-serving ego and to learn how to work for the good of the whole, which is embodied in the Deity. In his *Psychology Today* interview, Dr. Campbell applauded this kind of orientation to life, as well as severely criticizing those intellectuals who make pleasure seeking the number-one priority. Dr. Campbell said:

> People have been getting a false message for the last 100 years—namely, that physical bliss is obtainable, and that you are cheating yourself if you don't have it. We social scientists have been generating unhappiness with this unscientific, optimistic talk about happiness. We should join Buddha and St. Francis of Assisi and warn people that the direct pursuit of happiness is a recipe for an unhappy life. Perhaps we should teach that the first value is duty, not pleasure.

Giving greatest emphasis to performing your duty is, of course, one of the main themes of the *Bhagavad-gita* and is also an attitude that is awakened by proper Deity worship. The Vaiṣṇavas also maintain that genuine and deeply satisfying pleasure is an automatic by-product of performing one's duty in a state of God consciousness. However, Vaiṣṇavas also say that when duty is not linked to *bhakti* or personal devotion to God, duty becomes a dry, lifeless drudgery, which is easily abandoned to pursue the sensual pleasures that freely abound in the modern world. When duty is connected to *bhakti,* though, doing one's duty becomes an act of love that is joyfully performed. Even the most simple labor becomes a spiritually-surcharged act of love.

Shri Chaitanya spent most of the second half of his life residing in Jagannath Puri, and every year, right before the famous Jagannath cart festival, which we shall presently learn more about, Shri Chaitanya gave a magnificent demonstration of how *bhakti* transforms labor into acts of love and joy. At the start of the Jagannath cart festival, the Deities of Jagannath, Balarama, and Subhadra are taken in gigantic carts from Shri Mandir to the Gundica temple, more than a mile away. Before the festival began, Shri Chaitanya gathered hundreds of His followers at Gundica temple so they could thoroughly clean it and make it ready for the Deities' arrival. The story of the cleansing of the Gundica temple is told delightfully in the *Caitanya-caritamrta,* the biography of Shri Chaitanya written by Krishna dasa Kaviraja. By following Shri Chaitanya's example, the Vaiṣṇavas turned the cleansing of the temple into a festival itself.

Krishna dasa Kaviraja writes, "Śrī Cāitanya Mahāprabhu washed and cleansed the temple in great jubilation, chanting the holy name of Lord Kṛṣṇa all the time. Similarly, all the devotees were also chanting and at the same time performing their respective duties." Everyone was sweeping, mopping, scrubbing, and polishing walls, floors, ceilings, and altars. Yet, because Shri Chaitanya showed His followers how to work in the spirit of devotion, they were experiencing a spiritual bliss from their chores equal to any form of meditation or religious exercise.

In his monumental work, *Ways and Power of Love*, Pitirim A. Sorokin explains in detail how religious exercises and paraphernalia are among the most powerful devices known on earth to cultivate a sense of love and duty. Sorokin writes:

> When carefully studied and fully understood, the ritual and sacramental techniques of the great religions turn out to be among the most scientific and effective techniques for spiritual and moral transformation.

Their effectiveness, according to Sorokin, lies in their ability to go beyond "intellectual ideas and proofs" and to secure for an individual "the mediation and cooperation of emotional and affective factors."

Some people find the Vedic religion to be very baffling and overwhelming because of the incredible richness and complexity of its religious architecture, imagery, ceremonies, philosophy, and scriptures. Some people yearn for a simpler, more austere expression of spirituality, which is often found in many Protestant churches. However, there is a danger here. Sorokin points out that rich spiritual expression serves an indispensable need. Human beings are not simply intellectual creatures. For religion to be effective, all the senses, feelings, and the unconscious factors—all of the person—must be involved in the spiritual process, or else a person's spiritual sensibilities begin to wither away and atrophy. Spiritual preachings, then, become lifeless words that go in one ear and out the other.

Sorokin gives an excellent explanation of how emotional and affective factors make spirituality real. He writes:

> Being aroused, these factors awaken the forces of the unconscious and, guided by the altruistic ideas and precepts, they help to draft the power of the unconscious instincts, reflexes, and drives for service to moral values and ideals. Under this condition, the otherwise "cold" ideas of intellect become supplied with strong driving power. They begin to influence our mind, body, and behavior. Preaching now begins to be practiced; the enormous discrepancy between noble precepts and ignoble deeds narrows and sometimes vanishes. Persons and groups become now altruistic not only "ideologically" but also behavioristically. Herein lies the enormous importance of affective and emotional support of our ideas, precepts, commandments, and ideals.

Deity worship strongly incorporates all of the above-mentioned advantages of affective spirituality. The all-pervading, infinite Godhead has gracefully incarnated in Deity-form in the neighborhood temple or family shrine. Spiritual thoughts and emotions have a concrete focus, and, amazingly enough, the Deity reciprocates. As said before, Vaiṣṇavas are very reluctant to speak of their mystical experiences, but the vast majority of Vaiṣṇavas have seen and heard God communicate to them frequently through Deities. God is all-powerful and can choose any medium through which to communicate with His devotees. For the Vaiṣṇavas, the reality of this communication is unmistakable and accounts for the vitality and widespread practice of Deity worship throughout India and wherever devotees live in the world.

Two lions guard a temple entrance at King Indradyumna's Bathing Ghat.

The next quote from Sorokin illustrates even more devices of religion, all of which are also found in the Vedic way, and which help to make spirituality a potent, living experience:

> Important also in religious techniques are various physical, biological, and psychosocial stimuli used: they effectively change our bodily conditions and psycho-physiological processes. Use of . . . ritual fastings and feasts; specific postures of prostration, sitting, standing, or immobility; specific motions of crossing, raising hands, head-bending, or genuflection; religious dances . . . extensive use of the most moving music—and the great religious music is among the greatest music of humanity; similar utilization of poetical, beautiful, and dramatic language—and the great religious poetry and literature such as the Bible, the Koran, the Vedas, the Bhagavad gita, the Mahabharata, are among the greatest literary masterpieces of mankind; a vast array of stimuli of color and forms, of touch and sight, of smell and of other sense organs: all these contribute their share to the mobilization of the bio-emotional forces for the service of religious and moral values.

It's interesting to note that when Sorokin, who had an encyclopedic knowledge of world culture, mentions religious literature in the above quote, he chose to list three works from the Vedic tradition—the *Vedas* themselves, the *Bhagavad-gita,* and the *Mahabharata*. Also, Vedic religion has a storehouse of ways to use all of the above-cited techniques. This usage helps to explain why religion and God in India are more of a living experience for the general population than in the West. These techniques bring God and humanity into intimate communion, and people interested in a spiritual revival in the West or who are just interested in their own spiritual evolution could profit immensely by investigating these techniques with the guidance of a sincere and honest guru.

Jagannath Puri is known as a city of festivals. Sixty-two major festivals are held in Puri throughout the year. The most important one is the Jagannath Cart Festival or *Ratha-Yatra*. Well over two million people flock to Jagannath Puri each year to celebrate the Cart Festival. During the festival, the Deities are brought out of the temple and are placed on mammoth carts, one for each of the Deities. Jagannath's cart is 50 feet long and 30 feet wide. It is propelled by 16 wheels, which measure 7 feet in diameter. Baladeva and Subhadra's carts are also large, but somewhat smaller than Jagannath's cart. To give you some idea of the size and strength of these carts, over 2000 priests climb aboard them to serve the Deities during the ensuing parade.

The carts are pulled slowly by huge ropes manned by thousands of loving and enthusiastic devotees. Millions follow in the wake of the carts, chanting loudly, "Jai Jagannath! All glories to the Lord of the Universe!" The summer's heat does not wilt the crowd's ardor. Smiles are seen everywhere, as God mercifully comes out to give the divine *darshan,* or audience, to everyone, irrespective of caste, creed, or color. God, or Jagannath, is ever-willing to move toward the devotees to invite them into the most intimate pastimes of the divine. Jagannath wants all people to be happy and to celebrate the glories of spiritual life and kinship. The idea of God coming out or incarnating in the world to revive the spiritual consciousness of all beings fills the crowd with great joy and rejoicing.

A devotee offers prayers to Lord Jagannath.

The *Vedas* report that there are 8,400,000 different kinds of bodies in the physical universe, and again, only the human body gives the soul the opportunity to transcend birth, death, old age, and disease—the four miseries of material life. When freed from the material universe, the soul goes to live in a spiritual universe, which has even more variety than the material universe and is completely composed of eternal beings who are in perfect harmony with each other and the Supreme Being. Everyone is advised, then, to take the human form of life quite seriously, for it affords the soul its only chance to revive fully its original nature and potencies, which allows the soul to leave its temporary quarters in the physical universe to return home, back to Godhead.

Coming back down to earth, twentieth-century science has proven conclusively that plants and animals possess consciousness. In his insightful book *The Inner Lives of Minerals, Plants, and Animals*, Manly P. Hall, the founder of the Philosophical Research Society, reports,

> Minerals, plants, and animals have a wider area of mental and emotional activity than is generally recognized. In the mineral kingdom only traces can be found of human personality traits, but among plants and animals they are numerous.

A person only has to interact with the family dog to learn that animals have feelings and reactions akin to human ones.

A Vaiṣṇava priest draws water from a well.

The invention of sensitive scientific instruments has allowed scientists to record many conscious responses in plant life. Fittingly enough, the great pioneer of this research was an Indian physicist and plant physiologist, Sir Jagadish Chandra Bose (1858-1937), who hailed from the state of Bengal. His research showed that when threatened by injury, plants make subtle but detectable movements to avoid danger. When plants are trimmed and pruned, palpable reactions occur. To pluck a blossom from a plant produces a painfullike reaction. In commenting on Bose's research, Manly P. Hall writes, "Each plant has a will of its own and an instinctive impulse to survive." Bose even measured a death trauma similar to that of an animal in a plant.

Upon concluding his research, Bose wrote, "In surveying the responses of living tissue, we find that there is hardly any phenomena of irritability observed in the animal which is not also found in the plant." Western naturalists, botanists, and horticulturists have confirmed Bose's findings during independent research.

Without the benefit of Bose's scientific instruments, the English poet William Wordsworth (1770-1850) came to the same conclusions. In the following lines he beautifully captures the aliveness of all nature:

> To every natural form, rock, fruit, or flower,
> Even the loose stones that cover the highway,
> I gave a moral life: I saw them feel,
> . . . and all
> That I beheld respired with inward meaning.

Plants evidently respond to prayer and meditation as well. Reverend Franklin Loehr's 1959 book, *The Power of Prayer on Plants*, gave many indications that these spiritual exercises stimulated faster growth and better health in plants.

From the Vedic point of view, nothing can have life unless the divine is present to generate the life-force. That is why consciousness is said to be the principal sign of a divine soul existing within a living body, be it plant, animal, or human. Royal Dixon argues for the spirituality of plants in his book *The Human Side of Plants*. Dixon states:

> Spirituality is a condition of responsiveness to and membership in the universal spirit, the spirit of the Creator, the Infinite Substance, God.
>
> The assertion that plants have spirituality, have souls, has been held up to ridicule wherever and whenever made. Nevertheless many scientists of great reputation and ability, realizing that "the best part of our universe is hidden from the unassisted sight, and that the 'music of the spheres' altogether unheard by the ordinary ear," have given to the idea of plant spirituality more than a passing glance, with absolute conversion, in frequent cases, to the affirmative side of the question.

Since plants and animals have consciousness, contends Manly P. Hall, and therefore souls, the soul within them must be as eternal as yours or mine and survives the death of the body. Mr. Hall explains it this way:

> To those who assume that life, consciousness, and reality are all synonymous terms, there can be no death without compromising the existence of God. Many philosophically-minded people have come to the conclusion that there is no death. If this is true, it applies not only to man but to any creature that is capable of being destroyed physically. For if life is one, eternal and inevitable, then physical destruction can only occur on a level of phenomena.

Here Manly P. Hall is echoing the first lesson taught by Shri Krishna in the *Bhagavad-gita* and covered in Chapter 2 of this book: "For the soul there is neither birth nor death at any time. . . . The soul is not slain when the body is slain." From the Vedic standpoint, Mr. Hall correctly applies this principle to the essence of all life forms, not just human.

The Bada-deula, or Deity Hall, of Shri Mandir. At 215 feet in height, it is the tallest temple in the state of Orissa.

The fact that all living beings have souls makes all creatures equal members of the great family of God. Royal Dixon gives us an eloquent statement of this view:

> The spirituality of the man and the spirituality of the plant being of one source and one existence, ineffably link together the two natures into the one great chain of life, offering to each a sympathetic perception of the other, joining both in the eternal kinship of Universal Nature.

In the Christian tradition, St. Francis of Assisi naturally felt this kinship. One medieval Christian thinker wrote that St. Francis "was accustomed to call all living creatures his brothers and sisters, and it is reported that when he walked in the woods or fields, various animals were drawn to him as if by instinct."

Highly advanced spiritual people are gifted with this ability to feel a oneness of essence with all living beings, because they see beyond the body to catch the core of being that is within each creature—its eternal, immortal soul. Because they are not prejudiced in favor of their particular species of life, who have an exclusive monopoly on eternity as the chosen life form of God, their consciousness expands to embrace all of God's existence, and they enjoy the incredible ecstasies of divine, universal love. Seeing the spark of God—the soul—in the heart of every living creature has its reward. The pleasure derived from such a perception dwarfs any physical pleasure conceivable by the human mind. It is love infinitely multiplied.

Regarding the more cosmological reasons for ahimsa, His Divine Grace A. C. Bhaktivedanta Swami Prabhupada explains,

> The animals are also making progress in their evolutionary life by transmigrating from one category of animal life to another. If a particular animal is killed, then his progress is checked. He has to come back again in that form of life to complete the remaining days in order to be promoted to another species of life. So their progress should not be checked simply to satisfy one's palate. This is called *ahimsa*.

Advanced social thinkers have also valued the contribution that the concept of ahimsa can make to solving the world's economic, environmental, and political struggles. In their book *Toward a Human World Order* Gerald and Patricia Mische expand on this application.

> Similarly, the Hindu concept of "ahimsa" provides inspiration toward a global environmental ethic. Ahimsa, which means "non-harming", and "respect for life," values the sacred and the divine in all life forms. Other life forms are valued not for how they can be used, but in their *own right*. The human ethic that flows from that is one of respect and active non-violence in *all,* including environmental relationships. In accordance with the principle of ahimsa, consumption is limited to that which is essential for sustenance. Ahimsa is an important concept not only in the development of a personal ecological ethic, but also as a philosophic foundation for the development of global structures that reinforce respect for, rather than violation of, the delicate balance and relatedness of all life forms.

In the modern world many people bemoan humanity's increasing alienation from nature and natural ways of living. We are paying a heavy price for this alienation in the form of global pollution of land, air, and water; heart disease, cancer, and other degenerative disorders; and constant political tensions, skirmishes, and wars—any one of which may end up in nuclear holocaust. The peoples of the world desperately need to get back into step with Mother Nature. To the Vaiṣṇava, two keys for reaching this rapprochement are perceiving the omnipresence of God in nature and ahimsa.

In *Where the Wasteland Ends,* Theodore Roszak asks, "Why, one wonders, should it be thought crude or rudimentary to find divinity brightly present in the world where others find only dead matter or an inferior order of being?" The Vedic way has always held that perceiving God in nature is an absolutely essential element of spiritual consciousness. Contemporary Vaiṣṇavas heartily agree with Dr. Roszak when he suggests "that its resurrection is an urgent project of the times."

Jai Jagannath, the Lord of the Universe and all of His plants, animals, humans, devas, and other life forms—each of whom possesses and is animated by an individual, eternal soul!

Lord Krishna's Temple at Dwaraka.

CHAPTER 5: DWARAKA

Close-up of temple's intricate detail.

It is time to leave the east coast of India and traverse the subcontinent until we reach the western extreme of India and the holy city of Dwaraka. Dwaraka is far off the beaten path of the average tourist and even modern development. Consequently, Dwaraka retains an ancient purity and vibrancy.

Like Jagannath Puri, Dwaraka is an excellent summer resort. The maximum temperature at Dwaraka is 86 degrees, while the minimum is 78 degrees. Cool breezes blowing in from the Arabian Sea delight Dwaraka's residents and help to create an optimal living environment, an ideal location for Shri Krishna to have built His capital city around the year 3000 BC.

There are many scriptural records of Shri Krishna's extraordinary capital. The book *Immortal India* states, "Dwaraka is described in *Mahabharata*, *Harivamsa*, *Vayu*, *Vishnu*, *Bhagavat*, *Varaha*, *Skanda*, and other puranas. *Skanda* has forty-four chapters devoted to it." From these sources we learn that Dwaraka was perhaps the most amazing city ever constructed on earth.

When Shri Krishna was sixteen years old in the Supreme Personality of Godhead's manifest pastimes on earth, He overthrew and killed His uncle, Kamsa. Kamsa was an evil tyrant who threw his own father in jail to gain the throne and ruthlessly killed his sister's children because a heavenly voice prophesied that her eighth child would slay Kamsa. To take no chances, Kamsa resolved to kill *all* her children.

Kamsa's sister's eighth child was Shri Krishna. Surviving numerous attempts to assassinate Him and hearing of Kamsa's repeated persecutions of innocent and religious people, Shri Krishna went to the capital city of Mathura and fulfilled the prophecy.

When God personally kills someone, however, something wonderful happens. The slain person is touched directly by God, and that touch, no matter what form it takes, gives the soul a kind of spiritual liberation. Therefore, Kamsa's soul was freed, but his allies on earth were outraged by Shri Krishna's regicide.

King Jarasandha was Kamsa's main supporter and, immediately upon hearing of Kamsa's death, he gathered a formidable army and marched on Mathura to punish Shri Krishna. Of course, no one can defeat God, but Jarasandha tried and failed seventeen times. This wasteful expense of human lives and money was symptomatic of India at that time. The people were ruled largely by warlord-mentality kings, who overburdened the country by maintaining excessive military establishments. One purpose of Shri Krishna's appearance then was to relieve the earth of these martial dictators, starting with Kamsa and Jarasandha.

While Jarasandha was organizing forces for an eighteenth expedition, Shri Krishna's family, the Yadus, were now threatened by a powerful new king, Kalayavana. *Immortal India* reports that because the Yadus "were practically besieged on all sides, Krishna decided to come down and construct a strong fort near the sea in Saurashtra and so settled in Dwaraka."

When God the Father personally appears on earth, He brings with Him the full opulence and power of the spiritual world to attract souls to return there. Dwaraka was Shri Krishna's greatest manifestation of divine opulence during His incarnation. In his masterful summary study of the Tenth Canto of the *Bhagavata Purana*, or *Srimad Bhagavatam*, which chronicles Shri Krishna's life, His Divine Grace A. C. Bhaktivedanta Swami Prabhupada states that Shri Krishna

> first of all constructed a very stong wall covering ninety-six square miles, and the wall itself was within the sea. It was certainly wonderful and was planned and constructed by Viśvakarmā. No ordinary architect could construct such a fort within the sea, but an architect like Viśvakarmā, who is considered to be the engineer among the demigods, can execute such wonderful craftsmanship in any part of the universe.

Many ancient structures, like the pyramids of Egypt and South America, defy our sense of the possible for ancient peoples, while structures contained in Babylon have never been duplicated since the fall of that most amazing city-state. The modern dikes of Holland show us that reclaiming land from the sea and keeping back the mighty ocean are feasible. His Divine Grace explains that Shri Krishna's purpose was to build a fort "in a place where no two-legged animal, either man or demon, could enter." After completing the city, Shri Krishna moved the people of Mathura to Dwaraka, and then felt free to deal with all the warlords.

Dwara means "doorway" and *ka* means "eternal happiness." Therefore, Dwaraka is the place where you go to acquire the happiness of eternal life. The *Srimad Bhagavatam* explains the supereminent position of Dwaraka:

> Undoubtedly it is wonderful that Dvārakā has defeated the glories of the heavenly planets [the higher planets of the physical universe—not the supreme spiritual dimension] and has enhanced the celebrity of the earth. The inhabitants of Dvārakā are always seeing the soul of all living beings [Krishna] in His loving feature. He glances at them and favors them with sweet smiles.

The above verse not only explains the preeminence of Dwaraka among cities, but also expresses the positivity and intimacy that is characteristic of the relationship between the devotee and God in Vaiṣṇavism. When God is seen directly, God is a loving figure who "glances" at us and favors us "with sweet smiles."

Evidence of the friendly dealings between God, Shri Krishna, and the citizens of Dwaraka is also found in the narration of Shri Krishna's return to Dwaraka after a prolonged absence caused by the events leading up to and culminating in the Kurukshetra War. As Shri Krishna reentered His capital, relieving the anxiety of her citizens, "The Almighty Lord greeted everyone present by bowing His head, exchanging greetings, embracing, shaking hands, looking and smiling, giving assurances, and awarding benedictions, even to the lowest in rank."

Painting of Lord Dwarakadish (Krishna), the principal Deity of Dwaraka. (The actual Deity is not allowed to be photographed.)

Dwaraka's residents reciprocated Shri Krishna's affection with the following prayer:

> O creator of the universe, You are our mother, well-wisher, Lord, father, spiritual master, and worshipable Deity. By following in Your footsteps we have become successful in every respect. We pray, therefore, that You continue to bless us with Your mercy.

This prayer demonstrates several things about the Vaiṣṇava conception of God. God is addressed as "father" and "mother," meaning that the Supreme is a complete whole, who encompasses both the male and female natures in one Godhead. Our relationship with God has many facets and flavors. Also, Shri Krishna is the "worshipable Deity," which means that even while Shri Krishna was personally present on earth, His devotees also carried on Deity worship. His Divine Grace A. C. Bhaktivedanta reports: "The Viṣṇu Deity worshiped by the descendants of Yadu was installed in each house in the city." Deity worship, then, according to the Vaiṣṇava tradition, was personally sanctioned and supervised by God the Father-Mother, when Shri Krishna lived on earth 5,000 years ago.

The intimacy with God and techniques of spiritual expression available to the citizens of Dwaraka are available to all of us today through the cultivation of *bhakti*—spiritual, unconditional love.

One of the finest descriptions of Dwaraka occurs in the Tenth Canto of the *Srimad-Bhagavatam,* when the great sage Narada Muni, intrigued and attracted by stories of Shri Krishna's exemplary activities in Dwaraka, comes to that city to see for himself. When Narada arrives:

> . . . he saw that the gardens and parks were full of various flowers of different colors and that orchards were overloaded with a variety of fruits. Beautiful birds were chirping, and peacocks were delightfully crowing. There were tanks and ponds full of blue and red lotus flowers, and some of these sites were filled with varieties of lilies. The lakes were full of nice swans and cranes whose voices resounded everywhere. In the city there were as many as 900,000 great palaces built of first-class marble with gates and doors made of silver. The posts of the houses and palaces were bedecked with jewels such as touchstone, sapphires, and emeralds, and the floors gave off a beautiful luster. The highways, lanes, streets, crossings, and marketplaces were all beautifully decorated. The whole city was full of residential homes, assembly houses, and temples, all of different architectural beauty. All of this made Dvārakā a glowing city.

A powerful demoniac personality by the name Bhaumasura had stolen this number of nobility's daughters to satisfy his voracious sexual appetite. Shri Krishna fought and killed Bhaumasura, and then these young women pleaded for Shri Krishna to accept them as His wives. Even though these women had been forcefully abducted, in society's eyes of that time they were fallen persons since they had lived in Bhaumasura's house and had been enjoyed by him. While society would reject them, Shri Krishna appreciated their devotion and accepted them wholeheartedly. His Divine Grace A. C. Bhaktivedanta Swami Prabhupada writes, "The all-powerful Lord Kṛṣṇa accepted the humble prayers of these girls and married them with the adoration of queens." Shri Krishna's other eight wives were the most qualified and exalted princesses of India.

Shri Krishna's relationship with His wives shouldn't be compared to a mundane harem. When understood with spiritual vision, Shri Krishna's actions display the all-powerful and all-loving potencies of God. It was mainly to see how Shri Krishna conducted Himself with His wives that drew Narada Muni to Dwaraka. While visiting Shri Krishna's palaces,

> Nārada saw one single Kṛṣṇa living in sixteen thousand palaces by His plenary expansions. Due to His inconceivable energy, He was visible in each and every individual queen's palace. Lord Kṛṣṇa has unlimited power, and Nārada's astonishment was boundless upon observing again and again the demonstration of Lord Kṛṣṇa's internal energy.

While going from palace to palace, Nārada saw Shri Krishna perfectly handle all aspects of life, from domestic duties, like raising children and pleasing His wives, to conducting business, to recreational activities, to politics, and most importantly, to spiritual activities, like group worship and meditation, as well as acts of public service. When Narada finished his tour, Shri Krishna said,

My dear Nārada . . . , you know that I am the supreme instructor and perfect follower of all religious principles, as well as the supreme enforcer of such principles. I am therefore personally executing such religious principles in order to teach the whole world how to act. My dear son, it is my desire that you not be bewildered by such demonstrations of My internal energy.

So, we can see that rather than being an example of how one man exploits many women, Shri Krishna's relationships with His wives were exemplary in every way in an egalitarian manner. God has the power to expand Himself into as many divine forms as necessary to relate intimately to His closest devotees.

People without knowledge of God's potency ask, How can one person marry 16,108 wives and give them each a palace and expand to be personally with each of them? The Vaiṣṇava, however, takes this revelation in stride. After all, reasons a Vaiṣṇava, God is capable of carrying on a full and simultaneous relationship with every living being. God can and does relate every second to infinite numbers of beings. Just to demonstrate this to us earthlings, Shri Krishna kindly married *only* 16,108 of His most intimate associates to display the magnificence of divinity to our earthbound minds. Mundane intelligence is baffled by trying to understand God's manifest activities, but for the lovers of God, these activities stimulate the highest spiritual revelations and delights.

The egalitarian nature of Shri Krishna's relationship with His wives is also highlighted in the following quote from His Divine Grace A.C. Bhaktivedanta Swami Prabhupada's summary study, *Krsna*:

All the 16,108 wives of Lord Kṛṣṇa were princesses, and when each saw that Kṛṣṇa was always present in her respective palace and did not leave home, they considered Kṛṣṇa to be a henpecked husband who was very much attached to them. . . . Although each thought that she was the only wife of Kṛṣṇa and was very, very dear to Him, Lord Kṛṣṇa, since He is Ātmārāma, self-sufficient, was neither dear nor inimical to any one of them; He was equal to all the wives and treated them as a perfect husband just to please them. For Him, there was no need for even a single wife. . . . The queens of Dvārakā were so fortunate that they got Lord Śrī Kṛṣṇa as their husband and personal companion, although He is not approachable by exalted demigods like Brahmā.

This above quote also shows the incredible power of bhakti to control even God Himself. When the infinite, eternal Godhead is loved purely, Shri Krishna manifests an eternal Divine Form to the devotee, which allows the devotee to conduct intimate dealings with God, up to the ultimate standard of conjugal affection. God, the Supreme, self-sufficient Being, permits Himself to be controlled and directed by the love of advanced souls. Material power does not enter into this equation. Brahma, the demigod in charge of the creative mode of material nature, who is the engineer who created this material universe and has fathered all of its life forms, cannot directly approach Shri Krishna. From the material point of view, Brahma is certainly more powerful than the princesses who married Shri Krishna. Yet it was the sincere affection of the princesses, not Brahma's prowess, that opened the door to Shri Krishna's heart and gained for the princesses the priceless gift of bhakti. God is love, and God can only be known by love. The power of love to control God is one of the most intimate and key mysteries of Vaiṣṇavism.

The Chakra-Narayana Temple on the Arabian seashore.

Shri Krishna's personal relationships also illustrate the extreme difference in mood between Vaiṣṇavism and Shankaracharya's monism. Monists are fond of saying, "neti, neti," which means, "God is not this. God is not that." While such an analytical approach is useful in understanding the true nature of God, most monists become fixated by this point and always seem to be seeing how God is not present in the phenomena of the world. The Vaiṣṇavas are more positive and concentrate on seeing God's omnipresence in and behind every phenomenon. A favorite Vaiṣṇava aphorism is, "Not a blade of grass moves without the sanction of God."

Shri Krishna's wives and palaces are examples of the infinite manifestive powers of God. His Divine Grace A.C. Bhaktivedanta Swami Prabhupada writes,

> The Personality of Godhead means one who is full with all power, all energy, all opulences, all beauties, all knowledge, and all renunciation. Therefore, in the palaces of the Lord there was nothing wanting for fulfilling all desires of the Lord. The Lord is unlimited, and therefore His desires are also unlimited, and the supply is also unlimited. Everything being unlimited, it is shortly described here as *sarva-kāmam*, or full with all desirable equipment.

The above quote demonstrates what might be called "the abundance theory of God," as opposed to many other Eastern points of view, including monism and many forms of Buddhism, which might be termed "scarcity theories." For instance, in classical Buddhism, the root cause of all suffering is said to be desire. Vaiṣṇavas would contend that this statement is too broad and throws the baby out with the bathwater. For the Vaiṣṇava, desire out of sychronization with the Divine is the cause of suffering. Furthermore, God has infinite desires and infinite manifestive powers to satisfy these desires. God's desires are not motivated by some lack or scarcity in God's beinghood. That is the nature of material desire. God's desires come out of God's overflowing fullness and abundance and the wish to share that divine completeness with all the parts and parcels of God. When the soul's desires are aligned with God's desires, then the soul begins to enjoy the abundance of God on many dimensions.

Ebbing tides reveal ancient Dwaraka ruins.

The overwhelming weight of religious history is on the side of negation rather than affirmation, in favor of the "scarcity theories" over the "abundance theory." That is why His Divine Grace A.C. Bhaktivedanta Swami Prabhupada calls Shri Krishna's personal relationships on earth

> unique in the history of self-realization. Usually people understand that for self-realization one has to go to the forest or to the mountains and undergo severe austerities and penances. But the *gopīs* and the queens, simply by being attached to Kṛṣṇa in conjugal love and enjoying His company in a so-called life full of luxury and opulence, achieved the highest salvation, which is impossible to be achieved even by great sages and saintly persons.

It is impossible for human beings to duplicate or imitate Shri Krishna's actions on earth. Shri Krishna is God and can satisfy thousands of wives by expanding Himself into thousands of Krishna forms. We cannot even make ourselves into two, what to speak of thousands. But still, we can follow in the footsteps of Shri Krishna at Dwaraka and learn to dedicate everything we own and do to the service of God and humanity. This kind of dedication will secure for us true material and spiritual abundance. Life is not to be negated, but affirmed in the service of God. If you are mature enough to use mansions and great wealth in the unselfish service of God, then it is spiritual for you to possess mansions and wealth. Many people, however, become intoxicated by wealth, even to the point of killing themselves from alcohol, drug, sexual, and other abuse. If a simple life-style is most conducive to your spiritual evolution, be happy with simplicity.

Vaiṣṇavism recognizes that we have significant individual differences in personality and stages of evolutionary development. We must honestly appraise our individual circumstances and dedicate all we have, be it humble, middle class, or upper class, to the service of God. After all, as the story of the imprisoned princesses proves, it is not what you have but the intensity and purity of your devotion that determines your closeness to God.

Jesus taught the same thing in the parable of the pharisee and the tax collector. God was happier with a repentant tax collector than with the upper-class Pharisee, who was proud of his religious practices and set himself above other people. God is one, and humble devotion, be it in Palestine, India, or America, is the sure-fire, infallible attitude of salvation.

Another moral of Shri Krishna's activities in Dwaraka and on earth in general is that spiritual beings do not have to become contaminated by participating in the affairs of this world. The *Srimad Bhagavatam* states, "This is the divinity of the Personality of Godhead: He is not affected by the qualities of material nature, even though He is in contact with them."

Observers of human behavior are well aware of the strong influence a person's environment has on their thinking and actions. In the modern world, media bombardment of our senses and minds makes it hard to find a little peace and quiet, what to speak of self-realization. It is hard to contact and maintain our true selves in the plethora of influences around us. Yet, according to the *Srimad Bhagavatam,* "The devotees who have taken shelter of the Lord do not become influenced by the material qualities." By following in Shri Krishna's footsteps, we become antiseptic to the oceans of negativity and temptation all around us. We flow through life in pure spiritual consciousness. We know and keep to our spiritual centers, not being tossed to and fro by the churning waves of materialism. We know ourselves and are content—another priceless gift.

Sunset at Dwaraka.

The strong emphasis of Vaiṣṇavism on God-as-person and the transcendental, interpersonal relationship between Shri Krishna and individual souls, as well as the wealth of scriptural records describing God's personal relationships, have allowed great Vaiṣṇava scholars and saints to develop these subject matters into an extensive science. As part of this science, the Vaiṣṇavas have delineated five major, direct relationships between God and souls. While Shri Krishna exhibited all five of these relationships in Dwaraka, the overall impression of His life there has made one of these relationships the predominating flavor of Dwaraka. Let us briefly delve into this relationship and the one that precedes it, leaving the last three relationships for the next chapter, Vrindavan, which is the most dominant place for those relationships.

First of all, the Sanskrit word for the relationship, or exchange, between God and the soul is *rasa*. The subject of rasa is thoroughly covered by Shrila Rupa Goswami's book *Bhakti-rasamrta-sindhu*, or *The Nectar of Devotion*. This work surveys all preceding scriptures' contributions to this topic, going back 5,000 years. His Divine Grace A. C. Bhaktivedanta Swami Prabhupada, during his indefatigable efforts to translate Vaiṣṇava classics into English for the benefit of the Western world, also wrote a summary study of *The Nectar of Devotion*. Concerning the word rasa, His Divine Grace reports that it "is understood by different persons differently, because the exact English equivalent is very difficult to find." But, since His Divine Grace's spiritual master translated rasa as "mellow," "we shall follow in his footsteps and also translate the word in that way."

In the Eleventh Chapter of the *Bhagavad-gita,* Shri Krishna shows His friend Arjuna the universal form of God, which demonstrates how God, Shri Krishna, is present in everything. Upon seeing this mind-boggling form, Arjuna, in Basham's words, "falls to the ground in terror, unable to bear the awful splendor of the theophany. (Arjuna's) . . . chief feeling at the revelation of Kṛṣṇa's divinity is one of awe. . . ." In response to this revelation, Arjuna says,

> O great one, greater even than Brahmā, You are the original creator. Why then should they not offer their respectful obeisances unto You? . . . You are the father of this complete cosmic manifestation, of the moving and the nonmoving. You are its worshipable chief, the supreme spiritual master. No one is equal to You, nor can anyone be one with You. How then could there be anyone greater than You within the three worlds, O Lord of immeasurable power? You are the Supreme Lord, to be worshiped by every living being. Thus I fall down to offer You my respectful obeisances and ask Your mercy.

The above verses from the *Bhagavad-gita* catch the overall effect of Shri Krishna's manifest life on earth: it is so amazing, powerful, opulent, and heroic that it naturally inspires a devotee to the dasya-rasa, or the master-servant relationship. Even one of Shri Krishna's most intimate friends, Arjuna, when made aware of Shri Krishna's real position as the all-pervading Godhead, slipped into dasya-rasa and said,

> Thinking of You as my friend, I have rashly addressed You "O Kṛṣṇa," "O Yādava," "O my friend," not knowing Your glories. Please forgive whatever I may have done in madness or in love. . . . O infallible one, please excuse me for all those offenses.

As we shall see later, it is not God's desire for a soul to stay in awe and veneration in relationship to God. But when souls voluntarily enter the physical universe and forget their own divine nature, as well as the nature of God, dasya-rasa is a necessary and appropriate stage of respiritualization. This stage teaches the soul that its eternal relationship to the Supreme is as a part and parcel, who eternally serves the Whole—God.

However, it must be noted that Shri Krishna's personal associates, like Arjuna, have not entered the physical universe like most souls, who voluntarily misused their free will. Souls like Arjuna are always with Shri Krishna and accompany Him during his incarnations to assist God in fulfilling His divine purposes. Therefore, Arjuna might play various roles—even forgetting his true self and the position of Shri Krishna—to allow Shri Krishna perfect opportunities to give perfect teachings on these subjects. Still, in truth, for the Vaiṣṇavas and from the point of view of Shri Krishna, souls like Arjuna are eternally liberated companions of God who never forget.

Dwaraka is the emblem of dasya-rasa since while living there Shri Krishna exhibited Himself as the perfect king and master, whose every action is taken for the welfare and benefit of His subjects. Because Shri Krishna's executive rule had none of the imperfections and abuses associated with mundane monarchies, the population of Dwaraka always stood ready to serve Shri Krishna unconditionally. This fact is noted in the *Srimad Bhagavatam:*

> My dear Lord, Your personal associates, headed by Uddhava, are always awaiting Your order by standing at the entrance gate of Dvārakā. They are mostly looking on with tears in their eyes, and in enthusiasm of their service, they are not afraid even of the devastating fire generated by Lord Śiva. They are souls simply surrendered unto Your lotus feet.

Shri Krishna's pastimes were manifest at Dwaraka for nearly 100 years. During this time, various warlords attacked the city, but all attempts to conquer Dwaraka failed. Vaiṣṇavas attribute two meanings to this fact; that good always prevails over evil, and no one is equal to or greater than God.

When Shri Krishna was ready to close His manifest pastimes on earth, arrangements were made for all of His eternal associates and His abode to also disappear with Him. After Shri Krishna, His family, and associates completed this task, Dwaraka was consumed by the sea, and a major period of divine revelation in the history of Vaiṣṇavism also came to an end. Some four thousand five hundred years later, it would take another incarnation of Krishna, Shri Chaitanya, to reveal again some of the most intimate truths concerning Shri Krishna's incarnation. But until Shri Chaitanya revived higher knowledge of Shri Krishna, the world had to be content with dasya-rasa.

Dwaraka Temple.

Today, many groups of scholars and researchers in India are working on proving the historical existence of Dwaraka, using archeological evidence. Activity of this kind is more pronounced around Dwaraka than in other ancient cities of India.

The efforts of researchers around Dwaraka have been rewarded. The Archeological Survey of India's branch office in Dwaraka, which conducts excavations, has unearthed many artifacts. Some pieces have been dated by scientists as coming from the time of 3000 BC to 2000 BC. Archeologists generally call these findings evidence of the Harrapan Civilization, which corresponds in time and place to the advent of Shri Krishna. Discoveries thus far have ranged from fragmental bits of lustrous red wares (pottery) to stone pillars and sculptures to complete temple complexes.

Besides land excavations, numerous finds have been made in the sea around Dwaraka. As recently as in February, 1985, the National Institute of Oceanography had identified the ruins of an ancient city underwater a short distance from today's Dwaraka. According to reports, five different locations have been detected under the sea with remains of ancient civilization. All of this evidence is indicative of the presence of Shri Krishna's capital in this vicinity.

Sunrise over the Madana-Mohana Temple.

CHAPTER 6: VRINDAVAN

Madana-Mohana Temple.

We have left the splendor and opulence of Dwaraka and have entered the beautiful forests of Vrindavan. To get to this idyllic setting from Dwaraka, we journeyed inland in a northeasterly direction to the middle of northcentral India, just below Delhi and thirty-four miles from Agra and the Taj Mahal. Mother Nature creates most of the beauty and wealth in Vrindavan, not civilization. Dwaraka is the emblem of civilized beauty, while Vrindavan is the emblem of natural, divine beauty.

The authors must note at this point that describing Vrindavan to people who have never heard of it before or who have not understood its significance is the hardest task any communicator can take. Within Vrindavan and its Vaiṣṇava religious lore is the most esoteric, profound, sweet, and loving revelation of God in the history of religion. Here God is disclosed in an intimate, confidential way, which explores all the expressions of friendship, parental affection, and conjugal love. In fact, these three expressions of love are the next three rasas in the devotee's love relationship with the Mother-Father God and have only been revealed fully in Vrindavan 5,000 years ago when Shri Krishna spent His first fifteen years of manifest pastimes there.

Because of the difficulty in communicating the true import of Shri Krishna's pastimes in Vrindavan to those people unfamiliar with Vaiṣṇava thought and etiquette, practically no genuine information on these subject matters was available in Western languages until very recently. Dr. Norvin Hein of Yale University lived in Vrindavan and nearby Mathura from August 1949 to June 1950, totally immersing himself in the thriving and plentiful religious theater of this area. Dr. Hein also investigated fully the religious doctrines and literature behind the religious theater of Mathura-Vrindavan. From his research Dr. Hein concluded: "Only a meager literature is available in Western languages on the life and teachings of the Braj sects."

Braj is another word denoting the area of Mathura-Vrindavan. Actually, from the material perspective, Vrindavan spans 168 square miles and is called *Vraja Mandala*. Within this expanse is the town of Mathura, which in ancient times was a mighty capital city, and the pastoral village of Vrindavan, as well as a host of other villages, towns, ghats, shrines, temples, and unique natural wonders. Braj, or as it is spelled in ancient Sanskrit, Vraj, means to go. *Vraja* is a place where one goes. And in the context of this region and its close interdependence with cows and bulls, Vraja also means the place where you take cows—a pastureland. *Mandala* means circle, or an intricate design of various expanding and contracting concentric shapes which invokes and acts as a channel for divine energies and revelation. Spiritually, mandala means the creative designing and manifestive power of God. So, together, Vraja Mandala means a spiritual pastureland where God manifests His original nature, pastimes, and abode. For the devotee, Vraja Mandala is also a spiritual pastureland where the devotee feeds on the sacred food of God—unconditional love, or *bhakti*—in its natural and primordial setting. It is said that within the 168 square miles of Vraja Mandala, or Vrindavan, there is an exact replica, or incarnation, of the spiritual world on earth. For this reason, Vrindavan is considered the most sacred place in the world for Vaiṣṇavas.

According to the Vaiṣṇavas, Vrindavan is so potent that any good deed's positive result is amplified 1,000 times when performed there. Conversely, negative deeds performed in Vrindavan get the performer 1,000 times the bad karma. Therefore, Vaiṣṇavas have been advised to make only short pilgrimages to Vrindavan and while there to focus all their energies on pure, devotional activities. Vaiṣṇavas have heeded this advice, making Vrindavan the area most saturated by spiritual activities in the world all year round.

Before beginning our description of Vrindavan, the authors must acknowledge how unqualified we feel to present this subject. We have all visited and appreciated Vrindavan, but how can the infinite and eternal personality of Godhead be committed to paper by human beings? Because the subject matter of Vrindavan is so sensitive, Vaiṣṇavas consider it a great offense to misrepresent Vrindavan or to reveal the secrets of Vrindavan to souls unprepared to receive such revelation or who are just prejudiced and will commit verbal and mental offenses against Vrindavan.

Devotee walks the Parikrama (pilgrim) Trail.

Vaiṣṇavas wish all beings well. To commit an offense against Vrindavan can seriously impede a soul's evolution. Therefore, in order to avoid these kinds of offenses by unwitting people, Vaiṣṇavas have kept traditionally reticent about Vrindavan to outsiders. As Dr. Hein notes, Vaiṣṇavas have been ". . . distrustful of the capacity of outsiders to understand their teachings fully and sympathetically in the printed page." Of course, all of that changed with the advent of His Divine Grace A.C. Bhaktivedanta Swami Prabhupada's teaching mission in the West which at last count had produced over two hundred million pieces of literature in Western languages on Vaiṣṇavism, including substantial, confidential information on Vrindavan. It can be said that His Divine Grace A.C. Bhaktivedanta Swami Prabhupada brought Vaiṣṇavism into the twentieth century era of communications.

It must be emphasized that Vaiṣṇavas at no time desired to keep their religion a secret. Dr. Hein calls Vaiṣṇavas "warmly evangelistic in attitude." However, Dr. Hein also reports that Vaiṣṇavas prefer the personal approach in communicating their religion to others, and "their promotional work tends to be done in face-to-face meeting." In this way, a Vaiṣṇava can tell whether or not a person is receptive to the message and can reveal knowledge of love of God according to the listener's capacity and receptivity.

The first major Vaiṣṇava teacher to advocate and use modern means of communication to spread Vaiṣṇavism on a wide scale was Bhaktisiddhanta Saraswati Maharaja (1862-1936). Vaiṣṇavas use a drum called a *mridanga* in their religious music. Bhaktisiddhanta Saraswati nicknamed the printing press "the big mridanga," because of its ability to reach many people. His disciple, His Divine Grace A.C. Bhaktivedanta Swami Prabhupada, followed in his guru's footsteps, and, as just stated, was extremely successful in giving the Western world access to Vaiṣṇavism through the print medium, as well as beginning to engage audio and video mediums. Both of these holy men reasoned that since every invention uses the intelligence, laws, and raw materials provided by God, it ought to be used in God's direct service. This attitude is the quintessence of Vaiṣṇavism and bhakti. The devotee is always looking for ways to engage all of his or her resources and the things of the world to advance human progress and to increase the intimacy between God and all living beings.

In order to appreciate Vrindavan and the Vrindavan concept of God, the basic elements and practices of Vaiṣṇavism must first be realized. Identification with the material body and mind must be broken. The self and the self's true nature must be experienced. The potencies of the self and God must begin to be perceived. Understanding your own spiritual nature is a prerequisite for understanding God's nature, although progress is usually made simultaneously.

Next, the relationship between the self and God must be recognized *(shanta-rasa)* and actualized. Actualizing our relationship with God means entering *dasya-rasa,* the servitor stage. The person honestly asks God to allow him or her to perform real services for the good of the whole.

When all of this is done, then a person is qualified to enter Vrindavan and to begin tasting the higher *rasas,* or relationships with God.

Because of all the above, the authors feel very humble in the face of entering Vrindavan. It is not a thing to be done lightly. We shall do the best job we can, considering our inadequacies and the enormity of the task. Because great souls like Bhaktisiddhanta Saraswati Maharaja and His Divine Grace A.C. Bhaktivedanta Swami have paved the way, we dare to follow. We hope we can at least give the reader a little taste for the Vrindavan concept of God, because that taste is very sweet and pleasing. According to Vaiṣṇavas, a little taste of Vrindavan inevitably motivates a soul to move closer and closer to God, until full, unconditional love of Godhead and all life is reached. Because such a sublime result is possible, we carry on.

With all of the preliminaries taken care of, we are now ready to enter the sanctum sanctorum—the holy of holies—of Vaiṣṇavism on earth: Vrindavan.

It is written in the *Skanda Purana:* "Vrindavan is a vast and spacious area. It is full of hermitages and endowed with a wealth of nice forests." Although Vrindavan is only a few hours drive from the bustling metropolis of Delhi, the place has almost fully retained its pastoral and spiritual qualities. The basic amenities of modern life are there: running water, electricity, and so forth; but there are no factories or other major industrial or commercial facilities. Vrindavan's principal activities are the pursuit of spiritual life, farming, and the care of dairy cows. This pattern of life is archetypal of Vedic civilization. Dr. Hein calls it "among the oldest patterns of civilized living now extant."

We learn of Shri Krishna's Vrindavan in the *Srimad Bhagavatam,* compiled by Vyasadeva. The famous Tenth Canto of this twelve canto work describes Shri Krishna's 125 years on earth 5,000 years ago. George Hart rates the *Srimad Bhagavatam,* or, as it is translated into English, "The Most Beautiful Personality of Godhead," as "among the finest works of devotion ever written, being equalled in my opinion only by other works in the Indian language."

The Encyclopedia of World Religions reports that after the Vrindavan revelation, the Vaiṣṇava conception of God is "above all a God of love, and the ideal becomes intimate union and communion with the incarnate God, both in his timeless essence and in his ceaseless beneficient activity in the world." Let us now take a little journey into Shri Krishna's Vrindavan through the eyes of the *Srimad Bhagavatam:*

> Vṛndāvana forest improved from the rains and was replete with ripened dates, mangoes, blackberries and other fruits. Lord Kṛṣṇa, the Supreme Personality of Godhead, and His boy friends and Lord Balarāma, entered the forest to enjoy the new seasonal atmosphere. The cows, being fed by new grasses, became very healthy, and their milk bags were all very full. When Lord Kṛṣṇa called them by name, they immediately came to Him out of affection, and in their joyful condition the milk flowed from their bags. Lord Kṛṣṇa was very pleased when passing through the Vṛndāvana forest by the side of Govardhana Hill. On the bank of the Yamunā He saw all the trees decorated with bee hives pouring honey. There were many waterfalls on Govardhana Hill, and their flowing made a nice sound. Kṛṣṇa heard them as He looked into the caves of the hill.
>
> When the rainy season was not ended completely but was gradually turning to autumn, sometimes, especially when there was rainfall within the forest, Kṛṣṇa and His companions would sit under a tree or within the caves of Govardhana Hill and enjoy eating the ripened fruits and talking with great pleasure. When Kṛṣṇa and Balarāma were in the forest all day, mother Yashoda used to send Them some rice mixed with yogurt, fruits and sweetmeat. Kṛṣṇa would take them and sit on a slab of stone on the bank of the Yamunā. While Kṛṣṇa and Balarāma and Their friends were eating, they watched the cows, calves and bulls. The cows appeared to be tired from standing with their heavy milk bags. By sitting and chewing grass, they became happy, and Kṛṣṇa was pleased to see them. He was proud to see the beauty of the forest, which was nothing but the manifestation of His own energy.

Krishna's appearance shrine stands in front of the Grand Mosque of Mathura.

From the Vedic point of view, the Kali Yuga started 5,000 years ago when Shri Krishna left the planet. Shortly thereafter, the influence of the three higher rasas of friendship, parental affection, and conjugal love began diminishing rapidly. Without the nurturing and civilizing effect of these higher rasas, humanity began quarreling among themselves, whether it was husband against wife, neighbor and neighbor, or nation versus nation. However, with the advent of Shri Chaitanya Mahaprabhu in 1486, the higher three rasas were reintegrated into the living body of Vaiṣṇavism and the earth. Since that time, both the Eastern and Western worlds have made great progress in all spheres of life. The Vaiṣṇavas attribute this improvement to the rediscovery of Vrindavan and its meaning.

After the disappearance of Shri Krishna 5,000 years ago, Vrindavan was gradually forgotten along with the higher rasas. Five hundred years ago, Vrindavan was just forests and open fields. Although a record of Shri Krishna's pastimes existed in the Tenth Canto of the *Srimad Bhagavatam*, no one could tell exactly where many of those pastimes had taken place, and few people visited Vrindavan to contemplate them. Shri Chaitanya changed all that when He visited Vrindavan and with spiritual vision rediscovered many of the lost places of Shri Krishna's pastimes.

A most amazing rejuvenation occurred over the whole of Vrindavan's 168 square miles when Shri Chaitanya sent six of the most qualified men in India there to continue and complete His work. These men succeeded so well that they have been immortalized in the annals of Vaiṣṇavism as the "Six Goswamis of Vrindavan." Later in this chapter we shall learn more of these men and their work. For now, let us just say they rediscovered almost every spot in Vrindavan where Shri Krishna and His female counterpart incarnation of Godhead, Shri Radha, had enjoyed Their divine pastimes, including places where They had personal dealings with parents, relatives, and friends. Also, the six Goswamis oversaw the construction of temples and shrines at many of these holy places, as well as writing voluminously and brilliantly on the spiritual significance of the pastimes of Shri Radha and Shri Krishna in both popular and philosophical mediums. Contemporary Vaiṣṇavism owes an immeasurable debt to the unparalleled devotion and work of the six Goswamis.

Elegant, white marble shrine marks the appearance place of Shri Radha at Barshana.

A partial equivalent to Vrindavan in the Western tradition is the Garden of Eden. Here also, the earth, plants, animals, people, angels, and so forth are all related in love to each other and the supreme Godhead. Another similarity is a vegetarian diet for all beings, human and animal. In the first chapter of Genesis, verses 29 and 30, it is clearly stated that before the "ejection" of Adam and Eve from the Garden of Eden, all beings in the Garden ate only vegetarian food. God says:

> "I have provided all kinds of grains and all kinds of fruit for you to eat; but for all the wild animals and for all the birds I have provided grass and leafy plants for food"—and it was done.

After the "flood" disrupted this natural harmony, humanity began eating animals for food. According to Vedic cosmology, slaughtering animals for food creates inharmonious energies in the atmosphere, which promotes and encourages violence in other spheres of life. God makes the same analysis in the Ninth Chapter of Genesis. The beginning of this chapter is somewhat enigmatic and contradictory. In verse three, God says animals may be eaten: "Every moving thing that liveth shall be meat for you; even as the green herb have I given you all things." But the next verse reasserts the law of the Garden of Eden: "But flesh from a live animal and the blood of that animal shall not be eaten." Verses 2 and 5 introduce a new hostility within the human family and with other creatures:

> And the fear of you and the dread of you shall be upon every beast of the earth, and upon every fowl of the air, upon all that moveth *upon* the earth, and upon all the fishes of the sea; into your hand are they delivered.
>
> And surely your blood of your lives will I require; at the hand of every beast will I require it, and at the hand of man; at the hand of every man's brother will I require the life of man.

When these verses are analyzed together, it is obvious that the introduction of meat into the diet of humanity was being commented on by God; and the review was rather disastrous. God in the Bible echoes the Vedic message that shedding animal blood for food will bring humanity calamitous consequences. The different parts of nature will not work in harmony. Hostility, mutual aggression, and a hard struggle for existence replace loving cooperation. These are the classical symptoms of the start of the Kali Yuga. Even within the human family the mood turns ugly, and conflict between human beings on all levels from families to nations becomes endemic. The Old Testament and the *Vedas* agree that vegetarianism and love of nature are essential ingredients of a naturally God-conscious lifestyle. It is interesting to note that Vrindavan today is practically 100% vegetarian.

Unfortunately, the Old Testament gives scant information on the pre-5,000-year-ago lifestyle. Also, the Bible in general does not really give much of a detailed picture of God, God's abode, and God's activities. Because of this fact, some Christian experts sense a certain reluctance on the part of many Christians for wanting to go to heaven. The lack of detailed information about the spiritual world makes many people conclude, consciously or subconsciously, that it will be boring.

This trend again points out the importance of visualization and having a detailed picture and map in your mind of where you want to go. If you do not have a clearly defined goal of a better and transcendental world, the natural tendency is to continue desiring to live in the world you are familiar with. As we have learned, the Vaiṣṇavas feel the next birth or life will be determined by the state of consciousness at death. In order to go to God's abode, a person's consciousness must be absorbed in contemplating God's abode and/or activities related to it.

Quite frankly, it is hard to contemplate an abstraction or simply metaphysical qualities. That is why Vaiṣṇavas feel the Vrindavan revelation is so important. By the Mother-Father God's incarnation in Vrindavan—along with Their abode, activities, and so forth—humanity is given a detailed picture of divinity in action. By making this detailed revelation the centerpiece of one's religious devotions, the mind becomes very attracted to the spiritual world and the chances of that desire overwhelming all other desires at death is immeasurably increased. For a Vaiṣṇava, contemplation of Vrindavan and Shri Shri Radha-Krishna's activities in Vrindavan is the surefire passport to the spiritual world.

Radha Kunda.

First of all, the abode of God, as made clear in the description of Shri Krishna's Vrindavan in the *Srimad Bhagavatam,* is full and decorated with all natural beauties and potencies. Since God is the controller of all existence, is it any wonder that God would personally desire to live in a cornucopia of nature? Great, natural beauty is a fundamental attribute of God's abode. When these natural wonders are contemplated in relationship to Shri Krishna—God, those thoughts become transcendental, or spiritual, and actually place one in the spiritual abode of Vrindavan. Also, the inclusion of the beauties of nature in God's abode explains why Vaiṣṇavas so often use the manifestations of nature—flowers, food, fire, water, and so forth—in their spiritual life and ceremonies.

Like the entire earth planet, the Vrindavan of today is not as spectacularly beautiful as it was 5,000 years ago. But Vrindavan is still a paradise. *Vana* means forest, while *vrinda* stands for the most sacred tree in Vaiṣṇavism, the *tulasi* tree. Together, Vrindavan means "the forest where tulasi trees grow wild." This occurrence is rare and uniquely defines the Vrindavan area. The scripture, the *Gautami Tantra,* gives the following description of Vrindavan:

> The beautiful forest of Vrindavan is the object of praise of all the *devatas* [angels]. Fully enriched by a wide variety of blooming flowers, always echoing with the melodious warble of birds, and consisting of thirty-two sub-forests, each lovelier than the majestic realms of Vaikuntha [a spiritual dimension], it is a most worthy object of meditation.

In each of these periods of peace, the Vaiṣṇava government protected cows on an equal level with people. During the reign of Ashoka (273-232 BC), it was against the law to harm any animate being. Ashoka, who incorporated Buddhism into his Vaiṣṇava heritage, stands out as a giant among executive heads of state in history. Ashoka set up a model government that encouraged the physical and spiritual well-being of the people in unprecedented ways. Dr. Pitirim A. Sorokin asserts that Ashoka's policies were incredibly successful. For the last thirty years of his reign Ashoka enjoyed total peace, which continued for 30 to 40 years after his death. When comparing Ashoka's record to the historical fact that for the last several thousand years the average country has been at war 25% to 50% of the time, Sorokin writes that

> the period of uninterrupted peace for some sixty to seventy years achieved by the love-inspired, nonviolent, peaceful policy of Asoka is an exceptionally rare achievement in the history of all countries at all times.

Vegetarian diet and cow protection, then, might be two keys to solving the world's political crisis.

When you walk down a cowpath in Vrindavan, in some places your feet are cushioned by a fluffy, soft layer of earth dust several inches deep. You can imagine how Shri Krishna and His friends enjoyed walking barefoot on this very path with Their calves and cows, heading out for the verdant pasturelands. Vrindavan is so benign and gentle that in many places you do not even have to wear footgear for your protection.

Beautiful birds like the bright green parrot adorn the trees of Vrindavan and fill the air with their melodious songs. Peacocks, long the symbol of royalty in many lands, strut majestically throughout Vrindavan in great numbers. Their impressive train of feathers and the power of their morning and evening calls thrill the observer. Peacocks figure prominently in the early pastimes of Shri Krishna. It is said the peacocks taught Shri Krishna how to dance, and they inspire all people living around them to appreciate deeply their graceful and ecstatic movements.

The Vrindavan forests also have their tricksters and comedians—namely, the numerous and resourceful monkeys. While they adorably scamper to and fro, be on guard. They love to steal cameras, wallets, purses, and whatever else they can get their hands on. If you fall victim to their wiles, do not lament. For some sweets or bananas the monkeys will be happy to return your belongings.

In Vrindavan all the manifestations of nature remind the Vaiṣṇava of some aspect of God. For instance, one of the six Goswamis, Rupa Goswami, writes:

> see how this forest of Vṛndāvana is full of transcendental creepers and trees. The tops of the creepers are laden with flowers, and intoxicated bumble bees are buzzing around them, humming songs pleasing to the ear, which surpass even the Vedic hymns.

In the natural, God-conscious condition, all manifestations of life are perceived as divine and stimulate a spiritual pleasure greater than self-conscious human efforts at spirituality. Therefore, the buzzing of bees in Vrindavan is more reminiscent of God than the grandest of religious hymns.

The physical environment of Vrindavan, combined with the incredible volume and quality of spiritual activities conducted there, make it an easy place to see and be with God. A charming and true anecdote from Dr. Miles Davis' (Patita Pavana Das) book, *Touring The Land Of Krishna,* illustrates Vrindavan's spiritual potency. Over two decades ago, a gentleman from Scotland settled in Vrindavan. A local government official asked him, "Why have you come here? Can God not be found in your own homeland?"

The Scottish devotee replied by posing a question of his own, "Where do you come from?"

"Jaipur," was the answer.

"And how deep do you have to dig for water there?"

"About 150 feet," said the official.

"And how deep in Vrindavan before you hit water?"

"Only eight feet," said the official.

The Scottish Vaiṣṇava smiled wisely and said, "Similarly, it's easier to become God conscious in Vrindavan, because the holy *dhama* is the land of Shri Krishna, the Supreme Personality of Godhead."

Cows graze in a Vrindavan field.

In the *Varaha Purana* Shri Krishna Himself says, "there is no place which is as dear to Me as Mathura. Supremely beautiful and enchanting, Mathura is the place of My transcendental appearance." Dr. Hein reports that in a twelve month period of 1949-50 government sources calculated that 500,000 pilgrims, almost 1,400 every day, visited Vraja Mandala to take advantage of this spiritual atmosphere; and almost all of them worshiped at Shri Krishna's appearance place in Mathura.

The appearance place of Shri Krishna housed one of the finest temples of ancient India. The first structure was built by Vajranabha, the son of Shri Krishna's grandson, Aniruddha. It is estimated that the next temple was built around 400 BC. This magnificent temple was tragically destroyed by the invader Mahmud Ghazni in 1017-18 AD. The temple was rebuilt and razed several times during the following centuries. The last demolition was ordered by the intolerant Aurangzeb in 1669-70 AD. For three centuries pilgrims had no temple to visit on this site. Just in 1965, a coalition of religious-minded Indian entrepreneurs started construction of a new and fitting temple here to honor Shri Krishna's appearance place.

Buddhists also consider Mathura a special holy place. Buddha's most illustrious and advanced disciple, Sariputra, himself considered a fully illumined one, was buried here. In the past, Buddhist monasteries flourished in Mathura. Fifteen hundred years ago, the Chinese Buddhist monk, Fa-Hsein, visited the Buddhist monastery of Upagupta in Mathura, describing it as "an important center of Buddhism." Also, the first statue of Buddha in a standing posture was uncovered in Mathura.

Today, Mathura is the most heavily populated area in Vraja Mandala, containing over 150,000 people. The earth beneath Mathura has proven to be a treasure trove for contemporary archeologists. In a stunning, octagonal mansion built of red sandstone in Mathura's Dampier Park stands the Government Archeological Museum. Dr. Davis reports: "More than 10,000 ancient specimens of sculpture and terra-cotta are on display, arranged in chronological sequence with suitable labels and informative charts." Museums around the world proudly display items from this collection, which is the world's largest display of Vedic, Jain, and Buddhist artworks from the Kushana and Gupta periods.

From the vantage point of a sociologist, Dr. Sorokin comes to the same conclusion:

> Making us full-fledged coparticipants in the lives of others, love infinitely enriches our lives. . . . In this sense it fills us with *knowledge,* because coparticipation and coexperience . . . is the most efficient method of learning and the most fruitful way to truth and knowledge. In this sense the love experience leads to a true cognition and *love becomes truth*.

These giants of twentieth century psychology and sociology with all their wealth of research and experience can only confirm what Shri Krishna stated thousands of years ago—to know someone, you must love them unconditionally. The less love there is, the more deficient is one's knowledge. This point applies to knowing God, people, nature, or whatever else there is to know. In his book, *The Psychology of Science,* Maslow contends that microscopes, telescopes, and other scientific instruments will not give us an accurate picture of reality unless there is love in the heart of the scientist who is using them.

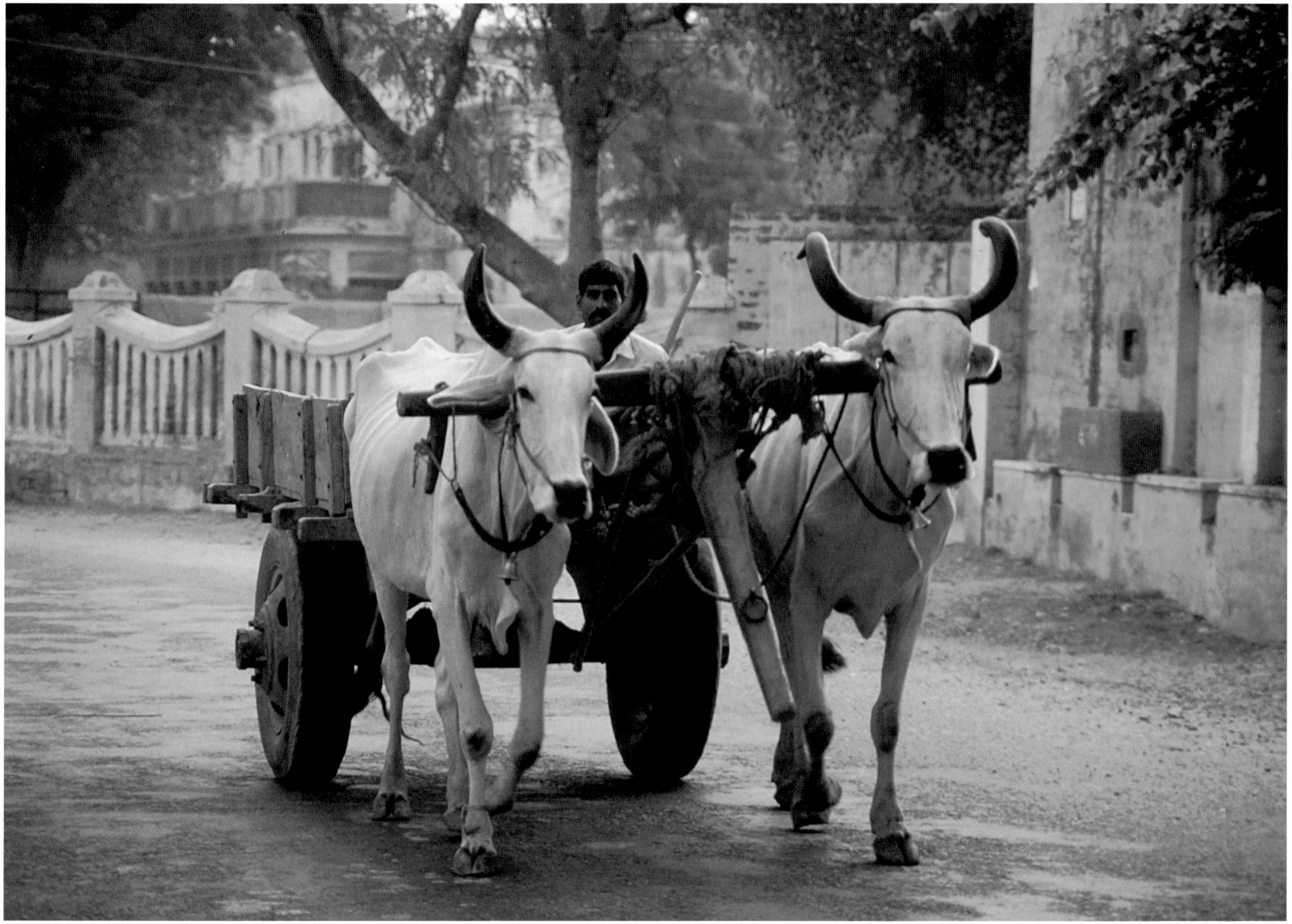

A bullock cart plies through the streets of Vrindavan.

After a day grazing his herd, a cowherder brings them home.

This fourth stage of love of Godhead is called *vatsalya-rasa,* or the relationship of parental affection for God. And what an amazing reversal this rasa represents! Normally, religious people look upon God as their parent and petition God for satisfying *their* needs. Here, the devotee has become so mature, empowered, and filled to overflowing abundance by cultivation of the previous rasas that there is an overwhelming desire to be *God's* parent. John F. Kennedy's most famous saying can be restated to express the mood of a devotee in vatsalya-rasa: "Ask not what your God can do for you, but what you can do for your God."

Shri Chaitanya explains vatsalya-rasa in this way:

> On the platform of parental love, the qualities of śānta-rasa, dāsya-rasa, and sakhya-rasa are transformed into a form of service called maintenance. . . .the devotee considers himself the Lord's maintainer. Thus, the Lord is the object of maintenance, like a son.

As rasas develop, each stage of advancement includes all the experiences and spiritual enjoyments of the previous rasa or rasas. Therefore, Shri Chaitanya says, "this mellow [of vatsalya-rasa] is full of the four qualities of śānta-rasa, dāsya-rasa, fraternity, and parental love. This is more transcendental nectar."

In our previous enumeration of Shri Krishna's qualities, recall that quality number 40 is "controlled by love." Therefore, since there are always devotees who want to relate to Shri Krishna in vatsalya-rasa, the infinite Godhead eternally manifests Himself as a transcendental child to these devotees. The Tenth Canto of the *Srimad Bhagavatam* states:

> Although Kṛṣṇa is beyond sense perception and is unmanifest to human beings, He takes up the guise of a human being with a material body. Thus mother Yaśodā thought Him to be her son, and she bound Lord Kṛṣṇa with rope to a wooden mortar, as if He were an ordinary child.

The general name for Shri Krishna's activities is *lila,*, or divine pastime. For the Vaiṣṇava these pastimes reveal the most esoteric secrets about the nature of God. For instance, the above incident of mother Yashoda binding Krishna illustrates how God is "controlled by love." As a child, Krishna would sometimes get into "mischief." One day Yashoda discovered that Krishna had broken a butter pot and was throwing away the butter to the monkeys! After a great chase, Yashoda caught Krishna and decided to tie Him to a grinding mortar as punishment. She picked up a rope but found it too short for her purpose. Time after time she went into the house and got more rope, but each time she tried to bind Krishna the rope remained inches short.

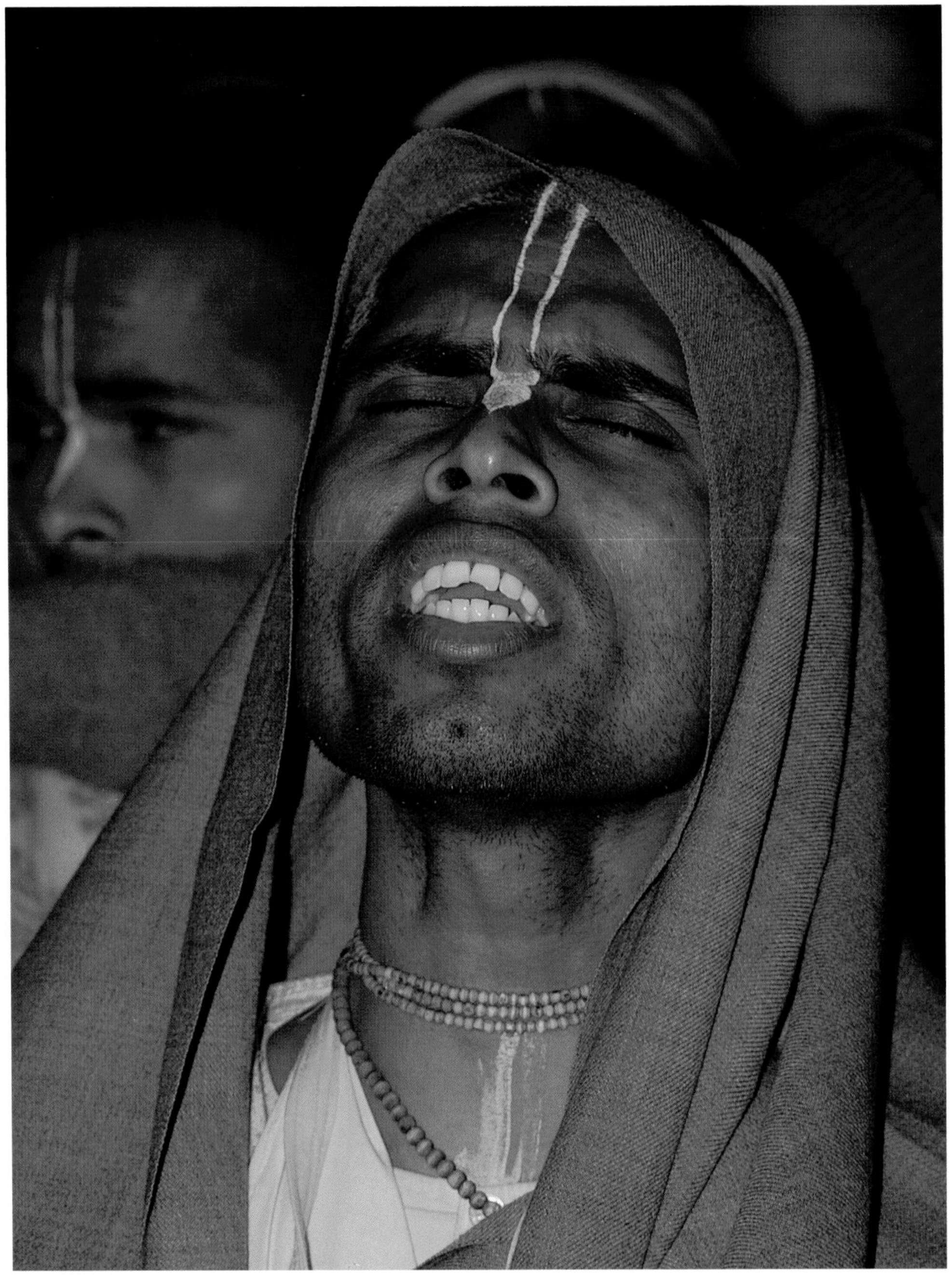

Lokanatha Swami leads the ecstatic chanting of Hare Krishna. On his forehead is Gaudiya Vaisnava tilak.

Some Indians and other people have grossly misinterpreted this lila, either out of ignorance or a sectarian desire to malign Vaiṣṇavism. They have accused Krishna of breaking all moral codes by making love to many women, some of whom were married, in the dead of the night. However, the facts of this lila are very different from this distorted picture. His Divine Grace A.C. Bhaktivedanta Swami Prabhupada writes: "Although such conjugal feelings [between Radha and Krishna] are not at all material, there is some similarity between this spiritual love and material activities." Unfortunately, this similarity has given the ignorant grounds to slander God's love. Vaiṣṇavas feel this behavior is deplorable, since it creates a false obstacle between innocent souls and this most attractive and intimate revelation of God's loving nature.

On that wondrous autumn night, Krishna played His transcendental flute and awakened Radha and the souls of all Her girlfriends, or *gopis* (cowherd girls). Regarding the potency of Krsna's flute, Jayadeva Goswami, a twelfth century saint and poet whose *Gita Govinda* is considered by Vaiṣṇavas to be the highest poetical expression of Radha and Krishna's love, writes: "The sound of Kṛṣṇa's flute charms the entire creation, animate as well as inanimate. The deer-eyed *gopis* of Vraja are so fascinated by it, that the *mandāra* flowers which decorate their coiffure fall down."

Yearning to exchange conjugal affection with Krishna, Radha and the souls of all the gopis flew to meet Him at Seva Kunja, the most sacred forest grove of Vraja Mandala. After they arrived, Krishna appeared to them and expanded Himself into as many Krishna Forms as there were gopis, and They spent the night performing the *rasa-lila*—the pastime of the sacred dance of love.

As His Divine Grace A.C. Bhaktivedanta Swami points out: "The rāsa dance is a completely spiritual performance." No immorality can be attributed to it. First of all, by earthly calculations, Krishna was only eight years old when it happened, and everyone was exchanging affection in spiritual, not material, bodies.

Vaiṣṇavas maintain that our human sexuality is an earthly reflection of this eternal, pure, and original love affair between the Supreme Male and the Supreme Female Personalities of Godhead, as exemplified by the rasa-lila. The intricacies and expressions of Radha and Krishna's madhurya-rasa and rasa-lila are infinite and can only be briefly hinted at in this book. This divine love has so inspired the Indian people and others that the greatest outpouring of poems, songs, plays, and philosophical literature on the subject of love of God in the history of the world has resulted from it.

A peacock stands near a soft, sandy foot trail through the groves of Vrindavan.

The Temples of Vrindavan and the Goswamis

> I offer my respectful obeisances unto the six Gosvāmīs, namely Śrī Sanātana Gosvāmī, Śrī Rūpa Gosvāmī, Śrī Raghunātha Bhaṭṭa Gosvāmī, Śrī Raghunātha dāsa Gosvāmī, Śrī Jīva Gosvāmī and Śrī Gopāla Bhaṭṭa Gosvāmī, who are very expert in scrutinizingly studying all the revealed scriptures with the aim of establishing eternal religious principles for the benefit of all human beings. Thus they are honored all over the three worlds, and they are worth taking shelter of because they are absorbed in the mood of the *gopīs* and are engaged in the transcendental loving service of Rādhā and Kṛṣṇa.
>
> —Śrīnivāsa Ācārya

Sanatana and Rupa Goswami were brothers from a wealthy and respectable family. Because of their genius and skill, the Nawab, the Muslim governor of Bengal, made them his chief ministers, and they served him ably for many years. With great difficulty they escaped the Nawab's service and joined Shri Chaitanya's movement. Shri Chaitanya asked them to "Establish devotional service to Lord Kṛṣṇa and Rādhārāṇī in Vṛndāvana. You should also compile bhakti scripture and preach . . . from Vṛndāvana." The brothers joyfully agreed.

When visitors from Vrindavan came to see Shri Chaitanya in Jagannath Puri, they "would praise Śrīla Rūpa and Sanātana Gosvāmī." Their renunciation and devotional fervor were of the topmost quality. The visitors would report:

> The brothers actually have no fixed residence. They reside beneath trees—one night under one tree and the next night under another. [They] beg a little food from the houses of the brāhmaṇas. Giving up all kinds of material enjoyment, they only take some dry bread and fried chick-peas. They carry only waterpots, and they wear torn quilts. They always chant the holy names of Kṛṣṇa and discuss His pastimes. In great jubilation, they also dance. They engage almost twenty-four hours daily in rendering service to the Lord. They usually sleep only an hour and a half, and some days, when they continuously chant the Lord's name, they do not sleep at all.

Vaiṣṇavas are advised not to imitate the renunciation of the Goswamis, since only highly advanced devotees who are directly nourished from the spiritual plane are able to do so. Still, their behavior is most inspirational and spurs devotees on to do their best in devotional service.

RADHA AND KRISHNA
Silk painting, Kishangar School, 18th century, Private Collection. Radha offers Krishna a lotus flower.

CHAPTER 7: PASTIMES OF KRISHNA IN INDIAN ART

KRISHNA-KALIYA
Silk painting, Kangra School, 18th century, Private Collection. Krishna dances on the head of the poisonous Kaliya Serpent and thereby saves the residents of Vrindavan from impending death.

The philosophy of Vaiṣṇavism, however, which serves as the basis for much of Indian art, stresses more perceiving the divine in the world, as well as the existence of an otherworldly transcendental abode. On this point Cooramaswamy writes, "This inseparable unity of the material and spiritual world is made the foundation of Indian culture. . . ." Dr. Basham also notes the integration of this world and the spiritual world in Indian art. He explains:

> The tendency of Indian art is diametrically opposite to that of medieval Europe. The temple towers, though tall, are solidly based on earth. The ideal type is not abnormally tall, but rather short and stocky. Gods and demigods alike are young and handsome; their bodies are rounded and well-nourished. . . . Occasionally they are depicted as grim or wrathful, but generally they smile, and sorrow is rarely portrayed.

In Indian art Basham finds "an intense vitality which reminds us rather of this world than the next, and suggest to us the warm bustle of the Indian city and the turbulent pullulation of the Indian forest."

The renowned French author Romain Rolland (1866-1944) marveled at how Vedic culture is so all-inclusive. He writes:

> There is no negation. All is harmonized. All the forces of life are grouped like a forest. . . . Everything has its place, every being has its function, and all take part in the divine concert, their different voices, and their very dissonances, creating, in the phrase of Heraclitus, a most beautiful harmony.

Rabindranath Tagore (1861-1941), the Nobel prize-winning poet of Bengal and himself a major force in the revival of classical Indian arts in the twentieth century, beautifully expresses the integrative and evolutionary spirit of Vedic culture in the following lines:

> Not my way of salvation, to surrender the world!
> Rather for me the taste of Infinite Freedom
> While yet I am bound by a thousand bonds to the
> wheel . . .
> In each glory of sound and sight and scent
> I shall find Thy infinite joy abiding:
> My passion shall burn as the flame of salvation,
> The flower of my love shall become the ripe fruit
> of devotion.

Therefore, we can see how many scholars, East and West, congratulate Vedic culture on being the best synthesis of the material and spiritual worlds known on earth.

Indian culture achieved this exalted status by conscious design. Vedic society always recognized the incredibly potent effect that popular culture exerts on people and social relationships. Therefore, Indian culture was involved in presenting ideal-type persons, especially incarnations of God, saints, and competent rulers as positive role models for the population. Consequently, India is considered to have one of the most civilized, stable, and law-abiding populations on an everyday level in the world. Even today, despite significant poverty, India has far less of a crime rate than industrialized countries. Family life is strong, and divorce is extremely rare.

Concerning the standard Indian social arrangement—the extended family—anthropologist Stephen A. Tyler writes, "Both psychologically and materially the combined resources of a joint family are more effective in meeting the world's demands and obligations than the isolated, independent nuclear family." And no doubt, the spirit of harmony and cooperation inculcated by Vedic culture is largely responsible for the success of the Indian extended family.

Modern psychology is also acknowledging the pivotal effect of culture. Dr. Assagioli writes, "Pictures and objects of various kinds (paintings, drawings, and all objects of art) often have a great suggestive power, especially upon those who belong to the visual type." Works of art for Assagioli are "living forces, almost living entities, embodying a power which has suggestive and creative power." Because of art's potency, Assagioli advocates deliberate use of it "for the further development of our personality." Of course, Vedic culture has followed this prescription of Dr. Assagioli for thousands of years with most salutary results. Only in the eighteenth century did the purity of Indian culture begin to be sullied by vulgar intrusions.

CIRA GHAT LILA
Silk painting, Kangra School, 18th century, Private Collection. Krishna teases the gopis by placing their clothing out of reach in a tree while they bathe in the Yamuna River.

KRISHNA AND THE GOPIS
Silk painting, Kangra School, 18th century, Private Collection. Krishna plays His flute on the bank of the Yamuna River in the company of the gopis.

Art was performed as a spiritual excercise. This discipline is called "Art as Yoga," or union (yoga) with God through art. Ananda Cooramaswamy explains that Vedic culture "was firmly convinced that an absolute Beauty (rasa) exists, just as others maintain the conceptions of absolute Goodness and absolute Truth." Therefore, art was a method of uniting with God's beauty and expressing it on the earth plane to the best of the artist's ability, augmented by the guidance of divine revelation in both scriptural form and personal meditation.

As stated before, the art and science of visualization is essential to Vedic and Vaiṣṇava spirituality and is especially developed and evolved in Vedic artists. The process of sculpting a Deity and the benefits thereof are explained by Shukracharya, one of the greatest of the ancient *gurus,* or teachers. First, there must be

> meditation on the deities who are the object of his devotion. For the successful achievement of this yoga the lineaments of the image are described in books to be dwelt upon in detail. In no other way, not even by direct and immediate vision of an actual object, is it possible to be so absorbed in contemplation, and thus in the making of deities.

Cooramaswamy states that the practice of visualization for devotees and artists are identical. He writes:

> The worshipper recites the *dhyana mantram* describing the deity, and forms a corresponding mental picture, and it is then to this imagined form that his prayers are addressed and the offerings are made. The artist follows identical prescriptions, but proceeds to represent the mental picture in a visual and objective form, by drawing or modelling.

By spiritual practice the artist, like the devotee, enters into a realm of living and eternal spiritual realities that propel forward their work like no earthly inspiration can. One of the best descriptions of this process is found in the *Ramayana,* another of ancient India's literary classics that describes the life of the prince incarnation who became king, Lord Rama. Valmiki, the author of the *Ramayana,* knew Rama's story well from oral tradition. But before writing he desired to realize its truth more profoundly. To do this, he sat

> with his face towards the East, and sipping water according to rule (i.e. ceremonial purification), he set himself to yoga-contemplation of his theme. By virtue of his yoga-power he clearly saw before him Rama, Lakshmana and Sita, and Dasaratha, together with his wives, in his kingdom laughing, talking, acting and moving as if in real life. . .by yoga power that righteous one beheld all that had come to pass, and all that was to come to pass in the future, like a nelli fruit on the palm of his hand. And having truly seen all by virtue of his concentration, the generous sage began the setting forth of the history of Rama.

SHRI NATHJI
Cloth wall hanging, Nathdwar School, 19th century, Private Collection. Portrait of the Deity of Lord Krishna at Nathdwar.

Krishna in Indian Art

Study of Indian art is simultaneously a study of Krishna, since Krishna is the single most important influence and depicted figure in Indian art. Writing in his book *The Life Of Krishna In Indian Art,* P. Banerjee states:

> The life of Krishna from childhood to his last days has been a source of perennial inspiration to the poets and the artists, as he represents the perfection of human character and endeavor. He is the embodiment of the intellectual and spiritual glory. Krishnaism permeates the entire Indian culture and thought. No other single individual has so much influenced the course of India's religion, philosophy, art, literature as the life and personality of Krishna.

Because God, Krishna, is an absolute being, anything related to Krishna or that reminds us of Krishna is also considered absolute and *is* Krishna. God is omnipresent and can be perceived in everything. But to a Vaiṣṇava, God is especially visible and a living presence in any artistic presentation of Divine Beinghood or God's incarnations in the world.

Related to the above principle is the following quote from the *Caitanya-caritamrta,* "The holy name of Kṛṣṇa, His transcendental qualities and pastimes, as well as Lord Kṛṣṇa Himself are all equal. They are all spiritual and full of bliss." Therefore, any artistic means to help us remember Krishna's name, form, qualities, or pastimes are also as good as Krishna Himself. That is the nature of the Absolute, or God. Any entry into awareness of the Absolute reveals all of the Absolute to the devotee. Herein lies another secret of bhakti yoga and Vaiṣṇavism.

RASAMANDALA—LORD KRISHNA'S COSMIC DANCE
Opaque watercolor on paper, Jaipur School, 18th century, Maharaja Sawai Man Singh II Museum, Jaipur. Krishna dances with Radha surrounded by Their loving attendants, the gopis.

Vaiṣṇavas are not surprised by individuality manifesting out of following the scriptures, since they contend that by following the rules and regulations of devotional art the artist communes with the living Godhead, who is ever-fresh and ever ready to give new insight on how to present the infinite. To a Vaiṣṇava, true individuality comes from living a spiritual life, whereas they would also say that the freewheeling life-styles and techniques of many modern artists only lead to superficial and largely meaningless individuality of no real depth or character.

While Krishna in many forms was sculpted by south India's artists, Dr. Basham reports, "The greatest and most triumphant achievements of Tamil bronze casting are undoubtedly the dancing Sivas, of which there are many examples dating from the 11th century onwards." Perhaps the best known and most controversial of these dancing Shivas is the "Puram Nataraja" acquired by the Norton Simon Museum of Pasadena, California almost a decade ago for about $1,000,000. The government of India was outraged by the questionable transfer of this priceless national treasure and after delicate negotiations, the Norton Simon Museum recently agreed to return it to India. From this incident the reader can imagine what price the finest specimans of Tamil bronze work could fetch in today's art market. These bronzes have always cut across cultural and ethnic barriers. Dr. Basham writes that "even the European can recognize in the finest specimens of the dancing Siva a truly religious inspiration, a wholly successful effort at depicting in plastic terms divine truth, beauty, and joy."

At this juncture, let us digress from art for a moment to discuss the relationship of Vishnu or Krishna to Shiva in Vedic society. Most followers of Sanatana Dharma worship either Vishnu-Krishna or Shiva as the Supreme Godhead. Followers of Vishnu-Krishna are called Vaiṣṇavas, while followers of Shiva are called Shivites. Within the Shivite movement, whose stronghold is south India, there are devotional and monist Shivites. Dr. Basham makes it clear that both Vaiṣṇavas and Shivites feel they are worshiping the same Godhead, but place their emphasis and focus on different aspects of that one Godhead. Traditionally, both parties have been tolerant and supportive of each other to a far larger extent than religious rivals in other lands.

Vaiṣṇavas consider Lord Shiva to be the most exalted and advanced devotee of Krishna, while Shivites hold a similar opinion of Vishnu-Krishna. Therefore, both parties revere the sacred art of their own and each other's schools. Vaiṣṇavas can and do express devotion to Shiva, since worshiping an advanced devotee of Krishna is considered an effective and recommended spiritual process. This longstanding friendship between these two giant Vedic trends, which, unfortunately, was occasionally punctured by intolerant outbursts, still remains one of the greatest examples of religious tolerance in world history.

Outside of south India two major schools of Indian sculpting were found in the ancient province of Gandhara (now in Pakistan) and Mathura and were known by those names. The Gandhara school persisted until the sixth century AD, while Mathura flourished as an art center up to the twelfth century when foreign invasions tragically terminated its artistic impetus and destroyed almost all of its ancient works.

Besides producing Vedic art, it is theorized that these two schools and the weight of the entire Vedic tradition exerted a tremendous transformative effect on Buddhist art. Originally, according to the *Area Handbook for India* and other sources, "Buddhist sculpture did not represent the Buddha in human form." Only symbols associated with stages of his life, like a wheel representing his teachings, were used. However, the Gandhara and Mathura schools produced the first of many fine sculptures of Buddha, the whole person, which obviously served more of a Deity function.

Devotional forms of Buddhism also evolved out of this trend. Therefore, the varieties of Mahayana Buddhism which spread out of India to China, Japan, Korea, and elsewhere in Asia owe an immeasurable debt to Vaiṣṇava and Vedic aesthetic and spiritual tastes. Without their personalizing influence, the world would not have a single sculpture of the human form of Buddha and would be deprived of a major category of world art that is universally appreciated but, unfortunately, beyond the scope of this book to present.

The *Area Handbook for India* states, "The greatest period of Indian sculpture is considered to extend from the fifth to seventh centuries AD, under the Gupta Dynasty." This strong line of Vaiṣṇava kings richly supported the devotional arts. Basham writes, "Guptan sculpture suggests serenity, security and certainty. It was at this time that India produced some of her most truly religious art."

GOVARDHANA LILA
Granite sculpture, Hoyshala Period, 9th century AD, Courtyard of the Vishnu Temple in Belur. Lord Krishna lifts Govardhana Hill with His left hand.

VENU KRISHNA
Ivory carving, Delhi School, 20th century, Private Collection. Krishna plays on His flute.

Typical of Akbar's universal spirit were the conferences he held at Fatehpur-Sikri from 1575 through 1582 with representatives of all religious groups within his empire. In the special "House of Worship" all-night debates were held to arrive at religious truth. From these meetings Akbar came to love Vaiṣṇavism, as well as Christianity and other faiths. Akbar was especially struck by the beauty of baby Jesus and commissioned paintings on this theme. An excellent *Madonna And Child* from this effort, painted around 1580, is found in the Harvard University Art Museum. The theme of God incarnating as a child was no problem for the artist, whom experts feel was a Vaiṣṇava, since he drew upon the artistic conventions of portraying Krishna as a baby to produce this work. Stuart Cary Welch writes that this artist "was so enthralled by the Christ Child that he interpreted him as a beguiling infant Krishna, merely substituting white skin for blue." This painting illustrates the eclectic and ecumenical spirit so promoted by Akbar and so characteristic of Vedic culture.

Mughal culture was very strong in the arts associated with book production—calligraphy, illuminated pictures, and jewel-like miniature paintings. These arts of Persian court life found new impetus when Akbar commissioned illustrated translations of Vedic classics, like the *Mahabharata* and *Ramayana,* using Muslim and Indian artists. Many of these illustrations can be enjoyed today at the Maharaja Sawai Man Singh II Museum of Jaipur, where Stuart Cary Welch says they still "radiate religious intensity."

While miniatures existed in India before any Islamic influence, they gained perfection as an art form during this period and have earned worldwide admiration. The Vedic acceptance of animals as part of the divine order influenced Mughal art, and animals got a more significant place in the Mughal landscape. The Vedic artist Basawan, who thrived at Akbar's court from 1570 to 1600, was especially skillful at portraying animals. In general the Vedic influence added depth, passion, and a wider range of emotional expressions to the more restrained and classically harmonious art of Persia.

LADU KRISHNA
Miniature bronze, Chola School, 17th century, Private Collection. Child Krishna dances with a ladu (an Indian sweet) in His right hand.

Kangra art attained its apex under the patronage of King Sansar Chand, who at the tender age of ten ascended the throne in 1775. While very interested and involved in political pursuits, he also loved the arts, especially painting. He directed the painting of Kangra's most famous *Gita Govinda* series while he was only fifteen or sixteen! In spite of never-ending political turmoil, Sansar Chand always kept up his interest in art, and, according to Stuart Cary Welch, under his guidance the Kangra school "attained Botticellian grace and refinement. . . . In time, the reputation of Kangra painting assumed almost legendary proportions, far beyond that of any other Hill schools." Sansar Chand is typical of how Indian monarchs combined cultural activities with their worldly duties, thereby assuring the Indian people of a rich and uplifting cultural life.

Lastly, four unfinished sketches from Orissa in the eighteenth or nineteenth centuries based on the *Gita Govinda* also deserve mention. These pictures are so aflame with spirituality that Stuart Cary Welch writes, "The fervent mood of bhakti, all-consuming devotion, permeates these sketches; every living thing seems to move as though aware of Krishna's imminence." Whoever this artist was, he truly achieved the heights of Vaiṣṇava art.

The Kishangarh school achieved its acme during the reign of another extraordinary monarch—Sawant Singh (r. 1748-64). Disgusted by the debaucheries he witnessed at the Delhi court of Emperor Muhammed Shah, Sawant Singh devoted himself more and more strongly to Vaiṣṇava practices back home in Kishangarh. He wrote devotional poetry, and, like a true Vaiṣṇava monarch, he retired seven years before his death to pursue single-mindedly spiritual life. The ideal Vedic executive does not wait for death to take him out of office, but cheats death by early retirement to gain spiritual immortality by totally immersing himself in bhakti yoga.

322

Kathakali dancers perform the pastimes of Radha and Krishna.

As far as human records show, dance in India has always been associated with God and the pulsating rhythm of cosmic life. In Chapter 6, "Vrindavan," we discovered that "all walking is dancing" in the transcendental abode. Therefore, Vaiṣṇavas have always held classical dance in the highest regard and have practiced it as a means of entering into God's divine rhythm and harmony.

Lord Shiva is the patron of classical Indian dance; hence, one of his popular names is Nataraja, or King of the Dance. In fact, India's scriptures say that by his cosmic dancing Shiva creates and destroys the material worlds at the appropriate times. In this respect, the Roman poet Lucian aptly caught the essence of Indian dancing in these words:

> It would seem that dancing came into being at the beginning of all things . . ., for we see this primeval dancing clearly set forth in the choral dance of the constellations and in the planets and fixed stars, their interweaving and interchange and orderly harmony.

Ananda Cooramaswamy sees Lord Shiva's dance as a "manifestation of primal rhythmic energy" and cites three meanings to it. First, it is

> Rhythmic Play as the Source of all Movement within the Cosmos . . . Secondly, the Purpose of his Dance is to Release the Countless souls of men from the Snare of Illusion. Thirdly, the Place of the Dance, Chidambaram, the Center of the Universe, is within the heart.

Interestingly enough, Shivites see these functions of Lord Shiva as indications that he is the supreme Godhead. On the other hand, Vaiṣṇavas see these functions as evidence that Shiva is an elevated and confidential associate of the Supreme Godhead; God, like any good executive, would delegate the job of creating and destroying the material universes to a ranking vice-president, while eternally remaining in the Supreme Abode beyond material flux. In any case, Vedic culture considers dance an eternal spiritual activity which elevates people who participate in it.

The *Rig, Yajur,* and *Atharva Vedas* all frequently refer to sacred, classical Indian dance. Enakshi Bhavani reports that dance "nearly always figured in ritual and sacred ceremony." This distinguished Indian dancer, whose book *The Dance In India* is an authoritative classic on the subject in English, also calls Indian dance "a Science, an Art and an Exposition at the same time."

"Indian dance demonstrates the deeply philosophical and highly religious moods of the Indian people." writes Kamaladevi Chattopadhyaya, the President of All India Theatre Centre, New Delhi. Classical dance is so important in India that it is given the foremost position of all the Vedic arts.

The Yakshagna Dance Troupe from Udipi, South India, does a traditional dance at UCLA under the sponsorship of the Asia Society.

The Yakshagna Dance Troupe at UCLA.

Dance has always been an integral part of Indian village life. Spontaneity in dance was cherished, but over the course of time dance evolved into a methodical performing art with various schools and strict disciplines. Over 2000 years ago, Bharata Muni wrote the *Natya Shastra,* or the Science of Dramaturgy (generally dated somewhere between the 4th and 1st centuries BC). Besides explaining the science of Vedic theater, the *Natya Shastra* also gave a comprehensive guide to classical Indian dance. In this work Bharata Muni says the engineer of our universe, Brahma, brought the entire science of Natya, dance and drama, to India and the earth in ancient times.

Many Indians consider Bharata Muni's manual to be so holy that they call it a "Fifth Veda," or the "Natya Veda," giving it an honored place right next to the original four *Vedas,* or sacred books. Enakshi Bhavani writes that Bharata Muni possessed "a mind that must have delved deeply into the mysteries of knowledge that comes with yogic meditation and contemplation." She also states that Bharata Muni retained "his inner visions of the beauty, perfect rhythm and noble attributes of the symbolic and divine dances . . ." to compose his manual. Amazingly enough, most classical dance in India still follows the outlines and rules laid down in the *Natya Shastra* over 2000 years ago.

Indian dance requires the disciplined use of the entire body and all of its means of expression. In the *Natya Shastra* ten postures of the body, thirty-six of the hand, nine of the neck, and thirteen poses of the head are delineated. The various schools of dance elaborated on these basic postures, each of which has a special and specific meaning, constituting a precise body language capable of telling complex stories to audiences familiar with these conventions.

Dr. Basham writes:

> The most striking feature of the Indian dance is undoubtedly the hand-gesture (mudrā). By a beautiful and complicated code, the hand alone is capable of portraying not only a wide range of emotions, but gods, animals, men, natural scenery, actions and so on.

Today, Indian dance uses hundreds of mudras, many of which are also employed in religious worship and in sacred art.

Each posture and body movement in classical Indian dance is said to create an effect far beyond aesthetic pleasure. Kamaladevi Chattopadhyaya writes:

> It was believed from earliest times that certain currents generated by repeated rhythmic movements of the body created moods and atmosphere that wrought powerful results affecting man and nature alike. Thus were evolved seasonal dances, festival dances, ritual dances.

Ultimately, through practice of the standard dance forms, Indian dancers could so awaken their spiritual devotion as to dance their way to heaven. In order to attain this elevated state of consciousness, the Indian dancer, according to Enakshi Bhavani, had to achieve "a true unison of the inner self and the physical being . . . immersed in the Divine Law." The dancer became "one with the world harmonies and attained an exquisite attunement with the one supreme circle of movement and balance existing in the universe."

In terms of actual dance Enakshi Bhavani explains that this attunement demands an

> essential co-ordination of footwork, bodily movement, hand gestures, placement of arms and movements of the head, eyes, eyebrows, and neck, with time beats of the drum. For this absolute co-ordination between sound and footwork, the creators of the Indian Dance ordained that there be a symmetry of count and metre between the finely intricate beats of time and every unit of the dance step and bodily movement.

This incredible coordination of Indian dance required the dancer to fuse body and mind together by means of devotion, or *bhakti,* to God. Then and only then could a classical Indian dance performance reach perfection and the desired effect.

The Yakshagna Dance Troupe at UCLA.

Before the advent of Buddhism in India, dancers were generally recruited from the upper classes of Indian society. Enakshi Bhavani reports: "Princesses and women of culture counted dancing as an accomplishment and a cultural asset, and they studied the art very seriously." And study they did. Classical dance is a holistic art and science, requiring well-educated and well-rounded performers for success. Therefore, prospective dancers from an early age had to learn not only dance but "dramatics, perfume-making, painting, music, singing, grammar, and the art of conversation." They naturally had to be literate and deeply learned in sacred philosophy and theology. Because of this highly developed background, Enakshi Bhavani writes, "No wonder the classical dance reached great heights in both performance and artistry."

The ascendency of Pali Buddhism in India after 500 BC interrupted the full and continuous evolution of classical Indian dance. This form of Buddhism stressed a more abstract form of spirituality and all of the arts declined during this period, especially since, according to Enakshi Bhavani, "Members of the higher strata of society and family members were forbidden to dance or to sing or to play on musical instruments."

Around the time of Christ, Vedic religion and culture rebounded to enjoy a strong renaissance, fueled by the immense popularity of the great Vedic classics *Ramayana* and *Mahabharata*. During the 1st and 2nd centuries AD this resurgence had gained new heights of achievement for the Vedic arts, including dance, which continued unabated for almost a thousand years.

The Chola dynasty (9th century to 13th century AD) gave new impetus to all the arts, especially dance, by rich patronage and devotion. Stone temple construction was a special tour de force of the Cholas, and they established schools of sacred dance in their newly built temple complexes. Temple sculptures of dancers in Orissa, Andhra, and all over south India highlighted the sacred status of classical Indian dance in this period.

Manipuri dancers perform in Bombay.

Under the weight of the British occupation of India and the secularizing effects of modernization, classical Indian dance suffered a dramatic decline in modern times. However, the Nobel prize-winning poet Dr. Rabindranath Tagore and others greatly repopularized classical Indian dance and again made it accessible to the masses of people. In the twentieth century classical Indian dance has regained a prominent place on the international stage due to the brilliant work of such dancers as Uday Shankar, whose dancing is applauded on four continents. His performance in the "Radha-Krishna Ballet" is especially appreciated for bringing to light the grace, power, and subtlety of classical Indian dance to contemporary audiences.

While classical Indian dance is quite spiritual, it also provides heart-warming entertainment and the excitement of great athletic prowess in the faster and more demanding styles. Many schools of dance are admired—Bharata Natyam, Kathakali, Manipuri, Orissi, Mohini Atam, Krishna Atam, and Bhagavat Mela dance dramas—and loved by the Indian people. To them the sacred dances represent divine beauty in motion. They are deliberate steps leading right into the kingdom of God.

We can hardly hope to do justice to all the schools of classical Indian dance in our limited space, so we have selected three exceptional schools for surveying which are important and representative of the rest—Bharata Natyam, Kathakali, and Kathak.

Bharata Natyam

E. Krishna Iyer calls Bharata Natyam "an art for eternity," because its practice today is virtually the same as it was thousands of years ago. It is the most common dance style performed throughout all of India, although the strongholds of classical Indian dance are south India, especially the cities of Tanjore and Madras. Bharata Natyam is "the mother art for most of the other classical dance systems of India," writes E. Krishna Iyer who also claims it is "the main source of inspiration for the allied arts of sculpture, painting, and icon-making." Although Bharata Natyam is a child of the temples, it is now extremely popular on secular stages too.

The derivation of the word "Bharata" to describe this system is most intriguing. Many experts claim it is a compilation of the first syllables of the three main elements of Bharata Natyam. The chart below from *The Dance In India* demonstrates this point:

BHA – VA	or	Mood	
RA – GA	or	Melody, Song	*BHARATA*
TA – LA	or	Rhythmic Timing	

A group of holy adepts known in south India as the *Nattuvanars* preserved the art of Bharata Natyam and also taught it to others. Their piety and skill are legendary and well-documented. The role call of some of its greatest heroes reads: Ponniah, Shivanandum, Vadivelu Pillai, Chinniah, and the most revered Muttuswami Dikshitar. Their mastery of music and dance was extraordinary.

While the Nattuvanars taught, the female temple dancers known as the *devadasis,* or the "Handmaidens of God," mostly performed Bharata Natyam. They received the rigorous and well-rounded training explained earlier in this chapter. Many would-be devadasis started training at the tender age of five. Inscriptions in the Tamil language mention that in the 11th century AD nearly four hundred devadasis practiced their art at the famous Shiva temple at Tanjore, while about one hundred were attached to the temple at Kanchipuram. The Chola monarchs definitely made the devadasis an established institution by paying them a salary for their dancing and other religious duties.

Twelve-year-old Bharat Natyam dancer in Guruvayur plays the role of Radha.

Kathakali

In his classic English book on Kathakali, K. Bharatha Iyer writes:

> Life on the Kathakaḷi stage is a dance. Kathakaḷi is a dance-drama; the drama and the dance are so blended that they exist throughout as inseparable, as a word to its meaning. There is hardly a moment when the dance ceases. . . . Even when the *naṭa* (actor-dancer) sits down and carries on the dialogue, the rhythmic movements of his arms, wrists, fingers, eyes and eye-brows continue the dance. Here dancing exists with its highest possibilities fully developed and employed, to express moods, to communicate thoughts, to heighten the effect of the dramatic, to enrich the lyrical tone and to build up and sustain the entire fabric of the drama on rhythm.

The trends of modernization have scarcely made any inroads on the naturally isolated state of Kerala in southwest India. Therefore, the Kathakali dance style indigenous to this area's villages continues to flourish without any impediments. Because villagers performed this art for other villagers and village life is so stable in Kerala, this state affords us one of the purest visions of ancient Vedic life and culture.

Kathakali literally means "story-play," and it is perhaps the most unique and distinctly Indian classical dance form. Also, it is very adventurous, avant-garde, and mysterious. The performances are based on incidents contained in sacred classics like the *Mahabharata,* and particularly the *Ramayana*. Many works are also based on Kerala's own ancient Sanskrit dramas, *Kutiyattam,* and pastimes from Krishna's life that were popularized in Kerala around AD 1650 in a dramatic form called *Krishna Atam*.

A Kathakali performer puts on green make up to play the role of Lord Rama.

As a Kathakali performance nears its climax, the forces of Good and Evil usually prepare for a mighty confrontation and battle scene. At the climax the villain, or *asura* (the opposite of a deva, or, in other words, a demon), is slain by the hero, oftentimes Lord Rama or Krishna. Then, the drums soften, the lamps flicker, and the catharsis of the audience and actors is complete. Everyone concerned has taken an incredibly long, eventful, and intense journey and is now ready to return to everyday life as the first rays of a new day break the horizon.

A Vrindavan play based on the pastimes of Radha and Krishna.

Kathak

"In North India, the classical dance found its fullest interpretation through the Kathak school," writes Sitara Devi. Kathak means "story-teller," and this dance style evolved out of the work of the traveling bards who roamed India communicating its sacred culture to the people. Many of the dance forms and versions of the sacred stories performed in Kathak had their origin in the Himalayan region, and Kathak remains the most popular dance form in Northern India.

In this region Krishna is fondly known as *Natavara,* or the "Divine Dancer," As all of the arts here primarily centered on relating Krishna's pastimes, operatic dance-dramas began to be performed, especially on the theme of Krishna's Divine Dance of Love, or the *rasa-lila* with the cowherd maidens (see Chapter 5). Vaiṣṇavas of the highest order called *rasudharis* devoted their entire lives to glorifying Krishna through music and dance. Eventually, these performances gained scientific and codified structure, becoming known as Kathak.

Kathak has its own language of hand signs and gestures. Enakshi Bhavani reports, "Instead of the statuesque posturing of the Bharata Natyam, the Kathak dancer moves up and down and sideways, whirls and pirouettes, punctuating each Paran [basic dance arrangement] with a perfectly timed precision." Bharata Natyam has 120 basic dance arrangements, or *parans,* while Kathak dancers must learn 100 *parans*. The fundamental elements of Kathak are its regulated postures (*mandalas*), fast turns (*bhramaris*), intricate dance steps (*gatis*), volatile hand gestures (*hastas*), and emotional interpretations (*abhinaya*). All of these must be done in perfect rhythm with the *mridanga* drum, which is a very popular instrument in devotional ceremonies. Of course, a Kathak performance itself is considered a profound religious ceremony and experience, like most other forms of classical Indian dance.

Sunrise at a Gaudiya Vaiṣṇava Temple in Mayapur.

CHAPTER 9: MAYAPUR

In commenting on this incident, His Divine Grace A. C. Bhaktivedanta Swami Prabhupada states that it is a perfect example of how Vaiṣṇava philosophy recognizes the importance of dealing with the varieties of life. Shrila Prabhupada admits, "Factually, in a higher sense, there is no difference between matter and spirit," but in our present condition, unless we make important distinctions and cultivate spiritual activities as opposed to greedy, materialistic activities, we will not be spiritually nourished or achieve the ultimate goal of life—love of God.

Little Nimai appreciated His mother's argument and said, "Why did you conceal self-realization by not teaching Me this practical philosophy in the beginning? . . . no more shall I eat dirt. Whenever I am hungry I shall suck your breast and drink your breast's milk." In this way at an early age Shri Chaitanya learned the basics of Vaiṣṇava philosophy, which He would present so convincingly to top scholars and the general public all over India in His later years. For more delightful details of Shri Chaitanya's childhood, the reader can look at Vrindavan dasa Thakur's biography of Shri Chaitanya named *Caitanya-bhagavata*.

Because Nimai's older brother had left home for the religious life of a sannyasi, or total renunciate, Nimai's parents were afraid to send Nimai to school, lest He get spiritual knowledge and follow the same path. However, His unruliness finally forced their hand and young Nimai started His education. Nimai excelled at academics with dazzling speed and brilliance. The *Caitanya-caritamrta* reports, "When the Lord was studying grammar at the place of Gaṅgādāsa Paṇḍita, He would immediately learn grammatical rules and definitions by heart simply by hearing them once."

O.B.L. Kapoor, an advanced devotee and scholar of Vaiṣṇavism, writes in his excellent book, *The Philosophy and Religion of Shri Chaitanya,* "Nimai's only passion at this time was study, to which he applied himself with single-minded devotion. An intellectual giant that he was, he acquired mastery over the different branches of Sanskrit learning at a very early age." But academic excellence did not bring maturity. Dr. Surendranath Dasgupta in his book, *A History of Indian Philosophy, Volume IV,* writes that Nimai "was indeed very gifted, but he was also very vain, and always took special delight in defeating his fellow-students in debate."

Shri Chaitanya Mahaprabhu inspires His closest associates and the people of Mayapur to perform kirtan, public chanting of God's holy names. Their joy often led to ecstatic dancing and parades.

Shri Chaitanya Chandradoya Mandir, the Mayapur headquarters of the International Society for Krishna Consciousness.

While still a teenager, Nimai's skill in debate won Him the title of "Lion in Debate," the equivalent of being the world champion. Regarding this kind of achievement, His Divine Grace A. C. Bhaktivedanta Swami Prabhupada writes, "As in the modern days there are many champions in sports, so in bygone days there were many learned scholars who were champions in learning." And these championships were earned in scholastic competitions. Curiously enough, this system of intellectual competition was responsible for Buddhism's rapid decline in India around the 8th century AD. If two spiritual teachers debated, the loser and all his students were obliged to become students of the winner. At this time Shankara began touring India, challenging all of the Buddhist teachers to debates. Even though Shankara was just a young man (he died at the early age of 32), he proved to be invincible at spiritual debate and practically all Buddhist teachers fled India rather than lose to Shankara. Naturally, this turn of events greatly reduced Buddhism's influence in India while fostering its growth in other parts of Asia.

In Shri Chaitanya's case, a Keshava Mishra of Kashmir, who was the *digvijayi pandit,* or "World Conqueror," came to Navadvipa to complete his conquest of India's scholarly world. This man's prowess intimidated the scholars of Navadvipa. Bhaktivinode discloses, "Afraid of the so-called conquering pandit, the *tol* [school] professors of Nadia left their town on pretence of invitation." Since Nimai was but a teenager and a loss by Him to the Digvijayi would not be so costly to Navadvipa's reputation, Nimai was left behind to meet the pandit's challenge. Unfortunately for the undefeated pandit, though, after a short encounter "he got defeated by the boy and mortification obliged him to decamp," writes Bhaktivinode.

These Deities of Radha-Madhava (Krishna) grace the altar of Shri Chaitanya Chandradoya Mandir.

During this period, Bengal and India in general desperately needed fresh spiritual impetus. T.V. Shastry calls this time a "dark period in the history of Bengal. The degeneracy of her people, evidenced in the social and religious practices, was their legacy from Buddhism at its worst" as well as deviant Hindu practices. The entire Indian "society was overridden with external form of worship in which spiritual feelings and clear understanding of the real goal of human life were absent," writes P. Banerjee. Also, Bengal had been ruled for nearly three centuries by Muslim rulers, many of whom were hardly sympathetic to Sanatana Dharma. To make matters even worse, the upper-class members of Indian society jealousy guarded their spiritual and social prerogatives, keeping the common people ignorant and repressed. In this dark situation, Nimai's uninhibited spirituality was truly a golden light illuminating the gloom.

Nimai's reputation soon spread throughout the Vaiṣṇava circles of Bengal. Many learned Vaiṣṇava preachers joined Nimai, and Bhaktivinode writes that Navadvipa "became the regular seat of a host of Vaishnava acharyas whose mission it was to spiritualize man-kind with the highest influence of the Vaishnava creed."

As explained in Chapter 6, "Vrindavan," Vaiṣṇavas are somewhat cautious about publicly displaying their emotional ecstasies because of fear of misunderstanding and of unwitting people committing offenses against it. Therefore, at first Nimai led His spiritual services in the private courtyard of His neighbor, Shrivasa, who was one of Nimai's most intimate associates and was even present at Nimai's birth. Kapoor reports that only Nimai's "close associates were allowed to participate. The doors of the house . . . were closed when the Saṁkirtanas (ecstatic group chanting) started and no outsider was allowed to enter." The site of this house is only about two hundred yards north of Shri Chaitanya's birthplace in Mayapur. Today, a picturesque temple commemorates the significance of this holy ground.

Devotees perform kirtan—public chanting—on the main road of Mayapur.

When Nimai was informed of the Kazi's actions, he decided to take a quick and resolute countermeasure. He told His followers that

> in the evening I shall perform saṅkīrtana in each and every town. Therefore you should all decorate the city in the evening. Burn torchlights in every home. I shall give protection to everyone. Let us see what kind of Kazi comes to stop our kīrtana.

Predating Mahatma Gandhi by several centuries, that evening's spiritual demonstration was the first mass incidence of nonviolent, civil disobedience in modern India's history and was totally successful. That evening all of Navadvipa was illumined by torchlight, and the chanting of Hare Krishna resounded everywhere. Shri Chaitanya personally led a massive chanting party of thousands of people to the Kazi's house.

After being assured of Nimai's peaceful intentions, the Kazi came out of hiding in his palace and talked to Nimai. The Kazi revealed that several mystical happenings like spiritual fire singeing the beards of his soldiers when they tried to enforce his ban and his own visions of a wrathful God had weakened his resolve. Actually, on the basis of the *Koran* itself the Kazi was a great offender. The *Koran* states, "And who is more unjust than he who prohibits the name of Allah being gloried in Allah's temples and seeks to ruin them? . . . For them is disgrace in this world: and theirs shall be great punishment in the next."

The fearless stance of Shri Chaitanya also indicated that He was entirely surrendered to the will and protection of God, which is exactly what Islam means, "submission to God." The 113th verse of the Second Chapter of the *Koran* confirms this point, "Nay, whoever submits himself completely to Allah, and is the doer of good, shall have his reward with his Lord. No fear *shall come* upon such, neither shall they grieve." To the Kazi's credit, he was aware of these things, admitted his fault, apologized, and even mentioned God's Vedic names.

Genuinely gladdened by the Kazi's change of heart, Shri Chaitanya said, "The chanting of the holy name of Kṛṣṇa from your mouth has performed a wonder—it has nullified the reactions of all your sinful activities. Now you have become supremely pure . . . you are undoubtedly the most fortunate and pious."

The Kazi cried upon hearing these words and said, "Only by Your mercy have my bad intentions vanished. Kindly favor me so that my devotion may always be fixed upon You."

Pleased by this response, Shri Chaitanya asked, "You must pledge that this saṅkīrtana movement will not be checked, at least in the district of Nadia."

The Kazi agreed, saying, "To as many descendents as take birth in my dynasty in the future, I give this grave admonition: no one should check the saṅkīrtana movement." In commenting on this promise, His Divine Grace A.C. Bhaktivedanta Swami Prabhupada writes, "even at present the descendents of the Kazi's family do not oppose the *saṅkīrtana* movement under any circumstances. Even during the great Hindu-Muslim riots in neighboring places, the descendents of the Kazi honestly preserved the assurance given by their forefather." This is but one of many examples of Muslims and Vaiṣṇavas living together harmoniously. On this note, it must be pointed out that one of the greatest saints of Shri Chaitanya's movement, Haridasa Thakur, was born into a Muslim family. After Advaita Acharya overcame fairly severe opposition, he had him fully accepted into the Vaiṣṇava family of Navadvipa. Soon, however, Haridasa's holiness became legendary, and no one could object to calling him a first-class Vaiṣṇava. Shri Chaitanya gave Haridasa the title of *namacharya,* or the greatest living example of how to chant God's holy name constantly and purely.

A traditional wooden ferry takes devotees across the Ganges River.

Harvest time in the fertile fields of Mayapur.

As we learned in Chapter 6, "Vrindavan," the eternal activities of enlightened souls in the spiritual world are singing and dancing. Therefore, when we sing, dance, and chant on earth, we are aligning ourselves with the highest dimensions of reality and enjoy innumerable benefits from this connection. God's unconditional love flows through us. Regarding chanting, His Divine Grace A.C. Bhaktivedanta Swami Prabhupada writes, "By chanting the Lord's holy name, one can derive all the stipulated energy synchronized from all sources." By making conscious the flow of unconditional love between the self and God, chanting allows us to actualize all of our potentials in a way that is regulated by a higher, divine intelligence. Growth and progress are far faster and more complete than if we tried by our limited intelligence and knowledge to manage this process. In Christian terms, singing, chanting, and dancing are excellent ways of allowing the Holy Spirit to work through us to create results that are beyond our individual capacities—an experience well-known in Black and other charismatic churches.

Many studies have proven the benefits of wholesome music. In *Ways And Power Of Love,* Dr. Pitirim Sorokin ennumerates some of these findings (please note, unwholesome music can have the exact opposite effects). Wholesome music

> increases bodily metabolism and muscular energy; affects volume, pulse, and blood pressure; lowers the threshold of sensory stimuli of different modes; stimulates emotions and moods according to the character of the music; influences internal secretions; reduces or delays fatigue; serves several therapeutic purposes, reduces patients' apprehension and fear, and often is the only medium through which the patient can be reached; increases industrial efficiency and output, and decreases industrial accidents; stimulates the spirit of cheerfulness and friendliness; decreases the feelings of tiredness, unpleasantness, and irritability in the working hours; sharpens the processes of attention and perception, decreases tensions, animosity, and antagonism.

Music is an essential ingredient of life's harmony, and Vaiṣṇavas have always used it consciously in their spiritual practices, deriving the above listed benefits as positive side effects of their devotion to Krishna.

Line of massive gopuras (gateways) at the Shri Rangam Temple.

CHAPTER 10: SRI RANGAM

Sculptures on a Shri Rangam gopura
The figures are from left to right: a Vishnu devotee, Lord Vishnu and His consort Lakshmi, and Saraswati (the Goddess of Learning).

The king of south India, Dharmavarman, was delighted by this turn of events. He felt that God really owned his kingdom anyway, and now God in the form of Shri Ranganatha was simply reclaiming His proprietorship. Dharmavarman constructed a gigantic temple on the island of the Kaveri on the site of where the present temple stands, and then installed Shri Ranganatha in it. After worshiping here for the rest of his life, King Dharmavarman went back to Godhead, attaining true salvation.

Some time after the reign of Dharmavarman, a terrible flood submerged Shri Rangam, and shifting sands completely buried the temple complex and Deity. Then, a dense forest sprang up over the site and for a long time, even the memory of Shri Rangam was erased from the south Indian mind. Finally, King Kili, a descendent of Dharmavarman, was resting one day under a tree and, unbeknownst to him, over Shri Rangam. The King was stunned by hearing a parrot chanting ancient Sanskrit verses glorifying Shri Rangam in the tree above him. Being open to divine revelation in all ways and forms, King Kili took this incident seriously. He ordered the area excavated, and his workers began finding Shri Rangam's walls. Then, in a dream God revealed to Kili the exact spot of the sanctuary. His workers quickly dug down and recovered Shri Ranganathaswami.

Auboyer tells us of King Kili's reaction to this miraculous happening: "Full of joy, King Kili had the forest cleared and the sand removed. He then built around the rediscovered sanctuary a temple with streets, enclosures and flower gardens." And, in an unbroken chain from the time of King Kili before the ninth century AD, Shri Rangam has flourished to this day.

A bathing ghat in an inner compound of the Shri Rangam Temple.

Ramanuja appeared in a brahmin family and was raised in an environment saturated with the teachings and lively holiness of the Alwars. In the book, *Outlines of South Indian History,* M.N. Venkata Ramanappa writes, "The progress of Ramanuja in learning was so rapid that it attracted the attention of his own great grand-father, Āḷavandar [also known as Yamunacharya], who was the chief Pontiff at Shrirangam." Alavandor was a vigorous Vaiṣṇava who attracted many learned disciples, who themselves became vigorous preachers of the faith. M. Yamunacharya writes, "Time passed with Alavandor happily in the work of watching and propagating the faith and writing a number of works."

In the past when Alavandor's teacher thought him ready, he was brought before Shri Ranganatha for the first time and had a marvelous spiritual vision. M. Yamunacharya describes it:

> He saw the holy image of Ranga as the treasure which the Universe enshrined. He exclaimed with feelings of bliss overflowing in streams of loving tears. 'O Blissful God, many days have I lost in the vain pursuits of the world. I mourn for this. Now, I have seen Thee. I shall be Thy servant hereafter. I feel reclaimed from the *death* of worldly enjoyments and initiated into the *life* of Thy service.'

Now, as his life's mission was nearing its glorious end, Alavandor was seeking a fitting successor. He went incognito to Kanchi to size up his great-grandson at school. When he saw Ramanuja, he remarked, "that bright and glorious central figure in the group possessing those fine shoulders broad and long like those of Shri Rama himself, that is Ramanuja." Happy with what he observed, Alavandor prayed:

> By thy favour, O Lord, the deaf hears, the lame runs, the dumb speaks, the blind sees and the barren woman bears. I have sought thee, grant me then that this Rāmānuja shall become the bearer of the torch of our Faith.

The Gateway To Heaven—the doorway to the sanctum sanctorum of the Shri Rangam Temple.

When Alavandor knew his passing from this world was imminent, he sent for Ramanuja, who, unfortunately, arrived soon after Alavandor's final departure. While paying respects to Alavandor's holy body, Ramanuja "discovered to his surprise three of the five fingers of the right palm of the sage remained closed," writes M. Yamunacharya. After questioning Alavandor's followers about what this could mean, Ramanuja discovered that the head of Shri Rangam had left with three desires unfulfilled—including the writing of an authoritative Vaiṣṇava commentary on the *Vedanta-sutra,* which is also named the *Brahma-sutra*. This commentary was especially important, since without it a religious school of thought was not taken seriously in the higher circles of Indian spiritual life. Shankara's commentary on the *Sutras* had firmly established the monist position, but now Vaiṣṇavism was considered inferior to Shankara's newer interpretation in intellectual circles because Vaiṣṇavas had no commentary to contend with Shankara's. Upon learning of this state of affairs, Ramanuja immediately vowed to achieve Alavandor's three desires if God and the sage blessed him. As this vow resounded in the hall, M. Yamunacharya writes, "the three bent fingers of the sage opened as if to say: 'aye.'"

Goshthipurna was stunned by this response. It stimulated an instantaneous reevaluation of his own position and he replied, "O that this idea never entered my crippled heart . . . which would not be moved with love for all mankind. Strange, I never felt the all-embracing love of Rāmānuja." At this point the student had become the teacher and the teacher gladly became a student and accepted Ramanuja's actions as being totally consistent with the meaning of the Ashtakshara Mantra. Goshthipurna then embraced Ramanuja and said, "Holy son, thou art mine, my own indeed thou art."

From that moment on, Shri Rangam would begin to function in the open manner of Ramanuja, and no longer would basic and holy mantras be kept hidden from the masses. The Ashtakshara Mantra of eight syllables—*oṁ namo nārāyaṇāya,* which M. Yamunacharya calls "the granter of every boon and promoter of devotion"—would now be openly chanted and taught. Narayana is another name for God, or Krishna. M. Yamunacharya gives us a good explanation of it. He writes that Narayana

> signifies 'we are in Him and He is in us.' *He is in us* implies the bond between Him and souls, the bond by which He is bound by His Grace to save us. *We are in him* implies that we can freely and wholly trust Him for all our welfare. . . . Absolute trust consists in thinking of ourselves as destined by Him to serve some mighty purpose of His.

Ramanujacharya (AD 1017-1137).

In *Outline of South Indian History* Ramanappa states that this episode distinguished Ramanuja "as a progressive reformer and a religious teacher by his love of the people of the oppressed classes." During his education, Ramanuja accepted as his teacher Mahapurna, who was of a lower caste than Ramanuja. While Ramanuja fully accepted Mahapurna as a transcendental personality beyond all social categories and worthy of the highest respects, Ramanuja's wife could not, and she offended the guru and his wife several times. Because of his wife's caste consciousness, Ramanuja abandoned householder life and was initiated into sannyas—the life of total religious dedication—at a relatively early age.

Throughout Ramanuja's career, M. Yamunacharya tells us, he felt it was his duty "to minister to the religious cravings of the lowest and humblest classes of people. . . . He opened the door of religious instruction to all those classes." Ramanuja was especially moved by the plight of the "untouchables," a category of people considered to have no social status whatsoever. He taught that everyone is a child of God and worked hard to erase the blot of "untouchability" from the Indian social system.

As has been intimated, Ramanuja studied with many Vaiṣṇava teachers to complete his training to take up the leadership of Shri Rangam. Because of this broad exposure, M. Yamunacharya writes that "Rāmānuja is described as the central gem in the precious necklace made up of the gems of teachers and disciples of the Vaiṣṇava apostolic." Now, with the blessings of all his gurus, Ramanuja was ready to assume his duties and start his mission.

Colorful sculptures of Garbhadaksya Vishnu and His associates adorn a threshold to the Shri Rangam Temple.

Terra-cotta Deities of Jagannath, Balarama, and Subhadra found in Tanjore near Shri Rangam.

The Vijaynagar kings generously patronized Shri Rangam. They reconstructed the seven concentric walls and built many towers. Most of this renovation work occurred during the 15th and 16th centuries, and present-day Shri Rangam owes much of its existence in structures, management, and festivities to these enlightened kings.

In AD 1510 Shri Chaitanya visited Shri Rangam and spent the four month rainy season quartered there at the home of Vyenkata Bhatta. His biography tells us: "While there, Śrī Caitanya Mahāprabhu took His bath in the River Kāveri and visited the temple of Śrī Raṅga. Every day the Lord also danced in ecstasy." At Shri Rangam the Lord met one of His "Six Goswamis of Vrindavan," Vyenkata Bhatta's son, who later became famous as Gopala Bhatta Goswami (see Chapter 6).

During His visit, Shri Chaitanya and Vyenkata Bhatta became close friends and used to enjoy long religious conversations sprinkled with humor and transcendental joking. Shri Chaitanya was gradually introducing Vyenkata Bhatta to the higher *rasas,* or relationships, with Krishna. Finally, Vyenkata Bhatta admitted, "Lord Kṛṣṇa and Lord Nārāyaṇa are one and the same, but the pastimes of Kṛṣṇa are more relishable due to their sportive nature." Vyenkata Bhatta was beginning to appreciate how Lord Krishna related to His devotees in friendship, parental affection, and conjugal love—rasas which were beyond the Narayana conception of God. However, Shri Chaitanya also affirmed in these conversations that it is offensive to consider one form of God better than another form of God. He said, "There is no difference between the transcendental forms of the Lord. Different forms are manifest due to different attachments of different devotees. Actually, the Lord is one, but He appears in different forms just to satisfy His devotees."

The Shore Temple at sunset.

CHAPTER 11: MAHABALIPURAM

The Shore Temple at sunrise.

Long before the time of Hippocrates (460-357 BC) the spices of south India—pepper, nutmeg, cardamom, and others—found their way to Greece, Phoenicia, and Rome through the beautiful, tropical port of Mahabalipuram. This trade prospered for well over 1,500 years, making Mahabalipuram a thriving metropolis, incredibly rich, cultured, and cosmopolitan.

The book *India* by Greystone Press states that the southern Kingdoms of India

> built great merchant and war fleets. Much of what they exported went to the Roman Empire. There are records of Roman fleets sailing from the Red Sea to India, and many Roman coins have been found in Southern India as well as the remains of a Roman colony and temple near Cranganore.

Ancient Chinese and Persian coins have also been discovered in Mahabalipuram's sands. Her people were courageous and adventurous. Waves of Indian emigrants departed from Mahabalipuram to settle in southeast Asia, Indonesia, Fiji, Java, and other Pacific locations. Because of their bravery, Vedic culture and art exerted a great civilizing influence over a vast area. The most startling monument of this immigration is the legendary temple of Angkor Wat in Cambodia. It is famous for its beauty and is the largest Vishnu temple in the world.

The Penance of Arjuna.

The concept of universal brotherhood was strong in ancient India. The *Laws of Manu* state, "This one is my countryman; this other is a stranger—so thinks the man of narrow mind and heart. The noble soul regards the whole wide world as kin." The scholars who wrote *India* consider this tolerant, assimilative tendency of Vedic culture to be responsible for its amazing longevity and resiliency. They write, "A unique source of strength for Hinduism is its extraordinary capacity for absorbing other religions. Instead of persecuting new creeds it assimilates them: it absorbs new concepts as a sponge absorbs water."

This Indian trait was not a result of expediency, but came from a genuine openness to new truth and a commitment to the evolution of human understanding. The authors of *India* write that throughout Indian history this tendency to assimilate worked so well that it made new inputs "sources of new strength." In this regard India and the United States have a lot in common. Both countries are perhaps the greatest living testaments to the power of the "melting pot."

Perhaps the most striking example of India's open-door policy is the history of the Jews in the Malabar region near Mahabalipuram. After the Romans devastated Jerusalem, the first group of Jews emigrated to Malabar around AD 70. They established a thriving, semi-autonomous community. K. Bharatha Iyer writes, "the charter of Bhaskara Ravi Varma conferred on the Jews valuable privileges and the head of the community was raised to a Nāṭuvāzhi (Governor)." Ironically, the Jews lived peacefully in India for almost 1,500 years until the arrival of the Portuguese in the sixteenth century. Iyer writes, "The Portuguese persecuted and compelled them to leave the town [Cochin] in 1565 when the Hindu ruling power had weakened." In spite of this harrassment by Westerners, in 1968 about one hundred descendents of the Jews still lived in Cochin—a marvelous confirmation of India's longstanding policy of protection for all peoples.

A yali (protector) stares out from the Vishnu Temple in Mahabalipuram's town square.

Archeologists consider Mahabalipuram "an archeological paradise." Casual snorkeling in the seas off Mahabalipuram can find the swimmer ancient coins, statues, and undersea ruins. By poking around in the sands, a person can also discover ancient relics. While many of the principal structures of Mahabalipuram have been uncovered, R. K. Das concludes that "more monuments, religious and secular, [are] buried underneath the high sand dunes of the neighborhood." Mahabalipuram is a perfect candidate for more archeological research.

Many of the monuments of Mahabalipuram are matchless and world class in quality, concept, and design. In Heinrich Zimmer's opinion the artists of Mahabalipuram "developed an ideal of the human form that was unique, something quite its own, when compared with the works of the rest of the Indian mainland." Her monuments are so special and numerous, writes Mr. Fergusson, that Mahabalipuram "has been visited and more often described than any other place in India."

Temple sculptures look out at the Bay of Bengal.

When merchants returned to Europe from Mahabalipuram, they always told their friends of a cluster of exquisite temples there, which the Europeans named the "Seven Pagodas." Even today, "Seven Pagodas" is synonymous with Mahabalipuram, although legend has it that six of the pagodas were lost to the raging seas in the tenth century. One pagoda, or temple, remains. Concerning this temple, Subramanyam writes, "Spanning twelve centuries of history and braving the corrosive onslaughts of nature, it stands as a symbol of the soaring aesthetic aspirations of the Pallavas."

Officially, this pagoda is called the "Shore Temple" and is famous worldwide. Actually, it is not a single temple, but a complex of three structures, two being dedicated to Lord Shiva, while the central compound is dedicated to Lord Vishnu. The Pallava Kings leaned primarily towards Vaiṣṇavism and Shivism, but, whichever way they were inclined, all aspects of the Godhead were worshipped and supported with the Shore Temple being a perfect example of their eclecticism.

Deep experience of a higher spiritual pleasure animated the Pallavas and their artists. Unless their communion with God was direct, vivid, and profound, they could not have achieved their tour de force in spiritual aesthetics. As Subramanyam writes, "An ethereal radiance appears to be at play everywhere, affecting everyone, the associates, the beneficiaries, and the adversaries, with varying intensity. The dominant note of . . . Pallava art is devotion, surrender." The goal was none other than "the transformation of life on earth in terms of the Divine," adds Subramanyam. To walk amongst these monuments is to participate in an unprecedented experiment in showing the mystery, beauty, and harmony of God to the range of the human senses.

Basham tells us that the artists who designed the Penance of Arjuna "had a sardonic sense of humour, for among the worshipping ascetics they carved the crafty cat, who performed penances to lure the mice to their doom." But for now, since the cat is deep in meditation, the mice play right before him without fear. The Penance of Arjuna is truly "a cameo of the cosmos."

A Sanskrit poet of the sixth century AD, Bharavi, had adapted the Penance of Arjuna story from the *Mahabharata* for his immensely popular poem of the time, *Kiratarjuniya*. Subramanyam reports, "It is believed that Bharavi must have inspired the Pallava kings to depict the same theme on the rock canvas." This fact, along with the sculpture itself, convinces most experts that Arjuna is indeed the person undergoing austerities in this most magnificent relief.

Outstanding among the monoliths of Mahabalipuram are the "Pancha Pandava Rathas," or the five (pancha) chariots (rathas) of the Pandava brothers. These temples are each carved out of a solid boulder and resemble massive chariots. Subramanyam assesses their importance in the following words, "Whether viewed as individual units endowed with a structural individuality and grace or as archetypes providing the model and inspiration for generations of temple-builders, the rock-cut shrines in Mamallapuram stand out as a class apart."

The Arjuna Ratha monolith with accompanying elephant. Both 7th century works are carved out of individual granite boulders.

Overview of the temple complex below Pakshi-tirtha.

Let us now tour some of the best cave temples of Mahabalipuram. First we have the Varaha Cave, which is right behind Arjuna's Penance. This temple is 33 by 14 by 12 feet and is known for three remarkable features: four panels of beautiful door-keepers, four excellent bas-reliefs inside, and an attractive frontage with an open terrace into which has been cut an oblong ablution tank with steps leading down to the water. The Varaha panel is on the northern inside wall. It tells of a time when the earth sank out of orbit and God in the form of a transcendental boar, Varaha, dove into the cosmic ocean to rescue the earth, symbolized in this sculpture by the Goddess of Earth. As Varaha emerges triumphantly out of the water, He holds the delicate Earth Goddess, who is seated on one of His knees.

Next we have the cave temple called Krishna Mandap, which is cut into the side of a boulder. Its main highlight is a sculpture of Krishna lifting Govardhana Hill, a subject we have covered in Chapters 6 and 7. Ramanappa writes, "This representation of the Govardhana scene is probably the best in India. . . ." The most charming feature of this sculpture is its depiction of the simple and innocent joys of pastoral life. While Indra sends down a torrential deluge and Krishna lifts Govardhana Hill, the residents of Vrindavan go about their lives unconcerned and unaffected by the crisis around them. Mothers care for babies, a cowherd boy plays his flute for bemused cows, and a milkmaid carries pots of dairy products on her head. These tableaus are near and dear to the experience of the vast majority of Indians over the long course of their history and make worshipers at this shrine especially affectionate for Krishna.

The temple at Pakshi-tirtha, where the legendary two white eagles land every day to eat prasadam.

Heinrich Zimmer gives this sculpture the highest praise. "What is most striking in this relief," he writes, "is the nimble, slender grace and dashing courage of the maidenlike Goddess. She appears as a young amazon . . . rushing at the clumsy demon who is greater in stature and strength than all the gods."

The subtlety of Pallava art is also greatly appreciated by Zimmer. He writes, "The works of this Pallava period, though vigorous, are very gentle; in representing brutal dramatic scenes, such as that of the present battle, they tend to avoid the moment of climax, and seek to suggest their point with restraint and indirectness." The sculpture shows the battle in mid-progress. The demon looks crafty as he reluctantly and stubbornly retreats, looking for an opening to deliver a telling blow. Zimmer states:

> The final triumph is not depicted. Yet it is obviously beyond question. The brilliant amazon, provided with the weapons of all the gods and stimulated by their hymns of praise, is the representative of all the affirmative forces of the universe. The demon is already hopeless; his massive head and club, suggesting darkness, violence, and resentment, are about to fall.

Another poem in stone.

For most of the Middle Ages the lucrative spice trade between India and the West had fallen into the monopolistic hands of Venetian and Arab merchants. They charged exorbitantly high commissions, and, when ship construction and navigation improved in Europe to the point of making long ocean voyages feasible, their European customers eagerly sent out fleets to search for new and direct trade routes to India, the land of fabulous wealth.

On one of these voyages Christopher Columbus "discovered" the Americas. Finally, in 1498 the Portuguese explorer, Vasco de Gama, reached the Malabar coast and landed at Mahabalipuram. Iyer writes, "This opened up a new and historic epoch of momentous consequence for India as well as for the entire East and that story is still unfolding itself."

A brahmin feeds prasadam to one of the two white eagles at Pakshi-tirtha.

East and West were again in direct contact as in the days of the Greek city-states and the Roman Empire. One interesting footnote to this renewed exchange is that the traditional boat used by the Indians at Mahabalipuram found its way to the West and is extremely popular today. In any Western yacht harbor we see many sleek "kattu marams," or catamarans in English. In the Tamil language *kattu maram* means "tied wood." The design of kattu marams is so sound that, with modern technology and construction materials, catamarans are some of the fastest boats on the seas today.

While India exported essential goods, luxuries, and knowledge to the West—"Arabian" numerals originated with Indian mathematicians but were taken to Europe by Arab merchants—and received gold in exchange for them, it wasn't too long before the West's superior military technology made the trade very one-sided. India would be severely traumatized and economically exploited by the coming colonial era, but would emerge from it in 1947 as an independent and united nation—something India had not been for a long, long time.

In the next chapter we shall see how one great Indian monarch of the modern era responded to this renewed contact with the West in the typically open and synthetic Indian fashion. But before we travel north again to visit one of the most beautiful cities of the world built in the modern era—Jaipur—let us take one little side trip to the outskirts of Mahabalipuram to meet two extraordinary eagles.

Atop the Vedagiri Hills near Mahabalipuram stands a famous Shiva temple called Pakshi-tirtha. *Pakshi* means "the birds," while *tirtha* means "a holy place of pilgrimage." Every day throngs of pilgrims brave the intense late-morning sun to climb a seemingly endless series of steps carved into the mountainside (the only way to reach the temple) to witness the daily noontime miracle of Pakshi-tirtha.

As noon approaches, two white eagles can be seen flying in from the north. The eagles circumambulate the temple three times, then land on a large boulder. Next, the temple priest feeds the birds a few morsels of blessed rice and a little water. After the eagles have finished their lunch, they take off and continue their southernly flight.

Ancient scriptures claim that these two eagles are no ordinary birds, but were actually yogis in their previous lifetime. Because of a discrepancy in their yoga practice, they had to take rebirth as eagles and are required to visit Pakshi-tirtha for millions of years. Certainly this story stretches the credulity of an educated, contemporary person, yet strong evidence exists to verify the eagles' daily visits for at least four to five hundred years! The *Caitanya-caritamrta,* Shri Chaitanya's biography written 485 years ago, refers to Pakshi-tirtha as a well-known holy place of that era, meaning the eagles also existed at that time.

Another strong evidence for the eagles' antiquity, though, was discovered by the Archaeological Survey of India in 1908 and published in the same year in the report of the Madras Government's Epigraphist. A group of inscriptions uncovered at Pakshi-tirtha dated 1664 and 1687 listed the names of more than ten Dutch army officers who personally witnessed the noontime meal and flight of the eagles. The list included the name of the Governor of the Coromandal Coast for that period.

The Chandra Mahal—City Palace—in Jaipur.

CHAPTER 12: JAIPUR

People stroll on one of the broad avenues of Jaipur.

One of the most inhospitable places on the face of the earth is the barren Thar Desert, which covers most of India's second largest state, Rajasthan. Spring turns the Rajasthani deserts into a furnace. The average temperature hovers around 100 degrees until the dreaded Loo winds begin to blow. Then the mercury jumps another fifteen to twenty degrees, and all people run for shelter. Special hats with built-in earflaps are donned by those few people brave enough to venture outside. As far away as Mathura and Vrindavan, Indians protect themselves from the Loo. There are instances of people being driven insane by a hot rush of searing Loo air, especially if it enters the ears. Hence, the region has developed its distinctive caps, which are designed to avoid this catastrophe. Nevertheless, the Loo is a menace as it whips up the surface soil into dust storms. In her book, *A Princess Remembers,* the Maharani of Jaipur, Gayatri Devi, explains that at this time, "The rivers dry up completely or shrink to thin, opaque trickles and all farming comes to a standstill while the people wait for the monsoon rains."

But the rains come, and especially the eastern side of the Thar desert enjoys a tremendous resurgence. Amid the rock and tracts of sand lie lush jungles, enchanting lakes, and fertile farmlands. Rajasthan is an area of extremes and intensities. By learning to adapt to its rigorous demands and responding positively to the land's abundant opportunities, the proud peoples of Rajasthan have distinguished themselves as being among the most talented and vigorous peoples of the world. Their courage, vision, resourcefulness, and cooperative spirit have been fully demonstrated time after time after time, especially over the course of the last five hundred years. Their story is a special chapter in world history.

Before Indian independence, Rajasthan was known as Rajputana, or the "Abode of Kings." It was comprised of twenty-two princely kingdoms. During the British occupation of India, these kingdoms retained semi-autonomous status. Their external affairs were controlled by the British, but the royal Rajput families governed the domestic affairs of their peoples in the traditional manner. Therefore, the native culture and refinement of the Rajasthani peoples have been preserved largely intact. *Fodor's India* asserts that Rajasthan "offers the visitor a spectacle of India in a way that cannot be matched by any other State in the Union." He later goes on to write, "Here . . . the traveler from the West will witness the pure splendor of the Orient."

The Rajput people and royal families trace their ancestry to the great martial clans of the immortal poems *Ramayana* and *Mahabharata*. They especially emulate the ideals of Lord Rama, who is considered to be the best example of an executive head of state totally dedicated to the people's welfare and service to God. In fact, Rama is worshiped as an incarnation of God who descended from the transcendental abode just to demonstrate perfectly the art of governance. Even to this day in India the ideal of perfect government is called Rama-rajya, and throughout history most Rajput monarchs sincerely have tried to live up to this ideal.

Far from being dictatorial or exploitative tyrants, most of the governing families of Rajasthan were renowned for their fair and beneficial rule. A warm and strong bond of love existed between the peoples of Rajasthan and their leaders, a bond forged by centuries of mutual hard work, sacrifice, and love of life. Neither the British occupation nor the advent of democracy could erase from the Rajasthani mind the memory of their rulers providing and caring for them like parents throughout times of prosperity and hardship. In the specific example of the 10,000 square mile area of Jaipur, we find case after case of excellent and far-sighted government equal in positive accomplishments for their people to that of any other government in the world. While speaking of the almost mystical union between the people and their rulers in states like Jaipur, Lord Curzon said, "The Native States have that indefinable quality endearing them to the people, that arises from their being born of the soil."

The Amber citadel.

A secluded bathing ghat in the old city of Amber.

Rather than fight the Mughals, Raja Bharmal gave his daughter in marriage to young Emperor Akbar. Their son, Salim, became heir to the Mughal throne, and he in turn also married a Kachwaha princess. By this intermarriage and the Mughal's deep appreciation of the talents and skills of the Kachwahas, a stable Mughal-Rajput axis was created, which, in Davar's words, "served as a firm support to the Mughal Empire for centuries." During the reign of Maharaja Man Singh (AD 1590-1614) of Amber, he distinguished himself as the ablest of all Emperor Akbar's military commanders. His name was a household word throughout the Mughal Empire, and he also served as peacetime governor of important districts like Kabul, Bengal, Bihar, and the Deccan.

Maharaja Man Singh was a devout Vaiṣṇava (in Chapter 6 we learned how he supported the building of the Govinda temple in Vrindavan). During Man Singh's time, Akbar was a fairly enlightened and universally-minded ruler, so the mixture of Mughal and Rajput cultures progressed smoothly with genuine, mutual benefit and enthusiasm. With King Man Singh of Amber standing beside Emperor Akbar as his military commander-in-chief, India was quite secure from any internal or external military threat, and the full energies of the emperor were devoted to increasing the material prosperity of the empire, while also subsidizing an artistic and cultural renaissance in India for all religious groups. In spite of Man Singh's prowess and exalted position in this vast empire of Akbar the Great, he remained a profoundly modest, cultured, and spiritual man.

An exquisite example of the inlaid marble tiles found throughout Chandra Mahal.

MAKING THE DREAM A REALITY

> Out of the silken darkness of a desert dawn
> emerged the dream of Jaipur city in the eyes
> of Sawai Jai Singh.
>
> Sawai Jai Singh had a vision of a heaven on earth,
> from the midst of the miseries of feudal disruption,
> and saw to the realisation of his vision
> in one of the few planned cities of the world—Jaipur.
>
> —Mulk Raj Anand

The book, *Homage To Jaipur,* begins with a twenty-four page biography of Jai Singh written by Mulk Raj Anand. The piece's poetic beauty, use of language in general, and philosophical depth equals in brilliance the biography's illustrious subject, Maharaja Jai Singh II. Although it is written in English, this biography is almost completely unknown in the West. Nevertheless, the authors of *Vaiṣṇava India* must acknowledge Anand's work as being one of the best written and enlightening biographies we have ever read.

Anand tells us that Jai Singh saw the building of his new city as a new beginning for his entire people. His primary goal was to transform the Kingdom of Amber, a feudalistic social body, into the State of Jaipur, a social body that preserved its ancient Vaiṣṇava culture, but modernized itself by the latest advances in technology, business, architecture, and the general progressing knowledge of humanity. Jai Singh hired 55,000 workers and craftspeople, paying them handsomely and promptly in gold over the course of fifteen years, to make his dream into a reality. The results were so successful that Anand writes, "You are one of the few feudalists of history in our country, whose philosophy the moderns can emulate. . . ." Ashim Kumar Roy reports, "Long before he died at the age of 56, Jai Singh had made Jaipur, as the state was by then called, one of the most important ones in Rajasthan both in area and prosperity."

When we assess how quickly and easily Jai Singh transformed his feudal, hill-fortress people into the thriving, lively, and cultured people of the vast Rajasthani plains, it has to go down in history as one of the most successful peaceful transformations of a people from the feudal to the modern worlds ever recorded. The trend of superlatives being achieved by the Kachwaha family continues with Jai Singh as it would continue on far into the future and right up to this very day, which is a story for the end of this chapter.

Anand explains the relationship between Jai Singh's astronomical research and his building of Jaipur. As Jai Singh observed beautiful order in the heavens and their circling orbs, he fervently desired to create a similar harmony in his own life, which was inextricably connected to the welfare of the people, whom he felt Govinda (God) had entrusted to him to govern wisely. Anand writes:

> And, more than everything,
> Sawai Jai Singh's astronomical researches demanded that
> as he had discerned order in the disposition of the planets
> in the macrocosm,
> so must he create a small order of his own microcosm.

Anand tells us that at this time Jai Singh's political power and creative vision were both getting stronger and stronger. However, Jai Singh's gaze now went from the stars to an oasis just seven miles down from the Amber Palace. On this site were six peaceful villages amidst groves of fragrant sandal, mango, rose-apple, champa, and palm trees. In between the trees grew an abundance of creepers. Here, Jai Singh wanted to build a "beautiful city in proportions through which the microcosm of the township may reflect, in essence, the order of the macrocosm," writes Anand. In other words, Jai Singh wanted to build a city where every person had their proper space and support to live a happy, prosperous, and spiritual life. Rather than using his absolute power for his own self-aggrandizement, Jai Singh used the security of his absolute power to meditate on social, economic, and political forms which would best serve the entire state. There is no doubt that Jai Singh enjoyed a high status and reward in Jaipur, but he more than earned his keep by providing some of the most effective and far-sighted leadership in the history of government.

E.N. Bacon in his book, *Design of Cities,* explains some of the joy to be derived from planning for more than yourself: "Through this sense of connection with a system greater than himself, man achieves aesthetic satisfaction. The more nearly universal the system, the deeper the satisfaction." By this standard Jai Singh was a most satisfied man, for he related intimately and well with all dimensions of reality, reaching the heights of universality—unselfish and altruistic actions for the good of all.

Another remarkable thing about Jai Singh was his enormously practical talent of translating his dreams and ideals into concrete realities like city plans, zoning, and passive solar designed buildings. A proclivity for architecture runs in the royal Rajput blood. Satish Davar explains why the Rajput nobility generally made great architects: "Abundance of building materials, extremes of climate, love of life and the dire necessity of fortifications made architecture a living tradition."

Besides studying the Vedic tradition's texts on building and town planning, the *Shilpa Shastras,* Jai Singh also investigated Western works in these areas. Jai Singh especially knew a lot about the design of Versailles and Luxembourg. In his excellent booklet, *Jaipur,* which is really a guide to Jaipur, Daulat Singh describes the architectural goals and efforts of Jai Singh:

> There was an urgent need for harmony. He must build a city where every public building is designed in harmony, all street fronts controlled and public activities zoned. His talented architect, Vidyadhar, rose to the occasion. No other city before Jaipur had received such detailed thought. It was an unprecedented attempt to achieve harmony of total environment.

Jai Singh was not bound by the past, but inspired by the past to make his own unique contribution to the world by applying the universal laws of life, Sanatana Dharma, to the particular circumstances of his time and environment. As a person, Jai Singh was the perfect blend of study and action, theory and practice, spiritual wisdom and worldly wisdom. Satish Davar writes that Jai Singh designed and built Jaipur "as a rational, futuristic city." Even today, the study of futurism, although an accepted academic discipline, is still considered the most avant-garde of all scholarly pursuits. But in the early 18th century, Jai Singh was not only a master of futurism academically, but he also built a fabulously successful city and state based on his futuristic studies.

In constructing Jaipur, Satish Davar tells us, the Maharaja showed "an astounding clarity of vision and an intelligent grasp of form and function. His logical mind constructed an inward looking environment, in which space and light are measured according to the laws of geometry, of mechanics, and optics." All of this care was taken to ensure that every resident had clear and easy access to the beauties and energies of nature. Jai Singh was convinced that a city designed to harmonize organically with the forces of nature would achieve heights of material and spiritual success. And, in the case of Jaipur, the Maharaja was correct.

Anand tells us that Jaipur is planned so that each resident "might be able to discover their own interrelationship with the universe, by living in intimate connection with the stars. . . ." Part of the design and zoning regulations gave each resident and each building access to sun and shade in the daytime and a clear view of the sky at night.

Portico of the office of the Head Curator, Dr. Das, of the Sawai Jai Singh II Museum.

Maharaja Madho Singh was the first monarch of Jaipur to leave India. In order to carry sacred Ganges water with him to drink during his voyage and visit to England, sterling silver, five foot high lotas (waterpots) were built. Here is one of them. They are the largest silver objects in the world.

As we approach the city's main gate, we find Jaipur, in Gayatri Devi's words, a city lying "on a plain, encircled by brown desert hills with fortifications and walls snaking over their contours." As we get closer, we might echo the Maharani's assessment that Jaipur is "the prettiest [capital] I had ever seen—an intricacy of domes and towers, lattices and verandas. . . . ." The people cheer again as Jai Singh's chariot, loaded with the Maharaja and fifty of his most trusted ministers, passes through the beautifully arched gateway, painted and inlaid with mosaic tiles, shining as resplendently as the Sun to whom it is dedicated. At the opposite end of the city stands a gateway named after the Moon. Sun and Moon gateways are a convention of Rajput cities.

Once inside Jaipur, we can see that the streets are lavishly wide, ordered, and straight. Jaipur is laid out in a grid system. Davar tells us Jaipur "has the distinction of being the first planned city in recent history that used a straightforward and precise grid pattern for its street-system." For the flat desert plain on which Jaipur stands, the grid system was a logical choice, but logic alone is never enough for a Rajput. Jaipur, like many Vaiṣṇava temples, is designed as a small replica of the universe. Dr. Ashoke Das writes, "Vidyadhar [Jai Singh's architect] divided his city into nine rectangular sectors symbolising the nine divisions of the universe." One advantage of "a nine-square sub-division of space," writes Davar, is that the central area can be reserved "for a privileged use and related visually and mathematically to the surrounding area as well." In this central square in Jaipur stands Jai Singh's palace and other public buildings.

Interestingly enough, New Haven, Connecticut, in the United States was designed in 1824 as a model city along the same pattern as Jaipur. In her book, *New Haven: A Guide to Architecture and Urban Design,* Elizabeth Mills Brown writes, "New Haven was laid out in the form of a large square divided into nine smaller squares—the central one reserved as common land. . . . This compelling diagram is recognized today as one of the earliest and most important in American planning history." From this statement we can see that the judgment and foresight of Jai Singh and his architect were sound and are confirmed by our most contemporary planners.

The streets of Jaipur are designed for aesthetics, comfort, free-flowing commerce, and the celebration of life. The main avenues are broad and expansive, being exactly 108 feet wide (108 is one of the most sacred numbers in Vaiṣṇavism). The smaller streets and passageways are 54', 27', and 13' 6" wide, respectively. The buildings along the main avenues are either four or five stories or fifty to fifty-five feet tall. The geometrical proportion of the building height to road width used in Jaipur is the same as used by contemporary government officials in determining zoning laws and equal access to sunlight.

The harsh Rajasthani climate, especially the desert sun and heat, demanded special attention in the architecture of Jaipur. Davar writes, "A sensitive handling of sun and space are important design criteria in desert settlements. It is essential to reduce the intensity of the sun for physical comfort and to give specific direction to controlled space for mental comfort. . . ." Therefore, Jai Singh told his architect "to study the relation of the sun at various times of the day, in the desert, and the airs of the different seasons," writes Anand. The resulting passive solar design of Jaipur makes the city comfortable to live in year-round.

Passive solar design means that little or no machinery or mechanical devices are used to create climate control. Rather, the position, design, and materials of the building naturally produce ameliorating effects on the weather. In the case of Jaipur, Davar reports:

> The building fronts were carefully modelled to keep the interiors cool, to allow only limited, glare-free light indoors and to get free circulation of breeze. Deep sun-shade obtained by continuous projections of inclined stone-slabs resting on triangular brackets are very effective in keeping large parts of the external wall in cool shade, when the sun is most direct and most intense. These sun shades (chajjas) at each level present strong horizontal lines re-inforcing each other and establishing a pleasing relationship with the street.

The Deities of Radha-Govindaji in Chandra Mahal. They are the presiding Deities of Jaipur.

An overview of the Jantar Mantar Observatory.

As Jai Singh passes these beautiful and practical facades on Jaipur's buildings, the celebration increases in intensity. The wide streets are packed with cheering, singing, and dancing people. Their spontaneous joy and creative expressions are every bit as important to them as the splendor and spectacle of the royal procession. Because of the streets' width, they have become, in Davar's words, "a dynamic stadium" that makes "a great contribution to the civic life of princely Jaipur." Festivities are so important to Jai Singh and his people that no trees line the streets to obscure the view. Davar tells us, "Trees were planted in clusters in parks, gardens, and public squares." The buildings along the main avenues are covered with public terraces, viewing balconies, and convenient rooftops for people to observe the highly developed Rajput and Vaiṣṇava ceremonial life, and, of course, to observe each other. The streets in Jaipur are not only for transportation of goods and people. As Davar writes, "The poetic and mythic function of the street was as significant as its rational or practical use."

Jai Singh's chariot is now passing through the main commercial sector of Jaipur. The Maharaja looks pleasingly at 160 new shops built from public funds. They have a homogeneous look and fit perfectly with the rest of the city. By means of a public auction, Jai Singh has sold these shops to his subjects, setting them up in the best possible circumstances for modern trade and business. Anand explains the far-reaching economic transformation this entailed:

> The way he [Jai Singh] advised Vidyadhar, to establish each lane and street and sector, as the venue of a creative craft and for the buying and selling of goods and services, shows Sawai Jai Singh's grasp of the need for change from the feudal rent-collecting set-up to the state as collector of taxes from the sale of merchandise.

The feudal economy of the Kingdom of Amber was being phased out in the new city-state of Jaipur.

Jai Singh devoted great care to the economic and work environments of his people. Living quarters were built above and behind the shops, so people did not have to waste time commuting and the extended family could support their business while not being far away from the responsibilities and joys of domestic life.

After the inspection tour, Jai Singh installed the Govinda Deity at an elegant shrine at a prominent location in Jaipur and finally moved into his personal palace at the very center of Chandra Mahal. Then, one night Jai Singh had a most unusual and portentous dream. In this dream Lord Krishna came to the Maharaja and kicked him out of bed. When Jai Singh awoke, he was startled to find himself lying on the floor. He knew that something was definitely wrong, and he immediately summoned together his brahmins and wisest ministers to seek out the dream's meeting.

When all of the facts were disclosed, the brahmins and ministers came up with the following interpretation. Although Jai Singh was doing banner service for God and the people, it was a mistake and a break in Vaiṣṇava tradition for the Maharaja to be located at the center of the city. This was the place traditionally reserved for God. In great humility Jai Singh promptly accepted this interpretation and moved out of his quarters that very day. He then had them converted into a gorgeous temple for Govinda, while Jai Singh built a new residence for himself overlooking Govinda's new home.

Jai Singh dearly loved Govindaji. Anand tells us that, by learning to sing and dance before Govinda, Jai Singh evolved "new rhythms for penetrating into your body-soul." Jai Singh was so attuned and receptive to God that God directly communicated with him to correct his mistake. Vaiṣṇavas, even exalted Vaiṣṇavas like Jai Singh, may make mistakes, but, as Krishna promises in the *Bhagavad-gita,* He quickly takes measures to bring the sincere devotee back on course. It is something like a cosmic, instantaneous feedback system. The more unfortunate thing would have been for nothing to happen after making a mistake. That would mean that an individual is not sensitive enough to receive information from God's feedback system, and, rather than mistakes being corrected, such a person's negative or destructive patterns would become entrenched and habitual. To receive a kick from God like Jai Singh did is considered very favorable and part of the unconditional love relationship with God. The sincere devotee accepts these signs as "love slaps" to get him or her back in harmony with the divine.

Jai Singh II's astronomical instruments were built for beauty as well as functionality, as seen in this citadel atop a yantra *in the Jaipur observatory.*

For the people of Jaipur today, the Govinda temple is still the center of attention. Hundreds of people attend even the early morning services at 4:30 AM. Whether they have to walk long or short distances, they come to pray and receive the holy darshan of Govindaji. Since so many Deities of Vrindavan like Govindaji now reside in Jaipur, it is almost like Jaipur is an extension of Vrindavan—and the city shares in the potent devotional mood of that most blessed city (see Chapter 6).

The commercial success of Jaipur now provided the basis for a cultural renaissance there under Jai Singh's patronage. *Homage To Jaipur* reports, "The increased prosperity of the state and the fame of its brilliant ruler . . . now began to draw large numbers of scholars, poets, astronomers, and painters, etc. to his court. . . ." Many of their masterpieces can be inspected today at Jaipur's Central Museum and the Maharaja Sawai Man Singh II Museum located in Chandra Mahal. We shall take a short tour of both of these museums a little later in this chapter.

A view of the stairs of the Samrat Yantra, or the Supreme Instrument, in Jai Singh II's observatory in Jaipur. For a complete description of the Samrat Yantra, see pages 527-528.

An aerial view of a section of the Samrat Yantra.

JAI SINGH, THE SCIENTIST

Because of Jai Singh's achievements in science, he is called the "Newton of the East." G.R. Kaye writes, "He conceived and carried out a scheme of scientific research that is still a notable example; and his influence is still a living one." All in all, Jai Singh built five observatories in India, so results from one site could be cross-checked with results from the other sites. The Englishman, Lieutenant-Colonel James Tod, who served the British Crown as a political agent in Rajasthan from 1806 until 1822, especially appreciated Jai Singh's dedication to science and knowledge in an otherwise chaotic and troubled time. Tod had developed a deep affection for the people, history, and traditions of Rajasthan. He was particularly fond of the Kingdom of Mewar and the city of Udaipur, which are the subjects of our next chapter and where Lieutenant-Colonel Tod performed most of his service. He so loved Rajasthan that he soon became its greatest historian, and our present knowledge of Rajasthani history owes an immeasurable debt to Tod's 1260 page book, *Annals and Antiquities of Rajasthan*. Regarding Jai Singh's observatories, Tod writes that they are "monuments which irradiate this dark epoch of the history of India."

The finest and best preserved of these observatories is the one within the Jaipur Palace precincts, located about 200 yards east of the minaret. Many experts consider this observatory to be the first example of modern architecture, and even today it looks futuristic and is a wonder to behold. The book *Sawai Jai Singh's Observatory* states, "Most of the instruments in the observatory look like massive geometrical figures in masonry. It has been described as a most surrealistic and logical landscape in stone."

Let us now take a look at some of the specific instruments in the Jaipur Observatory. The instrument that so struck Fr. Tieffenthaler is called the *Samrat Yantra,* or the "Supreme Instrument." Even today the Samrat Yantra provokes amazement. In his book *The Maharajahs,* John Lord gives us a twentieth century person's impression of it:

> In Brobdingnagian scale a gnomon ninety feet high with a flight of stairs up its hypotenuse serves the same purpose as the pin of a sundial; two hemispherical cups sunk into the ground and chased with symbols and notations are each the size of a big room; pillars, cones, curved buttressed pierced and incised, planes and arcs proliferate in a Chirico landscape as superhuman and alien as the heavens the contrivances were designed to measure.

The Samrat Yantra can calculate time within two seconds accuracy. *Fodor's India* states, "for sheer accuracy, it is difficult to beat even today." Besides being 90 feet tall, this building in the southeast corner of the Observatory grounds is 147 feet long, and the radius of each quadrant is 49 feet 10 inches. Also, part of the structure is built below the surface level.

Another instrument of Jai Singh's design is the Jai Prakash, which is named after its inventor. The Jai Prakash is affectionately known as "the crest jewel of all instruments." It consists of two complimentary hemispheres with a diameter of 17 feet 10 inches. On the concave side of the hemispheres are mapped out certain coordinates. Kaye writes:

> Crosswires are stretched north to south and east to west, and the shadow of the intersection of the wires falling on the surface of the hemisphere indicates the position of the sun in the heavens, and other heavenly bodies can be observed by 'placing the eye' at the proper graduated point of intersection of the wires.

Daulat Singh tells us the functions of the Jai Prakash: "With the help of the shadow of circular ring on marble, one can find out signs of zodiac, local time and the declination angle of the sun."

The Hawa Mahal, Palace of Winds.

Close-up of Hawa Mahal.

Since astrology is an ancient and venerable science in India, the Jai Prakash was especially esteemed for its use in making astrological calculations. However, it must be pointed out that the Indian system of astrology differs significantly from Western astrology. The zodiac used by the two systems disagrees, in this century, by about 23 degrees. Since one sign of the zodiac equals 30 degrees, the two systems vary by nearly one sign!

Originally, the Western, or Tropical, zodiac and the Eastern, or Sidereal, zodiac were identical. But because of various cosmic influences on the earth, there has been a westward drift of the point where the planes of the earth's equator and the plane of the earth's orbit (the ecliptic plane) intersect. This point determines the position of the zodiac in relationship to the earth. Vedic, or Sidereal, astrology has compensated for this drift, whereas Western, or Tropical, astrology has not adjusted for it. That this shift has occurred is a hard, scientific fact. In the astronomy textbook *Realm of The Universe,* George O. Abell writes, "Originally the signs of the zodiac had the same names as the constellations that they coincided with. Because of the precession [the technical name for the westward shift], however, the signs no longer line up with the constellations of the same names; thus the sign of Aries is now in the constellation of Pisces." This shift has taken place over "the past two millennia since the constellations and signs were named," writes Abell.

In his pamphlet *The Vedic Astrologer,* Tracy Ladd states the differences between Sidereal and Tropical astrology:

> The Sidereal astrologer fixes the planets as they traverse the heavens in relation to the signs and constellations in space, whereas the Tropical systems have little to do with the stars in space, thus attributing little or no effect coming from the rest of the universe.

Further on in his pamphlet, Ladd gives us an expanded explanation of Vedic Astrology:

> Vedic Sidereal astrology gives us a geometrical relationship between the planets, stars, and the living being here on Earth. As the planets traverse their orbits in relation to the heavens, they act as focal points for stellar energies and the planets' effects are thus blended with and changed by the energies coming from the different constellations in the zodiac before they reach us here on Earth. Man, as a part and parcel of the universe, has an intimate relationship with its totality, and the birth chart . . . gives . . . our exact relationship with the Cosmos.

Jai Singh certainly agreed with this theory, and it is one of the reasons why he went to such elaborate measures to build his observatories.

In general, Vaiṣṇavas like Jai Singh acknowledged the influence of the cosmos on their lives, but it must be pointed out that Vaiṣṇavas do not feel bound or absolutely determined by the cosmos. It is said that bhakti, or unconditional love of God, transcends the power of the cosmos and can largely overcome any negative celestial influences. Of course, negative or positive celestial influences are not the result of the caprices of nature, but are the result of a person's own past actions in previous lives and are therefore the tangible manifestations of a person's karma. To ignore karma is considered unwise if not foolish, since it is the hand we have dealt ourselves. The more we know about it, the better equipped we are to utilize our strengths and shore up our weaknesses. The ultimate purpose of Vedic astrology is not to enslave us, but to free us. By the power of their love, great saints and sages entirely transcend the cosmos and come under the direct guidance and protection of Radha and Krishna—God.

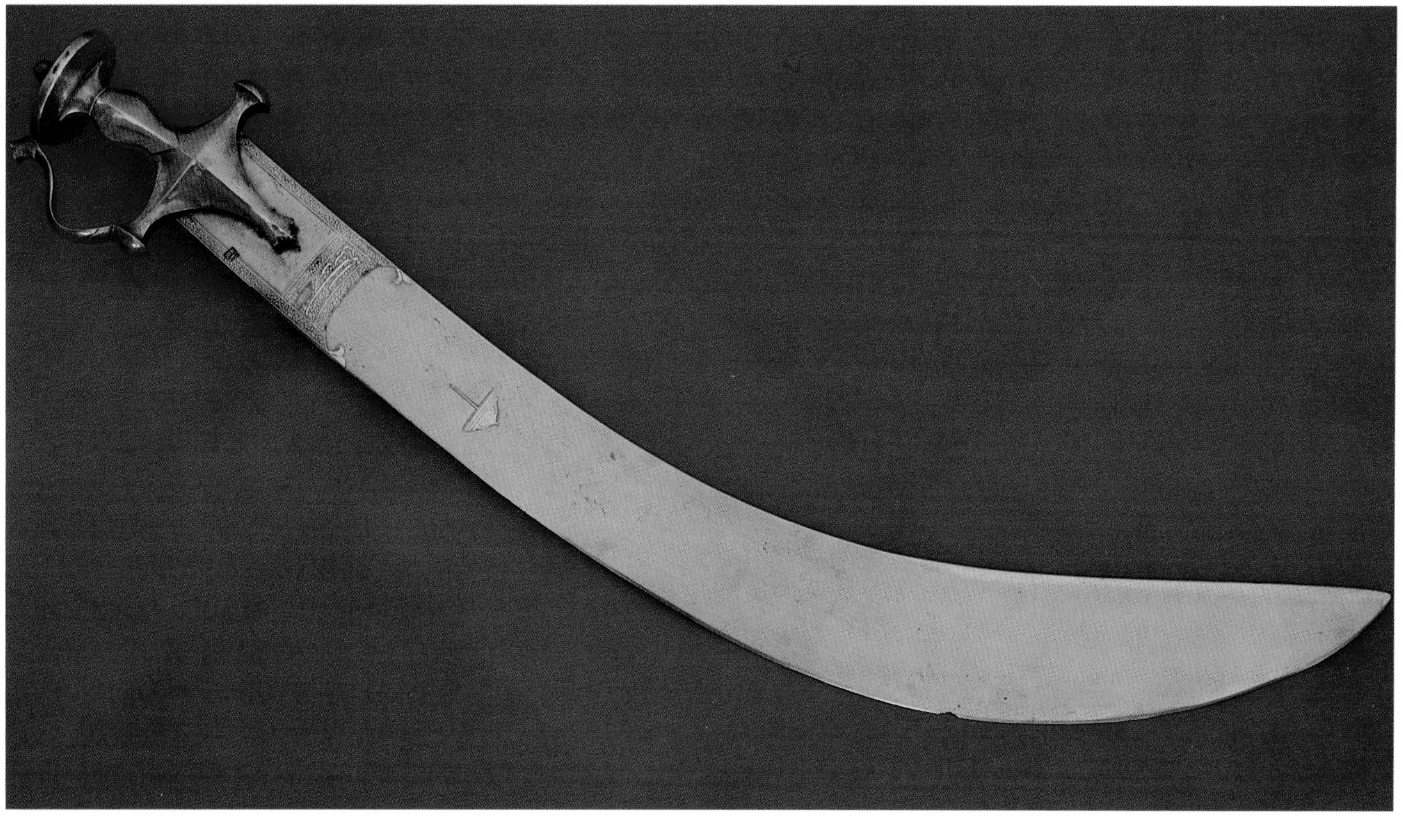

SWORD OF MAHARAJA MAN SINGH
Courtesy of Sawai Jai Singh II Museum, Jaipur. This sword is 33 inches long and weighs an astounding 22 pounds.

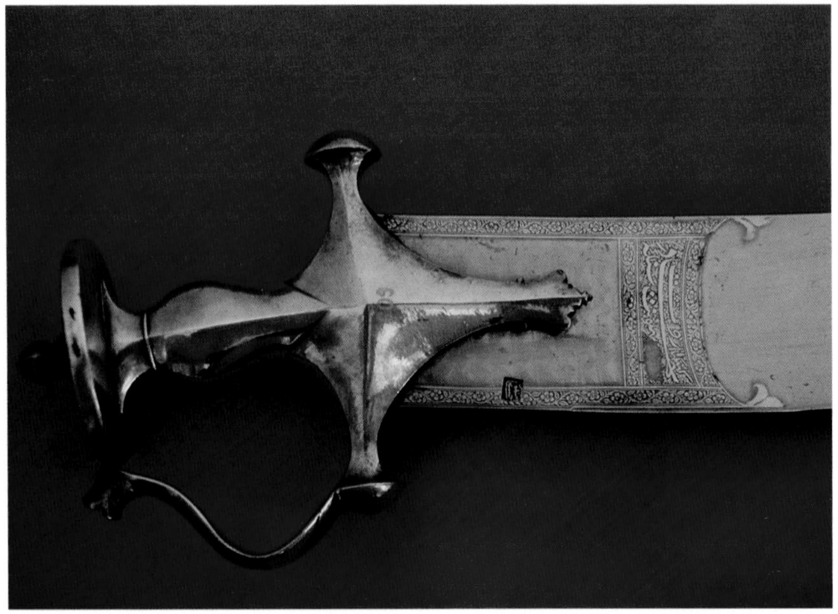

Close-up of Maharaja Man Singh's sword with the seal of Emperor Akbar's army forged into the blade. Courtesy of Sawai Jai Singh II Museum, Jaipur.

Another instrument in the Jaipur Observatory is the Dhruva Yantra, which shows the position of the Pole Star, or the geographical north. The Yantra Raj at the Observatory is most useful. B.L. Dhama, in *A Guide To The Jaipur Astronomical Observatory,* writes, "Every aspect of the ecliptic with reference to the heavens is easily represented [by the Yantra Raj], and a large number of problems involving the relations between altitude, azimuth latitude, longitude, time, and the positions of the heavenly bodies can be solved mechanically [with its help]." By the use of all the above described instruments of simple and ingenious design, Jai Singh was able to make accurate observations of the heavens and correct many of the faults in previously published astronomical tables in Europe, the Middle East, and India—and he did all this work right before the advent of modern technological equipment.

While to many of his contemporaries Jai Singh appeared like a giant genius, he always kept his work in perspective. In the introduction to his almanac he wrote:

> Let us devote ourselves at the altar of the King of Kings—hallowed be his name—in the book of the register of whose power the lofty orbs of heaven are only a few leaves; and the stars and that heavenly courser the sun, a small piece of money in the treasury of the empire of the Most High.

While Jai Singh's scientific expertise was atypical of Medieval India, ancient India apparently enjoyed strong scientific knowledge and accomplishment. For instance, the *Area Handbook for India* reports:

> Mathematics was a highly developed science in ancient India. Hindus claim credit for the origin of the concept of zero and of the numerals, which in modified form are now known to the world as Arabic numerals. The decimal system and certainly algebraic equations were also created by Hindu mathematicians.

Will Durant in his epic *Story of Civilization* praises the highly developed state of medical science in ancient India. He writes:

> Anatomy and physiology like some aspects of chemistry were by-products of Hindu medicine. . . . The doctors of pre-Christian India understood remarkably well the processes of digestion, the different functions of the gastric juices, the conversions of chyme into chyle, and of this into blood. Anticipating Weismann by 2,400 years Atreya (circa 500 BC) held that the parental seed is independent of the parent's body and contains in itself in miniature, the whole parent organism.

Nor, evidently, was technological development lacking. Ancient Vedic texts talk of thermometers, barometers, and even robots. P.N. Oak in his book *World Vedic Heritage* refers to the ancient Sanskrit text *Shukraniti* that deals, among other things, "with the manufacture of armaments such as rifles and field guns." According to Oak, eight different sources of energy for machines are also listed in ancient Vedic records: electricity, natural elements like water and fire, steam, "gems," air power, oil, solar energy, and magnetic power.

Various kinds of aircraft are also described, as well as the experience of flying. In the article "Technological Development in Ancient India" by Dr. A.W. Joshi, we learn that the description of flying in an airplane and seeing the horizon contained in the *Ramayana* were considered so authentic and vivid that Charles Berlitz concludes, in Joshi's words, that they "cannot be the result of poetic fantasy and can only come from the mouth of persons who have actually seen the horizon from high-up." Dr. Joshi then writes, "In a similar manner there is ground for strong belief that all other technological development mentioned in ancient Indian literature are accounts of true history."

Ancient Vedic cosmology also shows striking similarities to modern astronomy. The *Rig Veda,* one of the oldest Vedic texts, describes the earth as being spherical with, at any given time, half of it being illumined by the sun and the other half remaining dark. It is also stated in the *Rig Veda* that the earth and all other planets in our solar system orbit the skies because of the sun's gravitational system and that beyond our solar system are innumerable, sparkling stars. P.N. Oak concludes, "Thus the entire cosmic astronomy is most accurately described in ancient Sanskrit texts in the utmost detail."

After examining the ancient Vedic cosmology, the world's most renowned astronomer, Carl Sagan, in his equally famous book, *Cosmos,* writes:

> The Hindu religion is the only one of the world's great faiths dedicated to the idea that the Cosmos itself undergoes an immense, indeed an infinite number of deaths and rebirths. It is the only religion in which the time scales correctly correspond, no doubt by accident, to those of modern scientific cosmology. Its cycles run from our ordinary day and night to a day and night of Brahma, 8.64 billion years long, longer than the age of the Earth or the Sun and about one-half the time since the Big Bang. And there are much longer time scales still.

While Sagan attributes Vedic accuracy to "chance," the overwhelming weight of evidence points in a much different direction. Ancient Vedic civilization possessed advanced medical knowledge and procedures, an historical fact verified by the highest authorities like Will Durant. The language of ancient India, Sanskrit, is the most difficult and complex language known on earth. Modern students must study it full time for twelve years to achieve its first level of mastery. As the *Area Handbook for India* points out, Sanskrit literature "has a valid claim to be ranked among the world's greatest with regard to philosophical scope, variety of subject matter, accuracy and depth of insight, and, as the literature evolved, polish of expression."

Dr. M. Winternitz underscores the advancement of Sanskrit as follows, "In the earliest ages the Indians already analysed their ancient sacred writings with a view to philology, classified the linguistic phenomena as a scientific system, and developed their grammar so highly that even to-day modern philology can use their attainments as a foundation." Modern scholars have been baffled at how such a complex and sophisticated language was the spoken tongue of India thousands of years ago. If civilization as we know it only developed five thousand years ago, how could Indians speak and write in a language that exceeds in evolution anything used today? Where did it come from? Some scholars even give credence to the Vedic version of the origins of Sanskrit as a divine revelation to humanity. The followers of Sanatana Dharma would certainly concur and would say it happened millions of years ago. By 5,000 years ago, Vedic society had reached an extremely high plateau of civilization and then began a rapid decline. The more one studies ancient Vedic civilization, its language, philosophy, social sophistication, reports of technological advancement, and descriptions of modern technological equipment, one is forced to admit that this viewpoint is not only plausible, but just may be the only possible explanation of the facts. Given the wide and varied extent of the evidence, it would be foolhardy for contemporary civilization to not learn as much as we can from what survives of ancient Vedic civilization, whose vitality still produced geniuses of human accomplishment in the eighteenth century AD like Jai Singh II, the "Gazer of the Stars in their courses and comprehender of the Cosmos. . . . "

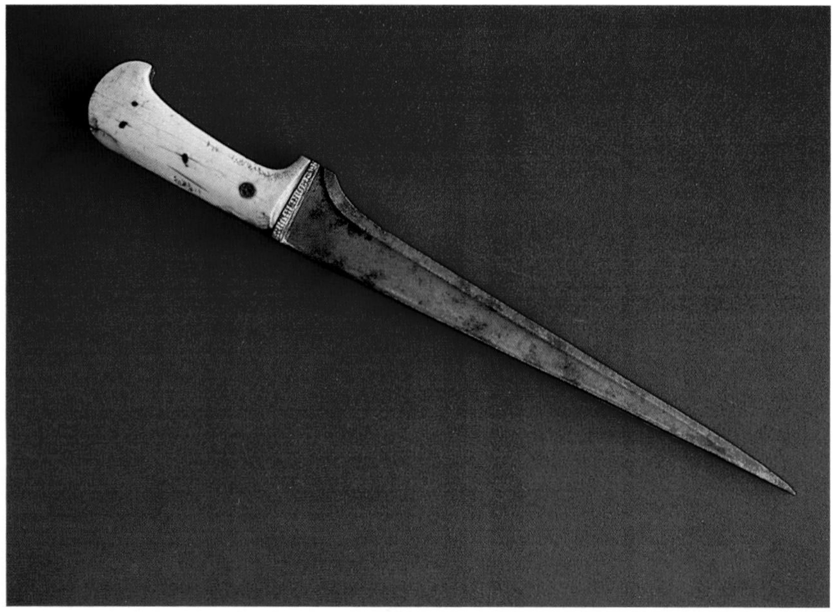

DAMASCUS DAGGER
Damascus steel blade with ivory handle from the 17th century, Private Collection.

CRAFTS, MUSEUMS, AND MODERN HISTORY OF JAIPUR

Anand writes that, after Jaipur was built, it became "one of the most flourishing craft-cities in the East. . . ." Since Jai Singh wanted the best for his city and was willing to pay liberally for it, the top artisans in all of far-flung India soon settled there. Davar tells us of the various kinds of crafts practiced in Jaipur:

> There was potters and utensil makers; brassware manufacturers and enamellers; weavers, dyers and embroiderers. Manufacture of vegetable dyes from dried flowers, fruit skins, leaves and herbs, and even rusty nails, was a local art. . . Builders, masons and specialist plasterers were renowned for their building art and their surface renderings with powdered marble. . . . An abundance of temples kept the image carvers busy. There were leather workers and tanners; jewellers and precious stone cutters. These skilled products, and those of the ivory carvers, reached distant courts as treasured possessions.

Soon, royalty all over the Indian subcontinent, Vedic and Muslim, sent their buyers to Jaipur to procure the finest products money could buy.

The enamelling industry is a good example of the high quality of work achieved in Jaipur. Enamelling in India can be traced back to pre-Christian times. Jamila Brijbhushan reports it "was one of the crafts that shared in the tremendous renaissance of the 16th century moving up in the 17th and 18th centuries from the realm of craft to that of art." Akbar's commander-in-chief, the illustrious Maharaja Man Singh, established the enamelling industry in Amber, which soon graduated from copying Mughal styles and colors to develop its own distinctive look. The maximum effect of color was realized by using only the purest gold for the carved ornamental base. Then, precious jewels were ground up to produce the richest colors for enamelling. Red came from rubies, green from emeralds, blue from lapis lazulis or blue sapphires, and so forth. Brijbhushan writes, "The colours sat in the grooves shimmering like sunlit water."

The intricacy of design engraved on small surfaces is amazing. "All the skill and expertise bestowed on miniature paintings were also lavished on jewelery," writes Brijbhushan. He continues, "The entire surface was one smooth whole, not even the most sensitive finger being able to find the trace where the metal ended and the colour began." Also, the naked eye was rarely "strong enough to take in all the miniscule detail laid before it," writes Brijbhushan. The largest and finest example of Jaipur enamelling is the famed Peacock Throne. However, today's enamelling work in Jaipur, according to Brijbhushan, "compares favourably with that produced in earlier centuries and quite often it needs a keen eye to distinguish one from the other." Contemporary Jaipur enamelling and other crafts find a ready international market and are a major source of foreign exchange for India.

The abundance and quality of crafts in Jaipur make it a "paradise of shoppers." Brassware is another specialty, and Beverly Beyer and Ed Rabey in the *Los Angeles Times* report that the brassware and silver shop of Allah Buksh and Son was "practically cleaned out . . . with one visit" by Jackie Onassis—and without her having to spend a fortune. Other interesting crafts worth mentioning are gold-thread embroidery and various forms of tie-dyes, which became very popular in the United States and Europe in the 1960s.

The prize pieces of Jaipur's arts and crafts can be seen by the public in the city's two principal museums. The Central Museum was completed by Sawai Madho Singh in 1886. Daulat Singh describes the Central Museum as a "lovely edifice of sandstone and marble in the Indo-Saracenic style, with beautiful marble kiosks, curvilinear caves and pink balustrades. . . ." The outer walls of the ground floor are home to an incredible collection of wall paintings, another specialty of Amber-Jaipur. Kanwarjit Kang writes:

> Nowhere else in Rajasthan has the tradition of painting murals remained as forceful as in Amber and Jaipur. . . . Here the mode of embellishing walls remained perpetually in vogue for more than three hundred years, beginning with the late sixteenth or early seventeenth century, to well nigh up to the thirties of the present century.

Excellent foreign wall paintings also grace these hallways.

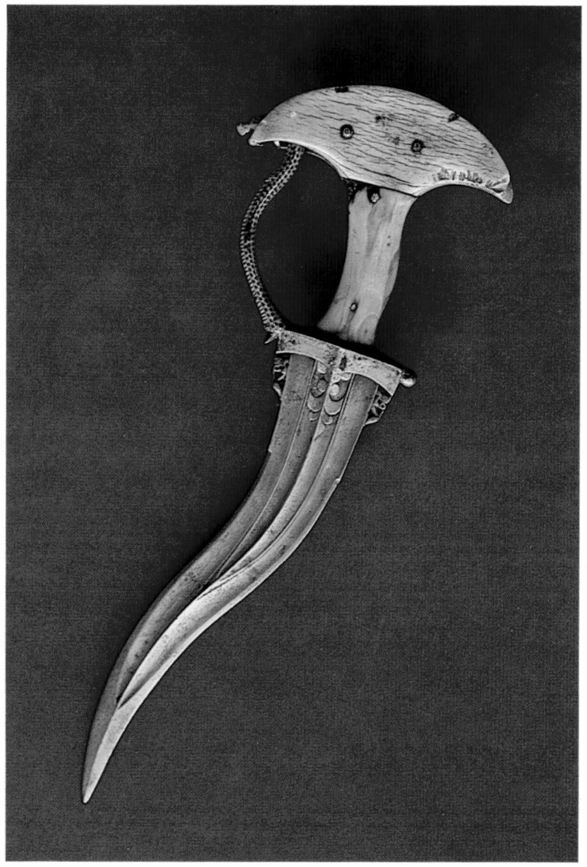

DAMASCUS DAGGER
Damascus steel blade with ivory handle from the 17th century, Private Collection.

Elsewhere in the museum are choice specimens of sculpture, textiles, wood and ivory carvings, brassware, pottery, china, weapons, and jewelery. Additionally, there are archeological, zoological, botanical, and ethnological exhibits. On display in the main hall is an exquisite collection of carpets. A 16th century Persian carpet with a garden motif acquired by Mizra Raja Jai Singh deserves special mention. It is 28 feet 4 inches by 12 feet 4 inches and has a classic richness of motif and design. Daulat Singh tells us this carpet is "regarded as one of the oldest and best of its kind in the World."

The incomparable personal collection of fine arts and crafts of the royal family of Jaipur went on public display for the first time in the City Palace, Chandra Mahal, in 1959. A section of Chandra Mahal was converted into a museum named after the last official royal ruler of Jaipur, the beloved Maharaja Sawai Man Singh II. Already by 1745 the royal family owned over 2,600 exquisite miniature paintings and almost 1,000 other titles, including illuminated manuscripts. Their collection was most eclectic. Asok Kumar Das reports that the subject matter included

> pictures of deities, portraits of Mughal emperors from Babur to Muhammad Shah, the Kachwaha rulers, past and present rulers of Udaipur, Jodhpur, Bikaner, Bundi and leading nobles, generals and feudatories. It also included pictures of Europeans, saints and holy men, birds and animals, and scenes of hunting, processions, wars and even ships.

The royal collection has been expanded with unswerving energy since the 1745 accounting. As Maharani Gayatri Devi writes, "The maharajas of Jaipur had for centuries been patrons of the arts and over the years their collections had been built up with connoisseurship and generosity." Now, two thousand of the finest specimens are exhibited in the equally imposing Hall of Public Audience, or the *Diwan-i-Am*. The large hall "with its double rows of grey white marble columns supporting scalloped arches (and with) the ceilings, pillars and arches . . . elaborately embellished with traditional floral motifs in gold paper and colours," writes Daulat Singh, is itself a work of art that is a most inspiring environment in which to inspect this unique art collection.

The favorite paintings of Maharani Gayatri Devi are "the many Mogul and Rajput paintings executed on the finest rice-paper, the lines traced with a single-hair brush and the paints mixed with the costliest and most brilliant ingredients: ground rubies, lapis lazuli, gold." The Maharani also especially loves the "huge, vivid, exuberant paintings of love scenes between Lord Krishna and Radha."

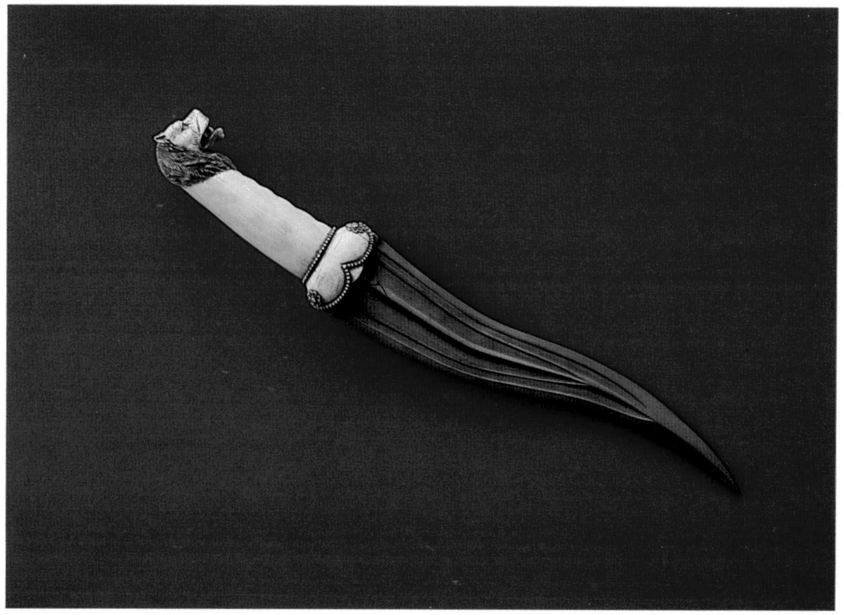

DAMASCUS DAGGER
Damascus steel blade with ivory handle from the 17th century, Private Collection.

The Maharaja Sawai Man Singh II Museum houses the royal library of 50,000 manuscripts. Maharani Gayatri Devi writes that some of the volumes date "back to the twelfth century," and:

> It is one of the most comprehensive private oriental libraries in the world. Almost every major language of India is represented—Sanskrit, Hindi, Urdu, Bengali, Marathi, Assamese, Oriya, Gujarati, Persian, Arabic—and the collection covers an enormous range of subjects, including Sanskrit scriptures, history, philosophy, Tantrism, poetry, drama, lexicography, music, erotica, medicine, and veterinary science.

Some scrolls in the collection have letters so minute in size that a microscope is required to read them. Other books, especially old epics, are written on palm leaves and the bark of betel nuts.

Another main section of this museum holds the Jaipur Armoury, which is, in Maharani Gayatri Devi's words,

> one of the finest in all India and contains almost every kind of ancient weapon imaginable, as well as such curiosities as guns designed specially to be fired from camel-back and such exquisite objects as the ceremonial swords still carried by the nobles.

All of the artistic and craft skills of Jaipur also went into these weapons of destruction. On this aspect of the armory, the Maharani writes:

> Until I saw the Jaipur armoury I never realized that the weapons of war could be so beautiful. There were powder-horns carved from ivory, embellished with complicated designs, or delicately fashioned from the shells of sea-urchins; they say it takes a whole year for a master craftsman to make one of these. There were golden daggers with handles of wrought crystal, guns with barrels bound with gold and butts inlaid with ivory and mother-of-pearl, ceremonial swords encrusted with precious stones, and daggers with handles shaped to resemble animal heads.

Fortunately, the once-warring Rajput princes no longer use these weapons in anger against each other, but have united in peace for the good of all India. Still, it is amazing to inspect how they combined the instruments of war with the finest aesthetics and creative vision.

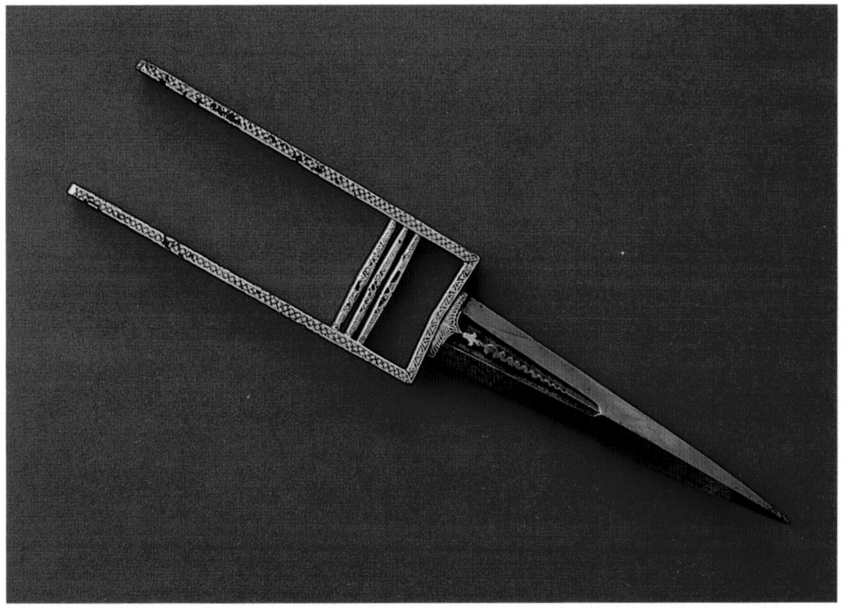

KATAR, TIGER KNIFE
Damascus steel blade, gold handle, 17th century, Private Collection. The Katar was used by Jaipur royalty to hunt tigers in one-on-one combat.

KATAR, TIGER KNIFE
Polished Damascus steel blade, gold handle with flintlock muskets flanking each side. Courtesy of Sawai Jai Singh II Museum, Jaipur.

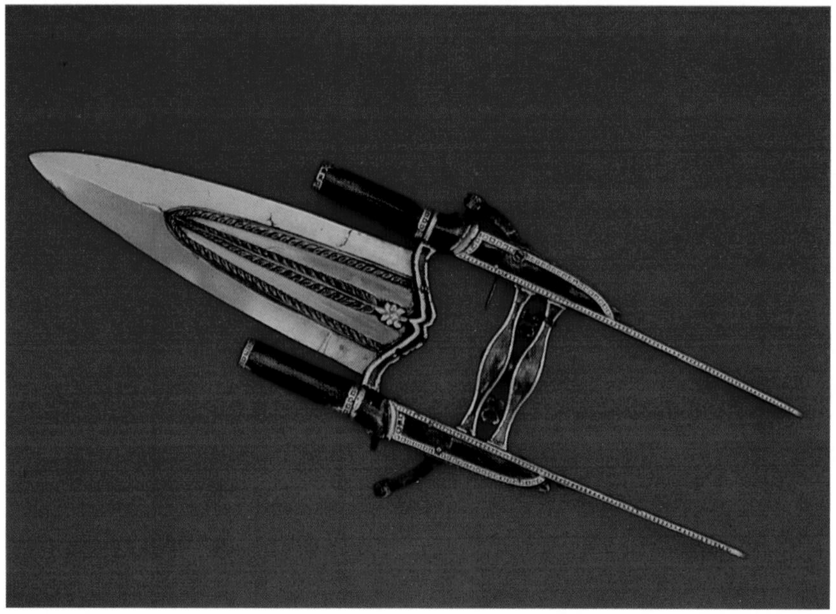

The success of Jaipur in crafts is also attributable to the Vaiṣṇava work ethic of seeing every activity as a direct service to God. Abraham Maslow calls this tendency of perceiving one's everyday work as divine service "unitive perception," and says that the Medieval Christian monk took it for granted. Maslow writes:

> It was possible for a monk in a monastery to say, "Yes, I'm digging potatoes for the greater glory of God." And this is a meaningful thing. This means you can be whatever you are. You can be a carpenter for the greater glory of God, too. And this opens up a whole world of the sacralizing of our activities of doing our jobs and not feeling that we're in a rat race. The kids frequently misunderstand us, you know. They think that we're caught up in something when we're really caught up in a love affair. They're apt not to see that we love our work.

Vedic and Vaiṣṇava cultures instilled this sense of higher service in one's daily occupation in practically all sectors of society, not only in monks or religious people. In an area like Jaipur that enjoyed both strong religious culture and a highly competent political leadership, the ancient Vedic social system and its divine sense of duty is most faithfully duplicated, and we can see that it still works wonders in the modern era, both in terms of quality of product produced and the prosperity and personal happiness of the workers. The genuine achievement of India has been creating a religious and social milieu for this attitude of divine service that can pervade the entire society and every worker, not just its religious elite. The fact that most Indians labored with this "unitive perception" and "sacramental vision" is another reason for the consistently high levels of culture and contentment in the Indian peoples over the vast majority of the last several thousand years.

Before turning for a look at the royal family in the twentieth century, let us quickly visit two more special places in Jaipur. First, we have the "Palace of Winds," or *Hawa Mahal*. This five-storey-high facade was added to the City Palace in 1799 by Pratap Singh (r. 1778-1803). "Pratap Singh was a poet of high order," writes V.S. Bhatnagar, "and made substantial contribution to poetry under the pen-name Vrajanidhi." He also was an outstanding patron of the arts and a builder of temples. His engrossing artistic leanings and originality can be seen in the Palace of Winds, which has become the most photographed sight in Jaipur. John Lord describes it as a "five-storey facade of curved, latticed windows looking strangely like a stone pipe organ." Of the pink sandstone Palace of Winds, Davar writes:

> Its intricate exterior wall, in its outline, looks almost like an oversized throne. Scores of semi-octagonal projecting balconies, large and small, are placed rhythmically in horizontal and vertical order, producing an effect of a vibrating exterior.

Each balcony was fronted by a perforated screen, behind which stood the royal women during processions and other public events. The entire Palace of Winds was constructed on an 85°, and not 90° angle—so the royal women could see out, but the people outside could not peer in. This strict segregation of the royal women from the rest of Jaipur society was mostly the result of the Muslim incursions into India. Many Indian women were abducted, and segregation was adopted as a means of defending them. As we shall see, the royal family itself was in the forefront of changing and liberalizing this policy in the twentieth century.

Hawa Mahal is especially beautiful at night. In the words of *Fodor's India,* the pink sandstone structure with "its honeycomb design glows in the evening like some fantastic nuptial cake." When the desert winds blow through the 170 screens and arches of Hawa Mahal, the visitor can easily understand its name.

Finally, to enjoy personally the royal life of Jaipur, we recommend you stay at the Rambaugh Palace Hotel. It is a former summer palace of the Maharaja of Jaipur, and its over 100 rooms give a guest a taste of the splendor of old Jaipur.

The dominant personality behind twentieth century Jaipur was Maharaja Man Singh II, or Jai. Although he was just a distant relative of the preceding Maharaja, Sawai Madho Singh, the ailing, heirless monarch chose to adopt Jai as a young boy and make Jai his handpicked successor. It seems that while Jai was being kept waiting to give a gold coin in tribute to the Maharaja, he grew impatient at the inordinate delay and, unlike his other brothers, pocketed the coin. The Maharaja was most pleased by Jai's independent attitude, and, upon his death on September 7, 1922, young Jai assumed the throne under a regency.

Young Jai grew up to be the most handsome, dashing athlete in India, his sport being polo. John Lord writes that Jai was "the most brilliant star in the galaxy of great Indian polo players of the 1930s." His team won the India Polo Association Championship Cup seven years in a row from 1933 to 1939. At only the age of twenty-two, he took Great Britain by storm, leading his team to a record-breaking, undefeated season, which John Lord states, "fixed [Jai's] reputation as a sportsman for the rest of his life."

The British writer, Rosita Forbes, described Jai as being "famous as a sportsman in three continents," and that he occupied "in the imagination of the Indian general public much the same position as the Prince of Wales did in the minds of workingmen (in England)." In no other way could Ms. Forbes suggest Jai's "universal popularity" in India.

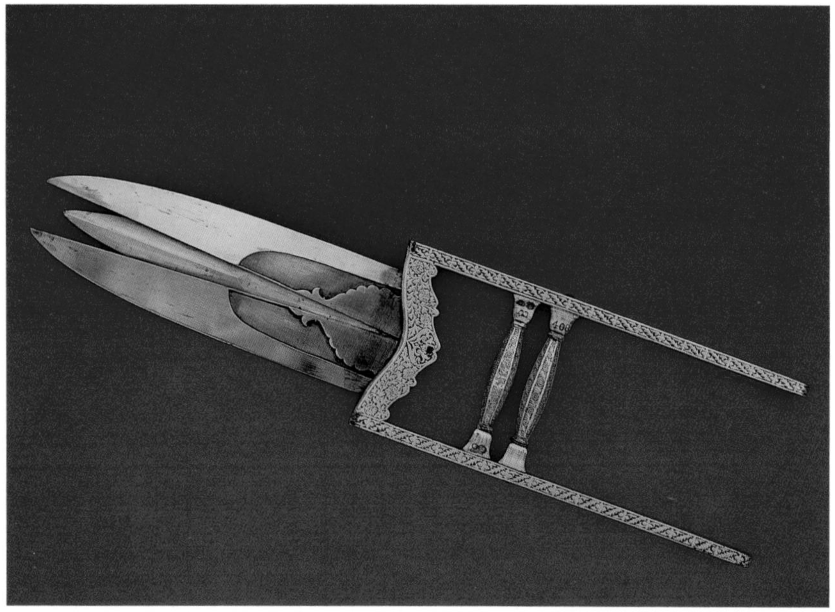

KATAR, TIGER KNIFE
Unique three blade scissor action mounted on gold handle. Courtesy of Sawai Jai Singh II Museum.

Jai's widow, the Maharani Gayatri Devi, writes that Jai's international image at this time was that of "a frivolous polo-playing glamour-boy, always seen with a beautiful woman on each arm. . . ." However, when Jai was in Jaipur, nothing could be farther from the truth. Jai, like all of his predecessors, took deep and personal concern "about the welfare and just government of his subjects," writes Gayatri Devi. The royalty of Jaipur never put a barrier between themselves and their people. Even Jaipur's founder, Jai Singh II, "often adventured from the precincts of his palace to pursue knowledge; to mingle with the people in their festivals. . .," writes Anand. Jai followed in this tradition, and, when he would often travel through Jaipur, writes Gayatri Devi,

> he spoke the local language and laughed and joked with anyone—farmers, shopkeepers, children on the street—and his attitude with all of them was startlingly different from the tenor of life in the palace.

The people also felt free to approach the Maharaja whenever they liked. Maharani Gayatri Devi continues her account of Jai's interaction with his subjects:

> All the people in Jaipur seemed to feel a special and intimate kinship with their Maharaja. . . . everyone in the city recognized his Bentley and his jeep and knew they could stop him on the street, or the pologrounds, or at the gates of the palace—anywhere—if they had a complaint, or wanted to bring some problem to his attention, or simply wished to ask after the welfare of his family and tell him about their own. It is a curious relationship . . . this special blend of concern, intimacy, and respect that the people of the princely states felt for their rulers. Jai . . . was always called "Father" by his subjects, and he embodied for them the special qualities of affection, protectiveness, and benevolent justice that they associated with the ideal father. It is a relationship that exists nowhere in modern independent India.

This reservoir of goodwill was largely fed by the consistently excellent administration of the Kachwahas. Jai followed in this tradition, and his extraordinary contribution was helping to lead Jaipur and India into the era of democracy and total independence. Like a good modern executive, Jai had no trouble in delegating significant authority. He convinced Sir Mirza Ismail, a Muslim who had run the state of Mysore with distinction, to accept the post of Prime Minister of Jaipur. Sir Mirza continued his superlative work in Jaipur and had nothing but praise for Jai, whom he described as

> an enlightened ruler, who, true to his promise, gave me his full support. What I liked best in Jaipur was freedom from intrigue. His Highness would not allow intrigue of any sort to raise its ugly head where he was concerned. He formed his own judgement, uninfluenced by busybodies, and acted on it.

In 1944, Jai and Sir Mirza inaugurated a constitutional monarchy system in Jaipur with a two-chamber, elected legislature with real power. In this way, Jai started the process of democratization "without violating tradition or endangering efficiency," writes Gayatri Devi. Jai was also a leading voice and negotiator in bringing the princely states into a united and free India. Almost one-third of India's territory and people were in the princely states, which, since they were not under British sovereignty, were also not required by law or treaty to join the new state of India. Jai and the Maharana of Udaipur quashed any attempts by the royalty to establish themselves independently of greater India. Jai knew from history that a divided India would invite intrigue and disaster for all of the people. Therefore, even though his people preferred overwhelmingly to remain under his able and just rule, Jai was willing to sacrifice his unique position and power for the common good. He personally was requested by the national government to negotiate with the hundreds of other princely states. He did and succeeded in helping to bring them all peacefully into India. The new constitution of India recognized his exalted position in Rajasthan by giving him an honorific position for life in the Rajasthan State Government. However, under Indira Gandhi's administration, even these honorific titles and other privileges were rescinded as part of the continuing democratization of India.

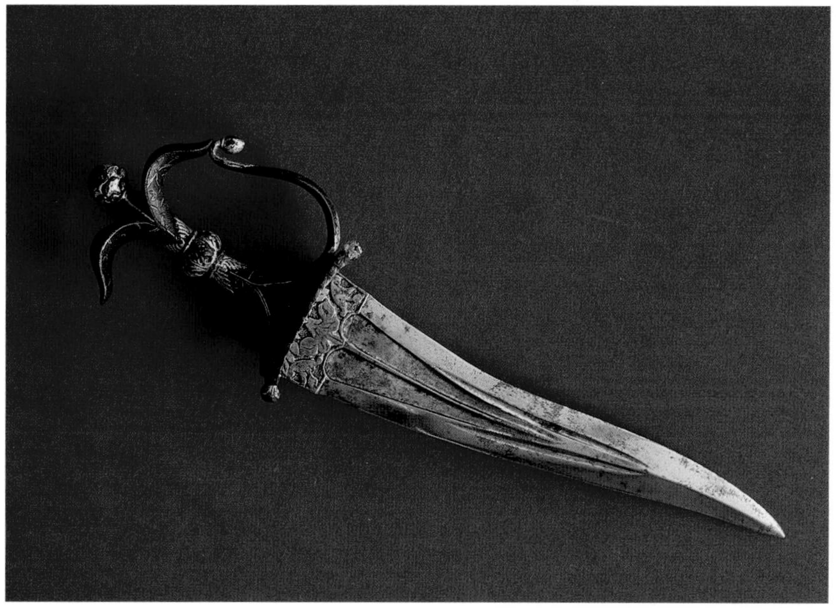

DAMASCUS DAGGER
Damascus steel with gold inlaid on the handle. Private Collection.

Palace guard wears a characteristically Rajput, orange turban.

When India became independent, Jai sent the following message to the people of Jaipur:

> An independent India will be called upon to shoulder great responsibilities; and I have every confidence that we, in Jaipur, will cheerfully assume our share of those responsibilities and assist, with the best that is in us, in the creation of an India which will take its rightful place among the free nations of the world.

This totally cooperative attitude on the part of Jai and most other monarchs did not go unnoticed. In the Government of India's White Paper on Indian states published in March 1950, Mr. Nani A. Palkhivala, who went on to become one of India's greatest lawyers, constitutional experts, and Ambassador to the United States, wrote:

> The edifice of democratic India rises on the true foundation of the co-ordinated effort of the Princes and the people. . . . But for the patriotic co-operation of the Princes, the tremendous change that has come over India for the mutual benefit of the People and the Rulers would not have been possible. . . . They may well claim to be co-architects in building a free and democratic India in which the people of the Provinces and the people of the States will enjoy alike the full measure of freedom and march together as citizens of free India.

Unlike most other aristocracies in the world, the Indian aristocracy fully contributed to the democratization and liberation of India, avoiding the ghastly consequences of civil war and revolution, while also preserving the strong social fabric and culture of ancient India into the twentieth century. For his efforts in this process, Jai deserves to be called one of the "Fathers" of modern India.

Unfortunately, the new government of India naturally had difficulties in relating warmly to the former princely rulers, whose place they had just taken in law but not in the affections of the people of the princely states. Therefore, a highly competent and experienced pool of administrators could not be fully utilized in the nation's service. Jai had to content himself with ceremonial duties and adjusting his large family and retinue to the new economic and social realities of India. Still, his sense of service kept Jai active in civic affairs. During World War II, he had faithfully aided the Allied cause in the Middle East and Asia, while the Jaipur infantry fought alongside the Americans in the bloody battle of Cassino in the Apennine snows of Italy. After the war, besides negotiating for a unified India, Jai also supported his wife, Gayatri Devi, in entering politics and running for Parliament, an unprecedented step for a royal woman much less a Queen of Jaipur. Jai also reentered official government service by accepting the post of Ambassador to Spain.

Against his doctors' orders, Jai participated in a polo match at Cirencester Park, England, on June 24, 1970. On that day, the man, whom *The Times* called "certainly the most respected and popular figure in the polo world of India and England of the last forty years," left his earthly frame. The outpouring of sorrow and affection for the fallen monarch was heartrending. An observer of the funeral ceremonies wrote:

> As his body lay in state on the night of 26 June 1970, in the famous Chandra Mahal just opposite Govind Devji's temple, in full view of the deity he loved so well, the entire city turned out to pay homage to him throughout the night, in an unending stream of sorrowful men, women and children.

The crowds were even larger the next day for the solemn procession to the royal cremation and burial grounds. Jaipur's population swelled, and more people attended the ceremonies than lived within the Jaipur city limits. Gayatri Devi writes:

> A crowd of more than half a million people lined the four-mile route to the cremation grounds of Gaitor. Many had started out from their remote villages the previous night, travelling as much as twenty miles by bicycle, bullock-cart, or on foot. As far as one could see, there was a surging mass of humanity come to pay homage to their beloved Maharaja, Sawai Man Singh.

Some mourners "clung precariously to trees and telegraph poles in an attempt to get a last glimpse of [Jai]," writes Gayatri Devi.

Perhaps the most fitting tribute to Jai came from Prince Philip and Buckingham Palace. With a heartfelt emotion Prince Philip wrote:

> All I know is that I gained immeasurably from his friendship in all sorts of circumstances. . . . To me Jai had a serene quality, a sort of cheerful calm, which may well have been exasperating for some but to me it was a most endearing and enjoyable characteristic. He combined with that a very rare quality in men, he was supremely civilized. Kind and modest, but with an unerring instinct for the highest standards of human ambition and behaviour.

Throughout their marriage, one of Jai's pet projects was urging his wife to take exemplary steps to gradually expand the role of women in modern Jaipur. The rigorous demands of World War II gave Gayatri Devi an open field for showing how women, even royal women, could perform services in a variety of capacities. At the time, noble women did not even receive a formal education in Jaipur and were far more restricted in their life options than either middle-class or lower-class women. Therefore, after surmounting many difficulties and resistances, in 1943 the Rani Gayatri Devi School opened its doors to forty daughters of nobility as a first step to enlarging the educational and vocational opportunities for all women in Jaipur. Today, the school attracts Indian girls from around the globe, and its graduates "become doctors, lawyers, and teachers," writes its proud founder.

What especially irritated Gayatri Devi after Indian Independence was the decline in the effectiveness of the local government. It pained her heart to see her former subjects physically suffer because the new, democratic administration did not meet the level of effectiveness of the former Kachwaha monarchy. Of course, given its record of excellence, it seems inevitable that almost any new government would be hard put to match the world-class administrative abilities and dedication of the Kachwahas. Still, when Gayatri Devi saw that the new government even neglected anti-famine measures during times of drought and the best-planned city in the world was beginning to suffer from urban sprawl and unmanaged growth detrimental to the people's comfort and environmental safety, she felt impelled to do something about it. She feared that impersonal bureaucracy could never replace the personal commitment of the Kachwahas to their subjects. She writes, "Emergency measures were neglected when there was no longer a personal involvement of the authorities with the people, and the villagers of Rajasthan suffered more terribly than ever before."

India's first democratic leader, Pandit Jawaharlal Nehru, had decided to place first emphasis on the industrialization of India. This decision was a departure from the economic philosophy of the late Mahatma Gandhi and other stalwart Congress Party leaders, many of whom now organized a democratic opposition to this policy. They called for more developmental aid to agriculture and the villages where the vast majority of India's people lived. Gayatri Devi was so impressed by the new Swatantra (Independent) Party's platform that she refused membership and a political candidacy with the ruling Congress Party and, with Jai's permission, joined the Swatantra Party. This news electrified the Indian media and public. Gayatri Devi was shocked at how her signing a membership card for a political party in a democratic country could create such an uproar.

Rambagh Palace, now a five star luxury hotel.

In April 1961, one of the founders of the Swatantra Party, Rajaji, was coming to Jaipur for a political rally, and Gayatri Devi was asked to give the first public speech of her life. The thought of delivering a public address terrified her, and she rushed to Jai for advice. He refused to let her off the hook. She writes, "He pointed out that as I had joined the party, it was my duty to work for it, and he gave me his permission to appear at the public meeting."

Gayatri Devi was soon to become a seasoned veteran of political speechmaking. Her party decided to contest elections for the first time in 1962, and she was nominated to be the Swatantra candidate for national Parliament, as well as being the party coordinator for all the party's candidates in Jaipur's 16,000 square miles. At first Gayatri Devi felt overwhelmed by the enormity of the task, but soon she skillfully tackled them, calling her first campaign "the most extraordinary period of my life."

Hers was to be no "front porch" campaign; soon she was traveling to the most humble villages in Jaipur to deliver her message. Back then, the Indian and world intelligentsia might have labeled her philosophy as too conservative. She favored a policy of Indian self-reliance, not Western-style industrialization. She admitted that India needed to be modernized, but she preferred the application of what we call today "appropriate technology," simple machinery and devices that are affordable by the masses and would increase production on a broad scale, rather than concentrating power and wealth in heavy industries for the benefit of a relatively small urban elite. This developmental approach achieved deserved worldwide attention and respect in 1973 with the publication of E.F. Schumacher's book *Small Is Beautiful/ Economics As If People Mattered*. There is no doubt that the policy of heavy industrialization practiced by India, Brazil, and other developing countries has failed to achieve the economic upliftment of the masses that the leaders had hoped for. As environmental problems proliferate, the "small is beautiful" philosophy of Gandhi, Gayatri Devi, and Schumacher might still prove to be the best strategy for caring for the material needs of most of the world's population. By no means is this debate over.

The Ashoka Capital in the courtyard of the Rambagh Palace.

A craftsman melts silver for fine jewelry work.

In any case, the people of Jaipur responded enthusiastically to Gayatri Devi's platform, although she was quick to add that, if elected, she would only be one member of Parliament and could not order the people's problems solved by fiat as in the old days. She would have to work within the democratic system of give and take.

Candidate Gayatri Devi was constantly amazed and pleased by the intense affection with which she was received on the campaign trail. She writes, "Everywhere I went I was met with the traditional welcome arches, with groups of women singing songs of welcome, with decorations—all the signs of celebration." She could only characterize the whole phenomenon "as a campaign of love." And the love went both ways. For the first time Gayatri Devi was able to share in the everyday environment and life of the people. She found their qualities most admirable:

> Seeing and meeting the people of India, as I did then, I began to realize how little I really knew of the villagers' way of life. The world is too apt to think of India as covered by a blanket of poverty, without any variation except for the very rich. Contrary to this picture, I found that most villagers, despite the simplicity of their lives and the cruel experiences of famine and crop failure, possess a dignity and self-respect that are striking and have a deep security in an inclusive philosophy of life that made me feel both admiration and, in a way, almost envy. Their attitude was far removed from the cringing poverty and whining beggars of the urban slums of Delhi, Bombay, or Calcutta.

The final days of the campaign found Gayatri Devi filled with anxieties. She was facing two major candidates from the Congress and Jana Sangh Parties, and she did not know how she would fare. However, when over 200,000 people cheered Gayatri Devi and Jai at an election rally the night before election day, she realized she would win. But she could not realize how large her margin of victory would be.

The Indian people love holidays and religious festivities, so it was natural that they would turn the most important days in a democracy—national election days—into another major cause for celebration. Gayatri Devi calls an Indian election "an uninhibited and joyful event." With characteristic Indian cheerfulness and style, writes Gayatri Devi:

> The women dress up and walk with their husbands and children to the polling booths, singing as they go. Villagers arrive in bullock-carts, the animals garlanded, the carts decorated with flowers and scraps of bright cloth, everybody on holiday, and, as always, entertainers, sweet-vendors, and storytellers set up their booths near the polling stands. . . .

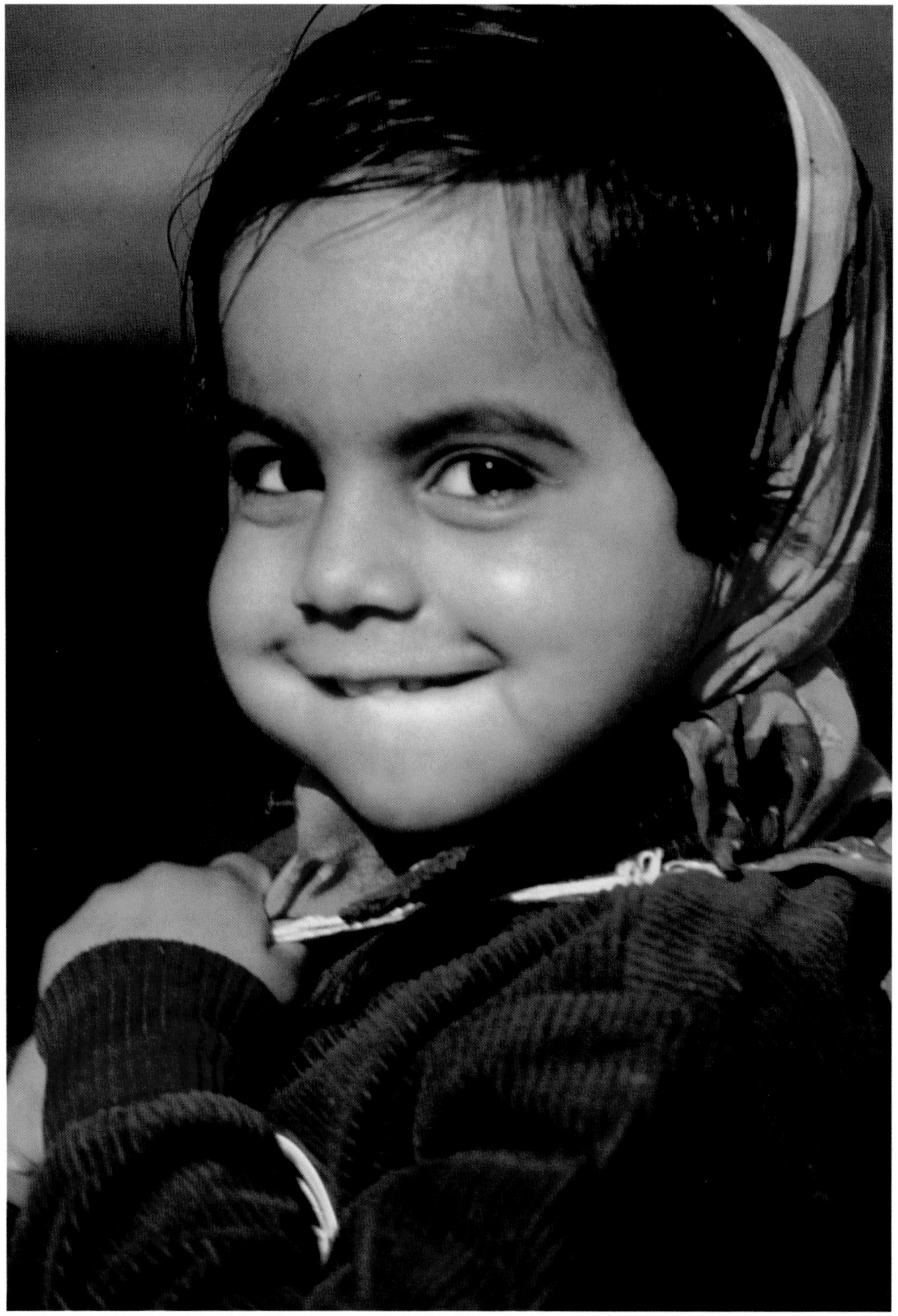

A smiling girl in Jaipur.

The election results were astounding. Only a single Congress candidate in all of Jaipur was elected. Gayatri Devi won her race by 175,000 votes over the next candidate. When she soon met President Kennedy in the White House during a visit to the United States, the President introduced her to an important group of Senators as "the woman with the most staggering majority that anyone has ever earned in an election." And the President was absolutely and factually correct. Gayatri Devi's 1962 election to the Indian Parliament stands today in the *Guinness Book of World Records* as the largest majority ever won by any candidate in any democratically contested election in the history of the world.

The newly elected Member of Parliament (MP) knew that her victory represented far more than a mere personal, political victory for herself. In winning by her world record margin, Gayatri Devi was continuing a loving relationship between the royal family and the people of Jaipur that had been going on for indeterminable centuries. The people of Jaipur were making a statement. They were taking advantage of democracy to affirm their satisfying, Vaiṣṇava way of life. Of course, it must also be admitted that a Rani winning by a world record amount in a democratic election is a supreme irony, but quite in keeping with the amazing Kachwaha ability to not only adjust but thrive on radically changing conditions.

Everyone in Jaipur knew that a vote for Gayatri Devi was also a vote for Jai, a vote for a respected and productive way of life, a vote for a sacred tradition, and a vote for prosperity. In many ways, MP Gayatri Devi's election was an affirmation by the voters of Jaipur of themselves and their way of life, of a Vaiṣṇava culture and heritage.

The Lake Palace in Jaipur, which serves as the summer residence for the queen.

568

Bubbles emulated his father in many ways, becoming both an excellent officer and polo player. At the time of India's independence, Bubbles was serving as the Adjutant to the President's Bodyguard, and, when his father passed on, Bubbles was colonel of a crack commando unit. Sawai Bhawani Singh, or Bubbles, is the fortieth Maharaja of Jaipur and does everything he can to maintain the incredible heritage that has been bestowed upon him for protection.

Our tour of Jaipur and its history is over. From Raja Bharmal's reign, 1547-73, to today is 439 years. For more than this length of time the Kachwaha family has provided the people of Jaipur excellent leadership. Man Singh built Amber, and Jai Singh II constructed Jaipur. The Kachwahas always moved forward, and the twentieth century saw them shine in the personalities of Jai, Gayatri Devi, and Bhawani Singh. How is this consistent record of achievement to be explained? No doubt the Kachwahas have good heredity, but the answer to this question must go far beyond genes. Over the past 500 years, the Kachwahas best represented the ideal of Vedic and Vaiṣṇava administrators. The family always held that God—Govinda Devaji—was the true owner and ruler of their kingdom. Each Kachwaha was very thoroughly trained in the principles of Vaiṣṇavism, as explained in this book. Certainly, the scientific application of Vaiṣṇava principles to personal life style leads to a higher and more efficient harmony of body, mind, and soul. Furthermore, this integrated, healthy person is then linked by an unconditional, personal loving relationship with God the Father and Mother, thus providing him or her with near-perfect guidance and intuition in life.

Palace Row in Udaipur on the bank of Lake Picchola.

CHAPTER 13: UDAIPUR

To stay at the Lake Palace Hotel and enjoy the natural, man-made, and divine wonders of Udaipur would certainly be a peak experience for almost anyone, as Lord Curzon, Rudyard Kipling, Arnold Toynbee, Jacqueline Onassis, and a host of other people have attested. But before we continue our tour of Udaipur, the capital of the Kingdom of Mewar built in the middle of the sixteenth century, let us go back in time to when the original capital of Mewar, the legendary city of Chittor, flourished. Let us look at that most venerable city and the mind-boggling history of its royal family and people.

Chittor is seventy-two miles northeast of Udaipur and today stands as a national monument to the finest and boldest martial spirit ever exhibited in India during the past two thousand years. The royal house of Mewar traces itself back historically to nearly the time of Christ, or at least from the second century AD. The authors of *Pratap The Patriot,* Balwant Singh Mehta and Jodh Singh Mehta, write, "Mewar was historically the most important of all the Rajput states for the history of Mewar for centuries remained the history of Rajputana, while at one period, it was almost the history of India." Amplifying on this point, Devilal Paliwal writes in *Mewar Through The Ages,* "[Their] sense of oneness and unity of purpose have had their indelible impact on the medieval history. The undaunting and chivalrous people of Mewar led by the heroic ruling classes of this land have produced unsurpassable examples of dauntless valiance and sacrifice that are rare in the entire human history."

The royal family of Mewar has the most impeccable background, also having descendence from Rama's son, Kush. The site of Chittor itself is one of the oldest and most populated areas in the world. In the book *Mewar Through the Ages* we learn that the hill of Chittor "must have sheltered some of the earliest stone age communities." Paliwal goes on to report, "From the point of view of human history, Mewar is one of the oldest regions of India. It has been occupied by man at least for a hundred thousand years, if not more." Various ancient sources attribute the first construction of the present fortress-city to the Pandava brothers, the friends of Krishna, five thousand years ago. In any case, by the second century BC, we have historical evidence of a flourishing city, state, and culture in Mewar, which was roughly the size of modern Switzerland with its capital in impregnable Chittor.

Chittor itself lies on a plateau 500 feet higher than the surrounding plain. The fortress-city is nearly three-and-one-half miles long and half a mile wide. The old city was enclosed by six miles of solid walls with bastions. Eleven gates gave access to the city, with the principal gate being the east gate. Chittor was largely self-sufficient in order to withstand sieges. Within the walls, writes Davenport, were "bazaars, schools, colleges, reservoirs, and granaries as well as many palaces, temples and towers."

The Lake Palace, now a five star luxury hotel.

580

Palace Row at night.

The late Maharana Bhagwat Singh (1955-1984) wrote that there are two main threads running throughout Mewar history:

> The first is the long continuity of the ruling family which traces its ancestry back at least to the beginning of the Christian era. The second is the devotion to the religion of Hinduism and the tenacity with which, through the centuries, the rulers and their people have defended this religion, together with the right of freedom, with so much bloodshed and sacrifice.

The threat to India and Mewar came from the lands west of the subcontinent. The Middle East had spawned the religion of Islam, and, for a mixture of religious, political, and economic reasons, varying Muslim confederations pushed militarily in all directions of the compass to bring new lands and peoples into their fold. In Europe the first mighty advance of Islam was only checked in the heart of France at Tours by Charles Martel in AD 732.

The initial eastern thrust of Islam into Asia was halted by the efforts of the mighty Rawal Khumman II (AD 813-833). of Mewar. Twenty-four times the Islamic forces of Al-Mamun, the Arab Caliph of Baghdad, tested the Rajput strength, but Chittor and Khumman held fast. Hugh Davenport writes, "Chittor became a rallying point for the Hindus," and "during Khumman's reign. . . the Mewar kings gained their reputation as guardians of Hinduism." For fifteen generations after Khumman, Mewar would find itself engaged in intermittent warfare to defend itself and India from these waves of invasions. Because of these struggles, writes John Lord, "At every step in Chittor there are places which are hallowed by the memory of brave and gallant Rajputs, both male and female, who have shed their blood to save their motherland. . . ."

The Mewar motto is: "God Almighty, the Creator, is always on the side of those who cling fast and unflinchingly to their faith and duty," writes Dave. The rulers of Mewar so lived up to their motto by exemplary acts that the people began calling them "The Avatar (Incarnation) of Rama." The Mehtas cite the following conclusion about Mewar's position in India: "The Hindus yield unanimous suffrage to the Ruler of Mewar . . . and called them 'Hindu-a-Sooraj,' or 'Sun of Hindus.'"

The royal family of Mewar was the first Rajput clan to gain the five essentials of a Rajput prince—a fort, a palace, a temple, a lake, and a garden. They never lost their position of preeminence, because they always used their assets to aid all of India in her struggle to remain free. In spite of Mewar's efforts, the Tartar Muslims under Muhammad of Ghur finally defeated a large Rajput army under Prithviraj III of Ajmer in 1192. This defeat at Tarain, a mere 26 miles from Delhi, was decisive in establishing the Sultanate of Delhi and giving the invaders effective control of a large part of India. Chittor and Mewar, however, were still independent and a leading force of resistance.

Naturally these were most troubled times in India. Because of cultural and religious differences, the invaders subjected the Indian people to their harshest treatment in history. The gentle, civilized tenor of Indian life was rudely interrupted by unprecedented attacks both on the civilian and military populations. Tod writes:

> Scenes of devastation, plunder and massacre commenced which lasted through ages during which nearly all that was sacred in religion or celebrated in art was destroyed by these ruthless and barbarous invaders. The noble Rajput, with a spirit of constancy and enduring courage, seized every opportunity to turn upon his oppressor. Every road in Rajasthan was moistened with torrents of blood of the spoiled and the spoiler.

In the thirteenth and early part of the fourteenth century, the Turks conducted a massive invasion of India. Finally, in 1303, Allaudin Khilji laid siege to Chittor for six gruesome months. Although his motives were primarily economic and political, Allaudin also desired to add Queen Padmini, "the lovely and accomplished wife of Rawal Ratan Singh, the ruler of Mewar" to his harem, states Dave. Although badly outnumbered, the Rajputs held firm. Allaudin offered to lift the siege in exchange for Padmini. No one in Chittor would even consider this proposal seriously, but a compromise was worked out. Under the protection of safe conduct, Allaudin could enter Chittor and see Padmini's reflection in a mirror.

An overview of Chittor.

After Allaudin took advantage of this proposal, trusting the Rajput sense of honesty and honor to prevent him from harm, Rawal Ratan Singh felt compelled to match his opponent's bravery by personally escorting Allaudin back to his lines. Davenport writes of the tragic results of this decision: "But once outside the gates he was surrounded and taken away to the Emperor's camp as hostage and liberty was made dependent on the surrender of Padmini." To leave the king in enemy hands or to surrender Padmini were both unacceptable, so Padmini in consultation with her uncle Gora and his twelve year-old son, Badal, designed a scheme to recover the king.

Padmini sent Allaudin a message agreeing to his terms on the condition she would come to him in a way befitting a Queen of Mewar, namely, in a magnificent procession accompanied by seven hundred maidservants carried in palanquins. Allaudin happily agreed and eagerly awaited to satisfy his desires.

The next day, seven hundred palanquins left Chittor. Each was carried by six wariors disguised as bearers, and inside were four more heavily armed warriors. Once inside Allaudin's camp, Gora, Badal, and the warriors sprang into combat. The carnage was immense on both sides, but Rawal Ratan Singh was rescued, although at the high price of many of Chittor's most able warriors and commanders. Allaudin's fury and frustration was now boundless. He stomped back to Delhi for reinforcements and returned to clamp down an even more furious siege on Chittor. Davenport writes, "The defenders found themselves faced with the choice of submission or death."

What happened next is one of the most shocking, heartbreaking, and courageous acts by any group of people in world history. Davenport calls it "one of the most gruesome events in the history of Mewar." The women were faced with the dilemma of entering harems and becoming the property of the conquerors. The men also faced a slavish future. For the people of Chittor an honorable death was far more preferable to a life where they had no freedom and would be refused the right to worship God as they saw fit. Therefore, all the women put on their bridal gowns, said good-bye to their relatives, and prepared themselves for the act of *johar,* voluntary death by fire.

The Vijaya Stambh—Victory Tower—built in Chittor by Maharana Kumbha (r. 1433-1468).

Perhaps the blackest moment in Mewar's history came when Kumbha was assassinated by his elder son, Udaisingh, in 1468. Udaisingh ruled Mewar for five years before he was driven out by his younger brother, Raimal, with the full support of the people and nobles. Further compounding his treachery, Udaisingh then went to the Muslim King of Malwa for help. Dave writes that Udaisingh "humbled himself by promising a daughter in marriage to the King of Delhi." Nature immediately intervened to stop this conspiracy. After leaving the meeting hall of the Sultan, Udaisingh was struck by lightning and killed. Dave writes, "Heaven manifested its vengeance to prevent this additional iniquity and preserve the house of Bappa Rawal from dishonour."

Mewar attained its zenith of wealth and power under the rule of Maharana Sangram (1509-1528). During this time, Mewar controlled almost all of Rajasthan. However, two new invaders, the Afghans and the Mughals, now began to hammer away at India and Mewar. Eighteen times Maharana Sangram was victorious in battle, but on March 12, 1527, the Rajputs were defeated at the pitched battle of Khanua. The Maharana was severely wounded and forced to retire. Upon his death a year later, his wounds numbered eigthty-four on his body, and he was missing an eye and a hand. Rajput kings could not be called back line or armchair warriors. They boldly led their troops into battle and fought alongside of them.

Overview of a residential neighborhood in Udaipur.

The temple of Lord Krishna built by Mirabai's husband, Prince Bhoj Raj, for her personal devotions.

Mirabai

The history of Mewar now intersects with the life of one of the greatest Vaiṣṇava saints of Medieval India—the devotional poetess, singer, and ecstatic—Mirabai (1498-1547). She was born a princess. Her father ruled the Rajput kingdom of Merta. Mirabai's mother died tragically young, and Mirabai was raised by her grandparents. Her grandfather, Rao Dudaji, writes Usha Nilsson in her book, *Mira Bai,* "was not only an able ruler and a well-known warrior, but he was also a devout worshipper of Vishnu." Because of Mirabai's intensely religious home environment and her own predilections, Nilsson concludes that "Mira Bai acquired a religious leaning from early childhood."

Mirabai also enjoyed the heights of blissful mystical and spiritual experiences from a very early age. While she was still a child, a wandering *sadhu,* or holy man, visited Merta and gave Mirabai a lovely Deity of Krishna. Davenport reports that Mirabai "spent much of her time in devotional prayer before a small image of Lord Krishna, known as Girdhar (Krishna as a cowherd) . . . ."

The current residence of the Maharana of Udaipur.

Behari describes Akbar's alleged entrance into Mirabai's temple: "The new arrivals were transfixed at seeing the delicate, innocent, and smiling face of the child of God, which seemed to welcome the new entrants and to shower her blessings upon them." When the singing and dancing reached its crescendo, everyone present could see divine light emanate from the Deity to surround Mirabai in a halo, as well as other miraculous manifestations of Krishna's personal divinity. Behari writes, "It was a great experience for the Emperor, and such occurrences were responsible for the tolerant nature and liberal views of the great Moghul." He gratefully touched Mirabai's feet in respect and left.

Word of Akbar's visit, however, soon spread quickly throughout Chittor. There was shock and scandal at the fact that a Mughal had actually touched a royal princess' feet. Akbar and Mirabai had met on the spiritual level beyond all the vain restrictions of society, but society was now judging Mirabai harshly by mundane political standards. Bhoj Raj was beside himself with rage. He chided her for allowing a Muslim to enter the temple and touch her. Then, he ordered his wife to "drown yourself and never show your face to the world again."

Mirabai was now in a quandry. As a Vaiṣṇava, she could never stop a sincere soul from entering God's temple, but as a Princess of Mewar, she had committed a great offence and was willing to pay the price. Therefore, she promptly left the palace and headed for the river to obey her husband's command. When she reached the river bank, she gathered all of her strength and started running for the water. But, just as she approached her jump-off point, a gentle yet firm hand grasped her from behind. She stopped and turned to see her Krishna, smiling at her in His full youthful charm. Overwhelmed by this vision of Krishna's beauty, Mirabai slumped to the ground unconscious.

Both brothers of Bhoj Raj who acceded to the throne, Ratan Singh and Vikramaditya, for various reasons, political and personal, opposed Mirabai's activities. This was a time of great military danger to Mewar and Chittor. The Mughal force was rising steadily, and the military peril increased daily. For thousands of years in India, the disguise of a wandering sadhu had been used most successfully by spies. Therefore, Mirabai's presence in Chittor, with her spiritual fame attracting numerous sadhus for generous hospitality, was perceived to be a political and military threat, as well as offending the social and cultural mores of Rajputana. The secular, military-political mentality collided head-on with the pure, open, and sweet spiritual mentality. Therefore, the Maharanas wanted to curtail Mirabai's religious life. However,
598 600 she refused to tone down her devotion or to stop seeing the devotees who came to her. She reasoned:

If the king is annoyed
I can leave his kingdom.
If Hari [God] is angry, where could I go?

This intransigence on the part of Mirabai infuriated the Maharana so much that he ordered several attempts to be made on her life. The following song of Mirabai notes three distinct attempts on her life:

Mira sang ecstatically of Hari's virtues.
The king sent her a serpent-basket
and placed it in Mira's hands.
When bathed and washed, she took a look,
she found an image of God.
A cup of poison was sent by the king;
it turned into nectar . . . .
A bed of spikes by the king was sent
ordering Mira to sleep on it.
When evening came and Mira went to sleep
She lay as if on flowers.
Mira's Lord is her eternal saviour
removing all obstacles.
Drunk with the mood of pious songs
she vows herself to Girdhar.

The newest of the many spectacular fountains in Udaipur.

The Royal Sun Emblem of the Maharanas of Udaipur.

Mirabai is often compared to St. Francis of Assisi, who said, "What are the servants of the Lord but his minstrels. . . ." Behari calls Mirabai, "the Apostle of this Divine Music called *Sankirtan*—the efficacious remedy for all mental, bodily, supernatural and spiritual ailments."

All of the relationships, or rasas, (see Chapters 5 and 6) with Krishna are covered in Mirabai's padas. However, as Nilsson writes:

> Mira Bai's bhakti is mainly of *madhurya bhava* [rasa]; in this she regards herself as a wife, beloved, and friend of Krishna. Her feelings achieve the same height, intensity, and absorption that the gopis had for Krishna. Therefore the largest number of her poems contain the expression of this love.

Echoing the *Bhagavad-gita,* Mirabai felt that her love for God had been going on for many lifetimes and incorporated the experience of reincarnation and the transmigration of the soul. She sings:

Our love is old, I cannot live without Him.
Our love is from the previous life,
it can't be abandoned now.
Mira's Lord is Girdhar
companion of all her lives.

In the following verse, Mirabai declares her constancy for Krishna and how she lived in the devotional mood of expectation, always open and ready for the appearance of her Divine Lover:

My eyes have acquired the habit
of looking at the Dark One [Krishna].
His sweet image is firmly
fixed in my heart.
Standing in my palace
I wait for Him to come.

A bronze statue of India's great freedom fighter, Rana Pratap, riding his famous horse, Chetak.

THE WARS RAGE ON

Maharana Vikramaditya not only was at odds with Mirabai, but managed to alienate almost all of Mewar. The Mehtas write, "On account of his arrogance and insolence, he became unpopular with the nobles." Taking advantage of this internal discontent and division, the Mughal Emperor Bahadur Shah laid siege to Chittor in 1535. The use of European artillery and explosives for the first time against Chittor proved fatal. As their situation became desperate, 13,000 women again performed Johar, and all of the warriors fought on the slopes until the last man.

Bahadur Shah's victory was short-lived. After only a fortnight, he was forced to retreat from Chittor, and Maharana Vikramaditya, who had escaped from Chittor before its fall, regained his capital. He remained as haughty and oppressive as ever, though, and was assassinated in 1536 by Banbir, who usurped the throne for five years.

After slaying Vikramaditya, Banbir waited for the cover of nightfall to dispatch Vikramaditya's younger brother and the last remaining heir, Udai Singh. A barber and personal attendant to the court by the name of Bari warned the boy's nurse of the plot. The nurse, Panna, is illustrious throughout all of India as the exemplar of personal sacrifice for how she met this threat to her royal charge. Colonel Tod writes:

> Aware that one murder was the precursor of another, the faithful nurse put her charge into a fruit basket and, covering it with leaves, she delivered it to the Bari, enjoining him to escape with it from the fort. Scarcely had she time to substitute her own infant in the room of the Prince when Banbir, entering, inquired for him. Her lips refused their office; she pointed to the cradle and beheld the murderous steel buried in the heart of her babe.

Close-up of a unique sculpture that decorates Jagannath Mandir.

When Pratap was faced with all the nobles democratically choosing him to be Maharana, he acceded to their wishes and reigned from 1572 to 1597. For the first fifteen years of his rule, he would be in almost constant combat with the forces of the Mughal Empire and Akbar the Great, who devoted special attention to subjugating Mewar and Pratap. The Mehtas write, "When almost all the Rajput princes were subdued, Pratap alone stood firm and kept his head high. He was, therefore, an eye sore to Akbar."

G. N. Sharma in his book, *Mewar and the Mughal Emperors,* gives an excellent portrait of Pratap:

> [Pratap's] personal appearance, early training and force of character amply attested and fulfilled the glory he was going to win. . . He was a great captain of war, tall, a most full and majestic figure with a high forehead, prominent moustaches and above all striking appearance with bright eyes which seemed to indicate great fire and determination within.

Colonel Tod gives us an accurate assessment of Pratap's predicament and goals when he became Maharana:

> Pratap succeeded to the titles and renown of an illustrious house, but without a capital, without resources, his kindred and clans dispirited by reverses: yet possessed of the noble spirit of his race, he meditated the recovery of Cheetore, the vindication of the honour of his house, and the restoration of its power.

Akbar's attempts to subjugate Mewar failed for the first four years of Pratap's reign. Then, on March 18, 1576, Akbar ordered Maharaja Man Singh of Amber to lead a large army of 80,000 soldiers against Pratap to finish him once and for all. Before the battle, Man Singh was hunting in the woods, unaware that Pratap had secretly slipped into the area. Pratap's scouts spotted the hunting party, and Pratap could have easily surprised and destroyed Man Singh in the forest. But this kind of sneak attack was unchivalrous by Rajput standards, and Pratap passed up this opportunity. Instead, he maneuvered his army into position to confront the main body of the Mughal invasion force. The actual battle took place on the plains near the pass of Haldi Ghati, about twenty-seven miles north of Udaipur.

RADHA AND KRISHNA
Silk Painting, Nathdwar School, 20th century, Private Collection.

As mentioned before, the Bhils once saved Pratap's family by hiding them in the Zawar Mines. Tod writes that the Bhils

> carried them in wicker baskets and concealed them in the tin mines of Jawara, where they guarded and fed them. Bolts and rings are still preserved in the trees about Jawara and Chawand to which baskets were suspended, the only cradles of the royal children of Mewar, in order to preserve them from the tiger and the wolf.

Pratap's only fear was for his family and the deprivations they endured, but his greatest fear—their capture—was never realized because of the Bhils' loyalty and perseverance.

Tod also gives us a fine picture of how the Bhils complemented the Rajputs in battle:

> Above and below the Rajpoots were posted, and on the cliffs and pinnacles overlooking the field of battle, the faithful aborigines, the Bhil, with his natural weapon the bow and arrow, and huge stones, ready to roll upon the combatant enemy.

After the battle of Haldi Ghati, Akbar personally assumed command of the systematic occupation of Mewar from Udaipur, which Pratap had quit for the hills. For six months, Akbar tried his best to end his Mewar problem, but Pratap's scorched earth policy and guerilla tactics stymied his efforts. Finally, on May 12, 1577, Akbar had to retire to his capital at Fatehpur Sikri.

For the next ten years, Pratap and the Mughals had a classic standoff. Pratap controlled the countryside, while the Mughals held the cities. In spite of the hundreds of years of atrocities inflicted on Mewar and India by the conquerors, Pratap remained, in the Mehtas' words, "free from communal bias. He bore no hatred or animosity against those who belonged to another race or religion . . . His fight was not against Turks or Mughals. It was a war of independence which he waged in the defence of his country."

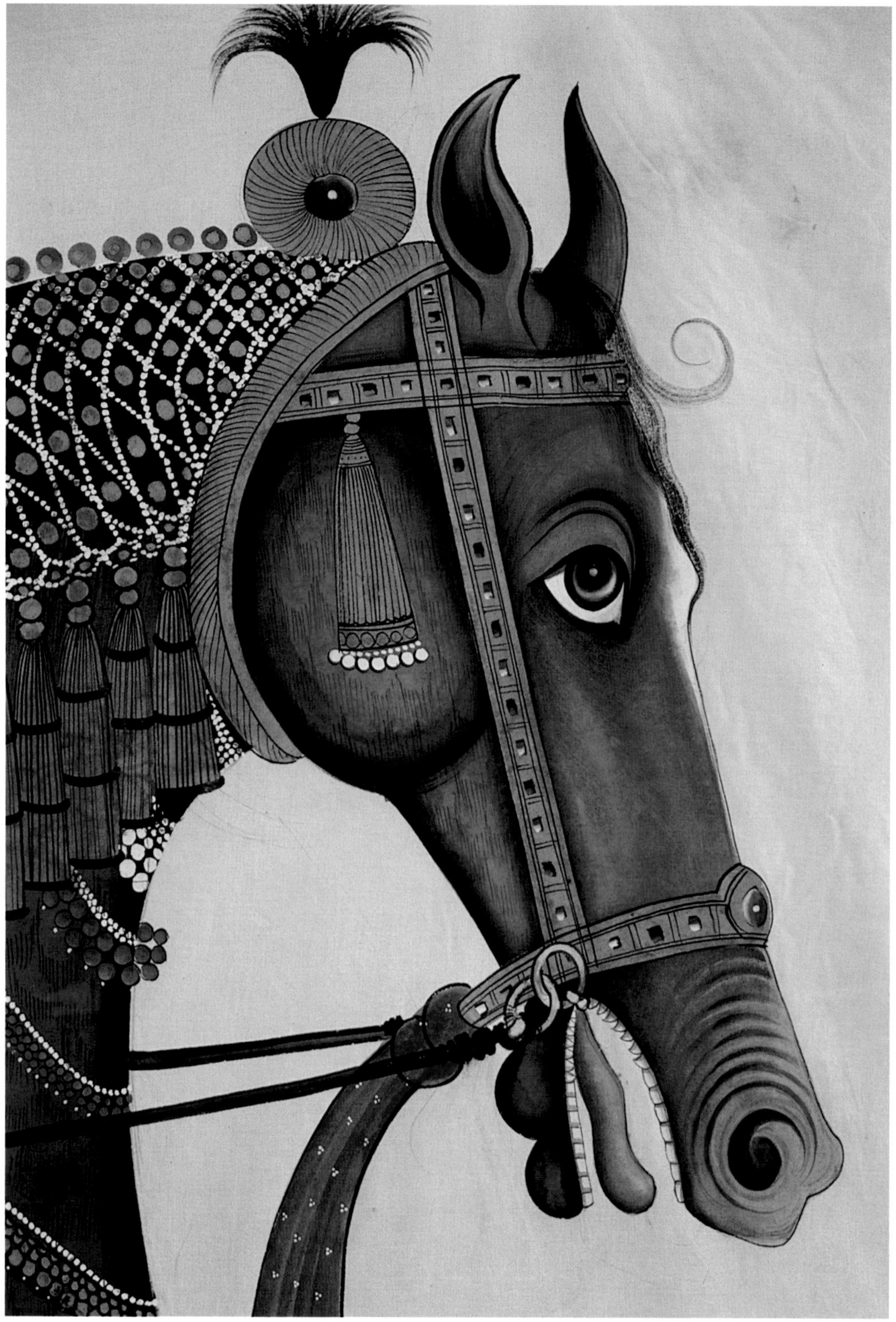

HORSE
Silk painting, Udaipur School, 20th century, Private Collection.

For the next several generations, Mewar prospered in peace. Davenport writes, "Because of their mutual respect, despite religious and political differences, the powerful Mughal Emperors and the Maharanas of Mewar lived together with fair tolerance during the reigns of Jahangir and Shahjahan." A highlight of this period was the reign of Maharana Jagat Singh I (1628-1652). As Mewar's wealth increased, this pious monarch donated heavily to the spiritual and cultural communities. The Mehtas write that "Hundreds of elephants, villages and gold and silver were given to them." Jagat Singh I started the Lake Palace. The famous Vaiṣṇava temple of Jagdish was also constructed by him in Udaipur and can be visited today. The sculpture work in the temple is remarkable. A fine bronze sculpture of Garuda, the winged, celestial carrier of Lord Vishnu with the Lord riding on his back, graces the entranceway. In the main sanctuary is an excellent stone Deity of God as Jagannath—the Lord of the Universe (see Chapter 4).

The peaceful coexistence of Rajput and Mughal was disrupted during the reign of the fanatical Aurangzeb (1658-1707), whom we have already met in the last chapter. Tod writes that "his bigotry outweighed his policy, and he visited the Rajputs with an unrelenting and unwise persecution." Aurangzeb probably vandalized more religious icons and temples than anyone else in recorded history. In 1680, he razed 63 temples in Chittor and 172 temples in and around Udaipur. Sadly, Aurangzeb inflicted this kind of senseless destruction over large areas of India.

Aurangzeb was resolutely resisted by Maharana Raj Singh (1652-1680), who won most of his battles against the Mughals. When Raj Singh ascended to the throne, he initiated the custom of *Tuladan*. Dr. G.H. Ojha reports that Raj Singh had himself weighed against an equal poundage of precious gems, which he then gave away in charity in typical Rajput grandeur. During a time of famine and pestilence in Mewar, Raj Singh employed his people in building the renowned Rajsamand Lake, which took seven years to complete. The irrigation capacity of this lake would help to relieve future generations from similar famines.

Along the bank of the lake were built nine marble pavilions. On twenty-five marble slabs in these pavilions were carved 1,017 Sanskrit verses, recounting the early history of Mewar. The Mehtas write, "This stone inscription is considered to be the biggest in the whole of India, perhaps, also in the world."

By a combination of guerilla warfare and massive engagements, Raj Singh was checking the Mughal advance. However, his vassals were upset by the resumption of debilitating hostilities and poisoned him in 1680. Undaunted by this setback, the slain Maharana's son, Jai Singh (1680-1698), took up the fight. In 1681, he surprised an army of 50,000 Mughal soldiers led by the Emperor's son, Prince Akbar, and gave them a crushing defeat. At this juncture, Prince Akbar rebelled against his father, who by now realized that he was getting far more trouble and grief than he had bargained for. Therefore, each side agreed to a peaceful settlement. In lieu of paying the hated "capitation tax," Maharana Jai Singh ceded some territory to Aurangzeb, and the Mughals withdrew from Mewar.

Like his father, Maharana Jai Singh was a great builder. In 1691 he converted a small, natural lake into a vast reservoir 30 miles in circumference by throwing up a dam in a mountain pass 30 miles southeast of Udaipur. Until the Russians constructed the Aswan Dam in Egypt, Jaisamand, or the "Sea of Victory," was touted as the world's largest freshwater, man-made lake.

From 1698 to 1818, Mewar fell into hard times and its darkest period. The Mughal Empire was disintegrating, but Mewar was unable to take advantage of this situation because of endemic internal conflicts. Undoubtedly, living under the constant threat and stress of the harshest wars had exacted a heavy toll. The cohesiveness of Mewar just seemed to have exhausted itself and evaporated. Then, another indigenous Indian kingdom, the Maratha Empire, turned from freedom fighters to looters, preying on Mewar and other Indian states. Davenport writes:

> To their astonishment the brave kings, nobles and people found themselves being called to arms to fight not the alien Muslims but their fellow Hindus. This broke their hearts. They fled to their hill fortresses and, despite efforts to rally them, the kingdom collapsed, its wealth was stripped, trade came to an end and the fields went uncultivated.

Artist at work in Udaipur.

Artist prepares pigments from organic materials.

In 1857, the first Indian revolt against British rule broke out in North India and Bengal. This "Great Mutiny" incited both sides to commit atrocities, often on a large scale. In Mewar, however, Maharana Swaroop Singh (1842-1861) rigidly adhered to the codes of Rajput chivalry. When a group of mostly British women and children appealed to him for protection, he exclaimed, "War is only for men." Then, he securely hid them in the Jagmandir Palace on an island in Lake Picchola. In 1623, Maharana Karan Singh gave the Mughal Prince Khurram refuge here also when his revolt against his father, Emperor Jahangir, collapsed.

The main palace of yellow sandstone on the island is three stories tall and has a round shape. It is lined with marble slabs, boasting a handsome and lofty dome crowned with the crescent of Islam. The Jagmandir is surrounded by large gardens and courtyards filled with beds of exotic flowers and fruit trees. The island is a paradise for bird-watchers and today is a popular tourist attraction. When Prince Khurram became Emperor Shah Jahan, it is thought that the design of Jagmandir greatly influenced him in the building of the Taj Mahal. In another demonstration of Rajput liberality, Jagmandir also houses a small mosque dedicated to the Muslim saint Madar.

Mewar entered the twentieth century under the leadership of Maharana Fateh Singh (1884-1930). He foresaw the coming evils of modern materialism and did his best to uphold traditional values, while also modernizing certain aspects of Mewar. Many roads, hospitals, schools, colleges, and the Udaipur-Chittor railway were constructed during his reign.

Maharana Fateh Singh loved simplicity and friendliness. The Mehtas write, "Abhorring the life of ease and pomp, he lived like a Rishi [a simple sage] though surrounded by the luxuries of the palace. He seemed to possess the most perfect manners in the world." Lord Curzon called the Maharana, "A ruler who lives a simple, exemplary life and devotes himself assiduously to the interest of his people." During the famine of 1889 and the plague of 1904, Maharana Fateh Singh mobilized massive relief projects to alleviate the people's suffering.

The lakeside view of the palace of the present Maharana of Udaipur.

Besides this folk art, Udaipur is also famous for its formal schools of painting, which have flourished here since antiquity. In these schools young artists still learn the traditional techniques of painting, especially the "Nathdwar" style. All the materials used are natural. Students and artists gather various kinds of clay and organic substances from the hills and lake shores to create their colors. The canvases are made of cotton or silk. All in all, art is an essential ingredient of life in Udaipur, making the entire city an open-air art gallery, entrancing the citizenry and visitors alike with beauty.

While the royal house of Mewar ruled in the name of Eklingji (Shiva), Vaiṣṇavism is the most popular religion in Udaipur and Mewar, and also enjoyed strong support from the royal family. Temples dedicated to Krishna, Vishnu, or other Incarnations of Krishna far outnumber any other kind of temple. The most famous Vaiṣṇava temple in Mewar is Nathdwara (the "Home of Lord Krishna)," which is 30 miles northeast of Udaipur. Colonel Tod writes of this temple, "It owes its celebrity entirely to the image of Krishna, said to be the same that has been worshipped at Mathura ever since . . . between eleven and twelve hundred years before Christ."

The Krishna Deity residing here, Nathji, was saved from Aurangzeb's iconoclastic fury in 1669 by Maharana Raj Singh. When the wheels of the chariot rescuing the Deity sank deeply into the earth in the village of Sihar and defied all attempts to extract it, a sage declared that this was a sign the Deity did not want to go any further and had reached His resting place. A shrine was built, and this humble village became the town of Nathdwara. Devotees from around the world come to Nathdwara for darshan of the full-length black stone Nathji.

In the town of Badoli are a group of Vaiṣṇava temples that Fergusson considered "the most perfect of their age that he had met with in that part of the country and in their own peculiar style, perhaps as beautiful as anything in India," write the Mehtas. Fergusson felt that one figure of Vishnu there was the most beautiful Vedic work he had seen in India. The happy coexistence of Shiva and Krishna worship in Mewar is most epitomized in the Hari-Hara temple in Bedla about two miles north of Udaipur. Hari is a name for Krishna, while Hara is a name for Shiva. The temple used to house a Deity of Vishnu (Krishna) and Shiva, but the Shiva Deity is now missing. Nevertheless, this temple demonstrates how a follower of Sanatana Dharma had no trouble in paying respects to all manifestations of the Godhead in a nonsectarian manner.

The temples of Udaipur and Mewar are very popular at night. The people gather there to sing devotional songs and recount the histories of their illustrious and noble ancestors. With a heritage as incredible as Mewar's, from the bravery of Maharana Pratap to the piety of Mirabai, it is no surprise that these stories continue to give almost endless inspiration and pleasure to the people of Mewar and anyone else fortunate enough to hear them.

Pillar of Heliodorus at Beshnagar.

CHAPTER 14: KRISHNA'S ANTIQUITY

The Capitol of Heliodorus Pillar.

Throughout this book we have referred to Krishna as having appeared on earth 5,000 years ago and have generally credited Vedic civilization and Vaiṣṇavism with great antiquity. But what hard, empirical proof do we have for this assertion? Certainly some archeological or other evidence must exist to confirm or deny these claims. In this chapter we shall survey the most prominent archeological discoveries that clearly demonstrate the antiquity of Krishna worship and Vaiṣṇavism.

First of all, detailed historical evidence of Vedic civilization is not that easy to come by, since the Vedic culture itself seems to have not valued the keeping of histories. In his book *Traditional India,* O.L. Chavarria-Aguilar writes of Indians: "A more unhistorical people would be difficult to find." Vedic civilization believed in recording the eternal and infinite. The ephemeral details of daily life (so much the concern of contemporary people) need not be recorded, since they had so little bearing on the larger, more significant goals of human life. Leisure time was to be used for self-realization, cultural pursuits, and worship of God—not rehashing current events or the past. Therefore, practically no histories, according to the Western concept of history, exist today about ancient India, because none were written.

Into this vacuum of historical data on India's past stepped the European scholars during the last several hundred years, and it is interesting to note how they first dealt with what they found. Religious scholars were especially shocked to observe the remarkable similarities between the lives and philosophies of Krishna and Jesus Christ. As a defensive reflex they automatically assumed that Indians must have come across Christianity in the early centuries after Christ's ministry and had assimilated much of it into their own religious tradition. This slant on Vaiṣṇavism was called "the borrowing theory" and gained many adherents in the West. Concerning this viewpoint, Hemchandra Raychaudhuri in his book *Materials for the Study of the Early History of the Vaisnava Sect* writes, "The appearance in India of a religion of Bhakti [devotion] was, in the opinion of several eminent Western scholars, an event of purely Christian origin. Christianity, according to these scholars, exercised an influence of greater or less account on the worship and story of Krishna."

Seven miles west of Mathura in the small and unimposing village of Mora, General Cunningham made another vital find regarding the historicity of Vaiṣṇavism. In 1882, on the terrace of an ancient well, he discovered a large stone slab filled with inscriptions. Although more than half of the writing had already peeled away on the right side, the remainder was legible. It was transcribed, and a facsimile of the inscription was published in the Archaeological Survey of India's *Annual Report*. The message was clear. Not only was Krishna worshiped in the centuries before Christ, but also His expansions or associates, especially "the five heroes of the Vrishni Clan." Scholarly research makes evident that these five are Krishna (Vasudeva), Balarama (Sankarshana), Pradyumna, Samba, and Aniruddha.

In 1908, a Dr. Vogel had the Mora Well slab removed to the Mathura Museum and tried to tamper with the translations of the inscriptions in order to throw the Vedic religion into a bad light. However, because the contents of the inscriptions had already been published authoritatively and were well known in academic circles, Dr. Vogel's efforts at creating
640 64 646 disinformation failed. The complex theology, metaphysics, and cosmology of Sanatana Dharma and Vaiṣṇavism definitely existed in an advanced state centuries before Christ. The Mora Well inscription is an important archeological proof of this historical fact.

In the village of Ghosundi in the Chitor district of Rajasthan is found the Ghosundi Inscription, which largely duplicates the message of the Mora Well Inscription. Kaviraja Shyamala Dasa first brought this evidence to light in *The Journal of the Bengal Asiatic Society*. Today, the inscription can be inspected in the Victoria Hall Museum in Udaipur.

The surviving part of this inscription relevant to this chapter reads as follows:

> [this] railing of stone for the purposes of worship is [caused to be made] in the Narayana-compound, [dedicated] to the Blessed Ones [bhagavabhyam] Samkarshana and Vasudeva, the gods, ******

The inscription is in a form of Sanskrit script called Northern Brahmi script, which dates the inscription as being from the second century BC in either the late Maurya or early Sunga periods. An almost identical inscription also was uncovered nearby and is called the Hathi-vada Inscription. These inscriptions also dispell the myth that Krishna was only revered by the *kshatriya,* or administrative-warrior, class of India, the class Krishna had appeared in. According to K. P. Jayaswal of the Archaeological Survey of India, these inscriptions demonstrate that brahmins, the priestly and intellectual class, also worshiped Krishna as the "Lord of all," and thus Vaiṣṇavism was entrenched in the entire Indian society.

Floral reef design on Heliodorus Pillar.

The same point is made in the famous Nanaghat Cave Inscription in the modern state of Maharashtra, where Vasudeva and Sankarshana (or Krishna and Balarama) are included in an invocation of a brahmin. Additionally, Raychaudhuri reports:

> The Nānāghāṭ Inscription shows further that the Bhāgavata [Vaiṣṇava] religion was no longer confined to Northern India, but had spread to the south and had captured the hearts of the sturdy people of Mahārāshṭra. From Mahārāshṭra it was destined to spread to the Tamil country and then flow back with renewed vigour to the remotest corners of the Hindu world.

On epigraphical grounds, this inscription is dated conclusively as coming from the second half of the first century BC.

A lot of numismatic evidence also corroborates the antiquity of Krishna. For instance, excavations at Ai-Khanum, along the border of Afghanistan and the Soviet Union, conducted by P. Bernard and a French archeological expedition, unearthed six rectangular bronze coins issued by the Indo-Greek ruler Agathocles (180?-?165 BC). The coins had script written in both Greek and Brahmi and, most interestingly, show an image of Vishnu, or Vasudeva, carrying a *Chakra* and a pear-shaped vase, or conchshell, which are two of the four main sacred symbols of God in Vaiṣṇavism. Many other finds of ancient coins also prove the antiquity of Krishna worship in India.

To summarize, today the weight of empirical evidence proves that Krishna and Vaiṣṇavism predate Christianity. Numerous literary, archeological, and numismatic sources build an unassailable case. Nevertheless, Vaiṣṇavism and Christianity still show amazing similarities. In the chauvanistic and sectarian atmosphere of the eighteenth and nineteenth centuries, these similarities led most Western scholars to adopt the now discredited "borrowing theory." But these attitudes did more than distort the truth. In the twentieth century they directly led to two world wars of unprecedented ferocity and destruction. Therefore, sensitive and caring people perceive these attitudes as being obsolete, and, instead of clinging to them, more intelligent people now seek the path of unity. Even in religion, one of the key contemporary attitudes is the ecumenical spirit, the desire to emphasize more our similarities with other peoples, nations, and religions rather than our differences.

If Westerners can drop their defenses and look at Vaiṣṇavism with ecumenical eyes, they will see a religion and a philosophy which undoubtedly through the Greeks helped to shape the soul of Western civilization itself and its largest religion, Christianity. Rather than being shocked by the similarities, we ought to rejoice in them. From at least our vantage point and in light of all the material presented in this book and from other sources, it is obvious to us that Christians and Vaiṣṇavas are worshiping the same original Godhead and are seeking salvation and solace from that Godhead through the same transcendental, personal loving relationship.

The early Western researchers into Vaiṣṇavism were correct in at least this sense: there are too many similarities between Vaiṣṇavism and Christianity for it to be mere coincidence. And since the "borrowing theory" cannot explain it, we suggest that both religions emanate from the same divine revelatory source—God. The message of Krishna in the *Bhagavad-gita* and the message of Jesus Christ in the New Testament are identical in essence: recognize the loving existence of your Divine Father and enter into a personal loving relationship with God. Each religion has developed this philosophy with different areas of strength. Vaiṣṇavism presents a far more systematic and scientific explanation of divinity and metaphysics, while Christianity in the West is proving more adept at putting the philosophy of God's love into practical action in areas like economic advancement, human rights, and political participation. If the ecumenical spirit grows and predominates in both East and West, then these two great religions can share their strengths openly with each other to create a civilization that would be far more evolved and cultured than anything that exists today. In the end the issue really isn't who borrowed what from whom. For a true Vaiṣṇava or Christian this issue is resolved simply—*everything* we have is borrowed ultimately from God. *God* is the original source, and God is one.

Palm leaf scroll from the 17th century of the Ramayana, *Private Collection.*

The purpose of this chapter is twofold—to give the reader a brief survey of Vedic and Vaiṣṇava literature and to suggest a path for further study in original Vaiṣṇava texts.

The history of Vedic literature from within the tradition itself severely contradicts most current anthropological theories on the evolution of the human race. Therefore, most scholars scoff *a priori* at the Vedic version and produce their own speculations about it based on sketchy empirical sources. Those people interested in the Western scholars' opinions on these matters can easily find them. However, knowledge of how Sanatana Dharma recounts its own origin is hard to find and will be presented exclusively here. While it is generally beyond the scope of this chapter, the reader should know there is an increasing body of empirical, logical, and other evidences to support the Vedic version of its origins. Should Indian scholars and scientists find enough evidence to prove the claims of Vedic civilization, the world would be forced into a major reconceptualization of its own origins and history that would be as revolutionary as Copernicus's discovery that the sun, and not the earth, is the center of our planetary system.

The word *Veda* itself means knowledge, and, as Will Durant writes, "a *Veda* is literally a Book of Knowledge. *Vedas* is applied by the Hindus to all the sacred lore of their early period; like our Bible it indicates a literature rather than a book." His Divine Grace A.C. Bhaktivedanta Swami Prabhupada writes, "Originally there was only one *Veda*. . .," and this knowledge was the primordial revelation of divine knowledge from beyond the earthly plane to the inhabitants of earth. We might say the *Veda* was a manual for the successful operation of spaceship earth. It fully explained how an individual and a society could relate harmoniously to all the different parts of nature to achieve prosperity and happiness. And the *Veda* must have been very sound, for it has certainly passed the test of time and created the most pleasant, peaceful, and prosperous civilization known to humanity for at least 5000 years of known history (and by deduction certainly existed far before 3000 BC).

Since Vishnu and Krishna are rarely mentioned in the four *Vedas,* some scholars say the *Vedas* do not support the Vaiṣṇava doctrine of Vishnu or Krishna being the supreme Godhead of Vedic religion. However, the purpose of the four *Vedas* is not to worship the supreme Godhead, but to delineate methods of piously achieving material goals. Therefore, contend Vaiṣṇavas, it is perfectly fitting for Vishnu and Krishna to receive scant attention in the four *Vedas*. Satsvarupa dasa Goswami's statement on this issue is typical of the Vaiṣṇava viewpoint, "Because the four Vedas deal mainly with material elevation, and because Viṣṇu is the Lord of liberation from material illusion, most sacrifices [in the *Vedas*] are to the demigods and not to Viṣṇu."

The few times that Vishnu and Krishna are mentioned in the *Vedas* are quite significant in establishing their supreme position. Concerning Vishnu, the *Rig Veda* states: "*oṁ tad viṣṇoḥ paramaṁ padam sadā paśyanti sūrayaḥ:* The demigods are always looking to that supreme abode of Viṣṇu." The *Atharva Veda* declares Krishna to be the original source of Vedic knowledge in the following quote: "*yo brahmānaṁ vidadhāti pūrvaṁ yo vai vedāṁś ca gāpayati sma kṛṣṇaḥ:* It was Kṛṣṇa who in the beginning instructed Brahmā in Vedic knowledge and who disseminated Vedic knowledge in the past."

As the above quote from the *Atharva Veda* states, Brahma, the original engineer of our universe, first received Vedic knowledge and created the universe by means of it. Vyasa, whose name means "the arranger" or "the compiler," never claimed authorship of the *Vedas*. He merely edited Vedic knowledge into forms convenient for people's use in the Kali-yuga. For this contribution, Vyasa is considered the original teacher, or guru, of this age, and even today a teacher's seat in India is called a "Vyasasana," or "the seat of Vyasa."

The *Srimad Bhagavatam,* like all Vedic literatures, reaffirms the divine origin of the *Vedas:* "That which is prescribed in the Vedas constitutes dharma, the religious principles, and the opposite of that is irreligion. The Vedas are directly the Supreme Personality of Godhead, Nārāyaṇa, and are self-born." In commenting on this verse, Shrila Madhvacharya, the founder of the Madhva-Gaudiya School of Vaiṣṇavism (which includes Shri Chaitanya) explains the intimate relationship between Vaiṣṇavism and the Vedas:

> The transcendental words of the *Vedas* emanated from the mouth of the Supreme Personality of Godhead. Therefore the Vedic principles should be understood to be Vaiṣṇava principles because Viṣṇu is the origin of the *Vedas*. The *Vedas* contain nothing besides the instructions of Viṣṇu, and one who follows the Vedic principles is a Vaiṣṇava.

A Vaiṣṇava, however, acknowledges the *Vedas* as only an elementary part of an entire body of sacred knowledge that must be accepted as a whole in order to understand the full purport of spirituality. The *Bhagavad-gita* warns the spiritual seeker against taking the four *Vedas* as the all in all:

> Men of small knowledge are very much attached to the flowery words of the Vedas, which recommend various fruitive activities for elevation to heavenly planets, resultant good birth, power, and so forth. Being desirous of sense gratification and opulent life, they say that there is nothing more than this.

The *Bhagavad-gita* admits that the Vedic formulas produce great material results:

> Those who study the Vedas and drink the soma juice, seeking the heavenly planets, worship Me indirectly. Purified of sinful reactions, they take birth on the pious, heavenly planet of Indra, where they enjoy godly delights.

His Divine Grace A. C. Bhaktivedanta Swami Prabhupada explains, "Once situated on those higher planetary systems, one can satisfy his senses hundreds of thousands of times better than on this planet."

However, the *Bhagavad-gita* then explains that in the long-run this Vedic path of pursuing the highest material pleasures is futile. It is like a vacation; once the vacation is over, it's back to work—the self returns to the earthly dimension to face again all of its dangers, challenges, and opportunities for ultimate spiritual salvation. The *Bhagavad-gita* states: "When they have thus enjoyed vast heavenly sense pleasure and the results of their pious activities are exhausted, they return to this mortal planet again. Thus those who seek sense enjoyment by adhering to the principles of the three Vedas achieve only repeated birth and death." From the Vaiṣṇava perspective, people who only accept the four *Vedas* as authentic Vedic religion and scriptures are psychologically fixated on an early stage of spiritual and human development.

Returning back to the subject of the origin of the *Vedas,* most Western scholars like Will Durant admit that the *Vedas,* especially the *Rig Veda,* are the oldest books known to humanity. Internal evidence from the Vedas themselves lend credence to this view. In *Hymns from the Vedas,* Abinash Chandra Bose writes, "Some astronomical facts derived from the Veda pointed by calculation to a date near 4000 BC." One solar eclipse described in the *Rig Veda* (V. 40. 5-9) has been fixed precisely by P. C. Sengupta to have occurred on July 26, 3928 BC. Regarding the divine benediction of Vedic knowledge to Brahma, the seasoned and knowledgeable scholar Will Durant writes that "this is a view which cannot be easily refuted." As stated earlier in this chapter, there is a large body of empirical evidence making the Vedic version of its origin quite plausible, if not probable.

Whereas the four *Vedas* deal with material advancement, the pupil sat closely to an Upanishadic teacher to receive philosophical and spiritual education. On this subject, His Divine Grace A.C. Bhaktivedanta Swami writes:

> When the activities for sense gratification, namely the *karma-kāṇḍa* chapter [the four *Vedas*] are finished, then the chance for spiritual realization is offered in the form of the *Upaniṣads,* which are part of different *Vedas*. . . . The *Upaniṣads* mark the beginning of transcendental life.

Transcendental life requires the awakening of transcendental senses to comprehend spiritual truths which originate from beyond the material dimension. Therefore, the Upanishadic teacher first makes his students realize the limitations of the material senses and intellect, thereby setting up the context for the development of spiritual senses within the student. Will Durant ably sums up this point:

> The first lesson that the sages of the *Upanishads* teach their selected pupils is the inadequacy of the intellect. How can this feeble brain, that aches at a little calculus, ever hope to understand the complex immensity of which it is so transitory a fragment? Not that the intellect is useless; it has its modest place, and serves us well when it deals with relations and things; but how it falters before the eternal, the infinite, or the elementally real!

The *Katha Upanishad* emphatically makes this very point: "Not by learning is the *Ātman* [self] attained, not by genius and much knowledge of books. . . . Let a Brāhman renounce learning and become as a child. . . . Let him not seek after many words, for that is mere weariness of tongue." Notice that Jesus echoed the Upanishadic message of "become as a child" in his teaching of his disciples. The meaning of this suggestion is clear; the mind and intellect must become as open, receptive, and accepting as a child's innocent mind before God and guru can grace the student with spiritual understanding. Before a child's innocence is attained, everything else learned is burdensome baggage.

Next, the Upanishadic teacher leads the student to turn his or her consciousness from inspecting the outer world to exploring the inner world of consciousness itself. Again, the *Katha Upanishad* states, "The self-evident *Brahman* [consciousness] pierced the openings of the senses so that they turned outwards; therefore man looks outward, not inward into himself; some wise man, however, with his eyes closed and wishing for immortality, saw the self behind."

Now the *Upanishads* look at what is the exact nature of "the self behind," both as it applies to the individual self and the whole of existence—God. Satsvarupa dasa Goswami considers the *Upanishad's* teachings on this subject to be its "main contribution" in that "they establish the Absolute as nonmaterial." He then goes on to elaborate on this Upanishadic lesson:

> The Upaniṣads describe Brahman as eternal, unmanifest reality from which all manifestations issue and in which they rest. Being inconceivable to material senses, Brahman is described as *nirguṇa* (without qualities) and *arupa* (formless). In the words of *Bṛhad-āraṇyaka Upaniṣad* (3.9.26), Brahman "is incomprehensible, for it is not comprehended."

Because the *Upanishads* emphasize the inconceivableness of the Supreme, they are most revered by monists, impersonalists, and followers of Shankarite thought. This emphasis also leads scholars like Will Durant to conclude that, "The Hindu thinkers are the least anthropomorphic of all religious philosophers." Will Durant is right. Neither monists, Shankarites, or Vaiṣṇavas ever feel that God is anthropomorphic or related in any way to an ordinary person. The *Upanishads* definitively and repeatedly make this point. However, the Vaiṣṇavas strongly contend on the basis of the *Upanishads* themselves that, by their denial of God's mundaneness, they do not affirm that God is impersonal.

The verses in the *Upanishads* that can be construed as an impersonal portrait of God are explained by Shri Chaitanya thusly, "Wherever there is an impersonal description in the Vedas, the Vedas mean to establish that everything belonging to the Supreme Personality of Godhead is transcendental and free of mundane characteristics." In translating and commenting on the nineteenth verse of the third chapter of the *Shvetashvatara Upanishad*, His Divine Grace A.C. Bhaktivedanta Swami expands on this key Vaiṣṇava understanding of the *Upanishads:*

> Although the Supreme Lord is described as having no hands and legs, He nonetheless accepts all sacrifical offerings. He has no eyes, yet He sees everything. He has no ears, yet He hears everything. When it is stated that the Supreme Lord has no hands and legs, one should not think He is impersonal. Rather, He has no *mundane* hands or legs like ours. "He has no eyes, yet He sees." This means that He does not have mundane, limited eyes like ours. Rather, He has such eyes that he can see past, present and future, everywhere, in every corner of the universe and in the corner of the heart of every living entity. Thus the impersonal descriptions in the *Vedas* intend to deny mundane characteristics in the Supreme Lord. They do not intend to establish the Supreme Lord as impersonal.

The story of why Vyasa compiled the last *Purana*—the *Bhagavata Purana,* or *Srimad Bhagavatam*—is most fascinating and indicative of the essence of Vaiṣṇavism. After Vyasa had compiled the four *Vedas,* 108 *Upanishads,* 17 *Puranas,* the *Vedanta Sutra,* and historical works like the *Mahabharata,* he was shocked to find himself totally depressed. He reasoned that, after such a great output, he ought to be elated or at least content, but he could not shake a pervasive sense of inadequacy. He said, "I am feeling incomplete, though I myself am fully equipped with everything required by the Vedas." While contemplating his dilemma, Vyasa reasoned, "This may be because I did not specifically point out the devotional service of the Lord, which is dear both to perfect beings and to the infallible Lord."

Vyasa's musings were interrupted by the sudden and unexpected appearance of his guru—Narada Muni. Overjoyed at seeing Narada at this most strategic time of need, Vyasa unburdened his mind to Narada, asking him to reveal the definitive cause of his despondency. Narada confirmed Vyasa's suspicions in the following words:

> You have not actually broadcast the sublime and spotless glories of the Personality of Godhead. That philosophy which does not satisfy the transcendental senses of the Lord is considered worthless. Although, great sage, you have very broadly described the four principles beginning with religious performances, you have not described the glories of the Supreme Personality, Vāsudeva.

Without unconditional love of Godhead—bhakti—life is ultimately futile, asserts Narada and all Vaiṣṇava teachers. In commenting on Vyasa's situation, His Divine Grace A.C. Bhaktivedanta Swami Prabhupada writes that Vyasa had

> certainly, as a matter of course, given descriptions of the glories of the Lord (Śrī Kṛṣṇa) but not as many as given to religiosity, economic development, sense gratification and salvation. These four items are by far inferior to engagement in the devotional service of the Lord. Śrī Vyāsadeva, as the authorized scholar, knew very well this difference. And still instead of giving more importance to the better type of engagement, namely, devotional service to the Lord, he had more or less improperly used his valuable time, and thus he was despondent. From this it is clearly indicated that no one can be pleased substantially without being engaged in the devotional service of the Lord.

The example of Vyasadeva is considered in Vaiṣṇava circles to be irrefutable anecdotal evidence that bhakti is absolutely essential. Who had achieved more than Vyasa, asks the Vaiṣṇava; yet, without giving bhakti its rightful emphasis, Vyasa, the knower of all material and spiritual knowledge, could not achieve any satisfaction. The lesson Vyasa learned in this incident is exactly paralleled in the New Testament. In one of St. Paul's most famous passages in I Corinthians, he writes:

> I may be able to speak the languages of men and even of angels, but if I have no love, my speech is no more than a noisy gong or a clanging bell. I may have the gift of inspired preaching; I may have all knowledge and understand all secrets; I may have all the faith needed to move mountains—but if I have no love, I am nothing. I may give away everything I have, and even give up my body to be burned—but if I have no love, this does me no good.

These verses are further indications that in essence Christianity and Vaiṣṇavism are identical.

Immediately after receiving his diagnosis from Narada, Vyasadeva began compiling the *Srimad Bhagavatam,* which deals exclusively with the intricacies of unconditional love of God. From all Vedic knowledge he culled whatever information, histories, and philosophy which supported the soul's loving relationship with the Supreme as being the ultimate goal of life. For this reason, the *Srimad Bhagavatam* is called "the mature fruit of the desire tree of Vedic literatures." It is also named "the literary incarnation of God. . . . It is meant for the ultimate good of all people, and it is all-successful, all-blissful and all-perfect."

The *Srimad Bhagavatam* also contains in its Tenth Canto the most extensive biography of Shri Krishna's incarnation on earth. From meditating on and entering into the rasas (relationships) enjoyed by Shri Krishna with His parents, friends, work associates, and spiritual confidants, the doors of bhakti are opened wide—and the devotee can experience the highest ecstasy of life. Finally, since the *Srimad Bhagavatam* is Vyasadeva's last and most heartfelt realization of Vedic wisdom, it is considered to be his definitive commentary on the *Vedanta Sutra* and the true meaning of life. For all of these reasons and more, the *Srimad Bhagavatam* is *the most important* Vedic scripture for most Vaiṣṇavas.

The main histories contained in Vedic literature are the *Mahabharata* and the *Ramayana*. Through oral recitations and dramatic presentations, the stories and lessons of these two great works have become embedded in the hearts of countless generations of Indians. As explained previously, the *Mahabharata* recounts the adventures of the Pandava brothers as they lose their regal inheritance, suffer through fourteen years of exile, and, with the help of Krishna, finally regain their inheritance in an awesome war against the greedy sons of Dhritarashtra.

In between the narrative of the *Mahabharata,* states Romesh Dutt, is found "an encyclopaedia of the life and knowledge of ancient India." Will Durant tells us that in the *Mahabharata,* "The Golden Rule is expressed in many forms; moral aphorisms of beauty and wisdom abound. . . ." Two examples of the Golden Rule found in the *Mahabharata* are: "Do naught to others which if done to thee would cause thee pain;" and, "But when an enemy seeks help, a good man gladly gives."

The *Vayu* and *Skanda Puranas* define a *sutra,* any *sutra,* as follows: "A *sūtra* is a code that expresses the essence of all knowledge in a minimum of words. It must be universally applicable and faultless in its linguistic presentation." Therefore, as His Divine Grace A.C. Bhaktivedanta Swami Prabhupada writes, "The *Vedānta-sūtra*. . . is the concise form of all Vedic knowledge."

The subject matter covered in the *Vedanta-sutra* is revealed in the following verse from the *Bhagavad-gita:* "That knowledge of the field of activities and of the knower of activities is described by various sages in various Vedic writings. It is especially presented in Vedānta-sūtra with all reasoning as to cause and effect." The field of activities is the world, the universe, the total environment affecting all actions. The knower of activities on the earthly dimension is the individual self and on the universal dimension is God. More than any other scripture, the *Vedanta-sutra* relies on logic and reason to validate its philosophy. This may sound like a contradiction from previous statements in this book, but, as Indian scholar Mysore Hiriyana writes, "The *Vedanta* never dispenses with reason, and the *Upanisads* are themselves full of arguments. All that is questioned is the final validity of reason in matters which do not come within its purview."

Because the *Vedanta-sutra* is written in philosophical codes, it is the scripture most vulnerable to subjective and misleading interpretations. Vedanta literally means "the final conclusion of all knowledge." In the *Bhagavad-gita,* the Supreme Godhead, the Personality of the Divine, whom we have met in this book under various names such as Krishna, Vishnu, Narayana, and others, says, "I am the compiler of Vedānta, and I am the knower of the *Vedas.*" Vaiṣṇavism asserts that the transcendentally personal Godhead is the ultimate source and goal of life. In order to preserve this understanding, Vyasadeva "compiled *Vedānta-sūtra,* and in order to protect it from unauthorized commentaries, he personally composed *Śrīmad Bhāgavatam* as the original commentary on *Vedānta-sūtra,*" writes His Divine Grace A.C. Bhaktivedanta Swami Prabhupada.

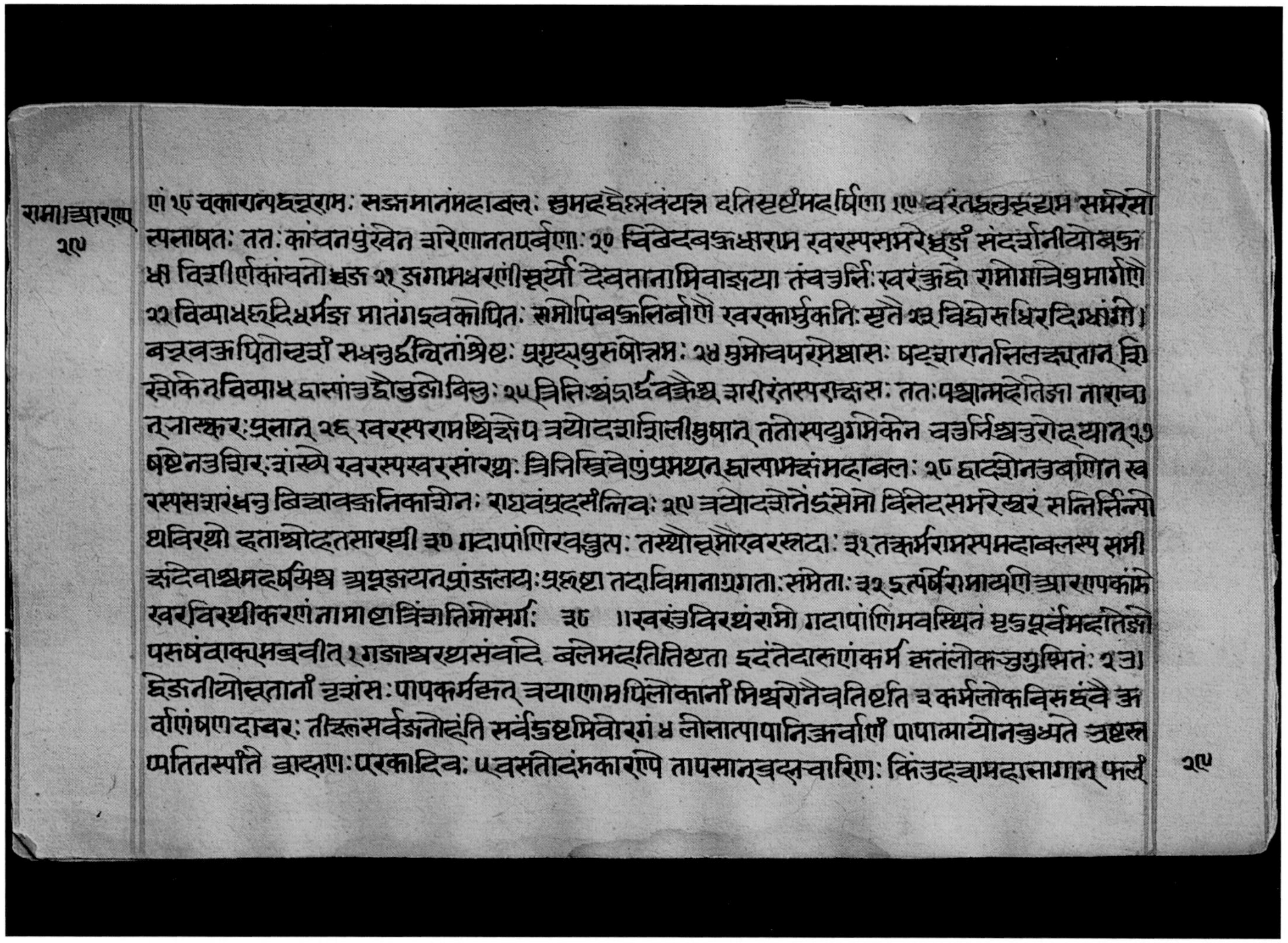

Rice paper scroll from the 18th century of the Ramayana, Private Collection.

LATER VAIṢṆAVA LITERATURE

Besides the early classical Vedic literature, each of the four major schools of contemporary Vaiṣṇavism have accumulated small libraries of original writings over the centuries elaborating on their own particular point of view. We cannot even hope to survey this vast ocean of Vaiṣṇava literature here, but must content ourselves with identifying some of their highlights.

In Chapter 10, Shri Rangam, we have already covered Ramanuja and the school of Shri Vaiṣṇavism. The Kumara School of Nimbarka and the Rudra School of Visnuswami also have their literatures, but considered more important by most scholars are the writings of Madhva (1238-1317), the founder of the Brahma-Madhva School. He personally wrote "thirty-seven works in all, of which only six are minor ones. . .," states B.N.K. Sharma in his book *Madhva's Teachings in His Own Words*. Madhva reclaimed the theistic *Srimad Bhagavatam* for Vaiṣṇavism.
Sharma writes that Madhva's

> commentary on the *Bhāgavata Purāṇa* is a reinterpretation of the crucial verses and contexts of that Purāṇa which had been given a monistic [impersonal] turn by earlier commentators. With an astonishing wealth of interpretative literature. . . Madhva has brought out the unmistakable Theistic significance of such passages.

Madhva's poetical masterpiece is his epitome of the *Mahabharata,* which Sharma considers quite modern in its scholarly approach. The *Anuvyakhyana* is Madhva's philosophical masterpiece, and it critically examines and compares all schools of thought's commentaries on the *Vedanta-sutra*. A contemporary of Madhva's time was Jayadeva Goswami, whose poem, the *Gita Govinda,* about the loving pastimes of Radha and Krishna, is considered a masterpiece of world literature and has been discussed previously in this book. The Vaiṣṇava poets Vidyapati and Chandidasa are also quite worthy of reading, especially since they and Jayadeva exerted a strong influence on Shri Chaitanya and His followers. From this general period, Sridhar Swami's commentary on the *Srimad Bhagavatam* is also worthy of special note, since Shri Chaitanya considered it the best of all time.

Shri Chaitanya was a direct spiritual descendant of Madhva and His school is called the Brahma-Madhva-Gaudiya School. While He only personally wrote eight verses, Shri Chaitanya inspired His disciples to write a veritable ocean of delightful Vaiṣṇava literatures in both poetry and prose. This body of literature represents the flowering of medieval and early modern Vaiṣṇavism and is perhaps an unprecedentedly large and high-quality literary outpouring of spiritual sentiments. The role of the "Six Goswamis of Vrindavan" in this literary tidal wave has already been recounted in Chapter 6.

In the Eleventh Canto of the *Srimad Bhagavatam,* Krishna Himself expands on the ultimate meaning of the *Vedas* to His dear friend Uddhava:

> What is the direction of all Vedic literatures? On whom do they set focus? Who is the purpose of all speculation? Outside of Me no one knows these things. Now you should know that all these activities are aimed at ordaining and setting forth Me. The purpose of Vedic literature is to know Me by different speculations, either by indirect understanding or by dictionary understanding. Everyone is speculating about Me. The essence of all Vedic literatures is to distinguish Me from māyā [illusion]. By considering the illusory energy, one comes to the platform of understanding Me. In this way one becomes free from speculation about the Vedas and comes to Me as the conclusion. Thus one is satisfied.

In commenting on the above verses, His Divine Grace A.C. Bhaktivedanta Swami points out the three phases of development in spiritual life delineated by the *Vedas:*

> The *Vedas* are composed of *karma-kāṇḍa, jñāna-kāṇḍa* and *upāsanā-kāṇḍa*. If one analytically studies the purpose of the *Vedas,* he understands that by *karma-kāṇḍa,* sacrificial activity, one comes to the conclusion of *jñāna-kāṇḍa,* speculative knowledge. After speculation, one comes to the conclusion that worship of the Supreme Personality of Godhead is the ultimate. When one comes to this conclusion, he becomes fully satisfied.

The futility of mere speculation to comprehend the *Vedas* is declared in the Tenth Canto of the *Srimad Bhagavatam:* "But those who speculate to understand the Supreme Personality of Godhead are unable to know You, even though they continue to study the Vedas for many years." Without proper spiritual guidance, the *Vedas* can be a labyrinth or an endless maze.

The danger of taking demigods to be the Supreme in the *Vedas* is duly noted in the *Padma Purana:*

> There are many types of Vedic literatures and supplementary Purāṇas. In each of them there are particular demigods who are spoken of as the chief demigods. This is just to create an illusion for moving and nonmoving living entities. Let them perpetually engage in such imaginations. However, when one analytically studies all these Vedic literatures collectively, he comes to the conclusion that Lord Viṣṇu is the one and only Supreme Personality of Godhead.

The ultimate view of the *Vedas* is transcendental monotheism, but presented with a rich and satisfying complexity and detail worthy of an infinite reality.

In the early sixteenth century, Shri Chaitanya reiterated the ultimate devotional goal of the *Vedas*. He said, "In the Vedic literatures, Kṛṣṇa is the central point of attraction, and His service is our activity. To attain the platform of love of Kṛṣṇa is life's ultimate goal. Therefore, Kṛṣṇa, Kṛṣṇa's service and love of Kṛṣṇa are the three great riches of life."

The original Vedic authority for this universe, Brahma, who received the *Vedas* by aural reception, reached the same conclusion. The *Srimad Bhagavatam* reports:

> The great personality Brahmā, with great attention and concentration of mind, studied the Vedas three times, and after scrutinizingly examining them, he ascertained that attraction for the Supreme Personality of Godhead Śrī Kṛṣṇa is the highest perfection of religion.

Go to the root of existence—Vishnu, Krishna, God—for all of your needs. For a Vaiṣṇava, this is the greatest advice he or she can give to any person. This is the greatest charity, the most valuable gift, the supreme revelation. As the *Bhagavad-gita* states, "All purposes served by a small well can at once be served by a great reservoir of water. Similarly, all the purposes of the Vedas can be served to one who knows the purpose behind them." Love of God is the supreme purpose behind the *Vedas*.

Our journey through Vaiṣṇava India is now over. We hope we have given our reader a clear picture of the ultimate goal of life in Vaiṣṇavism—unconditional love of Godhead. Whatever faults are in this presentation are the full responsibility of the authors. For whatever good is in this book, we thank the previous acharyas, gurus, and intellectuals of the world for giving us the knowledge and insight to build on.

Let us conclude by stating the one enormous advantage we people of the latter half of the twentieth century enjoy over all previous generations in comprehending Vaiṣṇava India—we have the library of writings of a pure devotee of Krishna, His Divine Grace A.C. Bhaktivedanta Swami Prabhupada, freely available at our fingertips to light up our way on the spiritual path. The contemporary Vaiṣṇava world and Western scholars are nearly unanimous in praising Shrila Prabhupada's integrity, unalloyed devotion, and skill in presenting Vaiṣṇavism to the West and rejuvenating it in India. If by our humble efforts we can encourage even one soul to drink the nectar of Vaiṣṇavism through Shrila Prabhupada's writings, then all the effort and expense involved in writing and publishing *Vaiṣṇava India* would have been well worth it.

THE END

Alauddin Khalji: the ruthless sultan of Delhi who ruled from 1296 to 1316. By the sword, Alauddin conquered almost all of India and initiated a harsh and efficient system of taxation. He enforced strict morality and took extreme measures to stop any opposition, Muslim or Hindu, to his absolute control.

Alavandor: "one who comes to rule, protect, or save"; another name for Yamunacharya. See *Yamunacharya*.

Al-Mumun: the seventh Caliph of Baghdad who ruled from AD 813 to 833 and is considered the most magnificent of the Abbassidan Caliphs. He was extremely generous and liberally patronized the arts. While a successful military commander, he could not best Mewar. He created instability in his empire by denying the divine origins of the *Koran* and attempting to force his heretical Islamic views on his subjects.

Alwars: a name for the God-intoxicated saints of south India who emphasized intuitive realization and ecstatic love of God.

Amba Mata: "mother"; another name for Durga. See *Durga*.

Ananda: an intense spiritual bliss which is considered to be an intrinsic quality of the soul and God.

Andhanari: a plastic representation of Shiva and his female counterpart, Parvati, where their bodies are intertwined to show the intimate complementarity of the male and female energies.

Andhra: an ancient dynasty centered in the Andhra valley between the Krishna and Godavari Rivers in the Deccan. Andhra was a stronghold of orthodox Vedic civilization and culture from its founding in 60 BC to its mysterious demise over 400 years later. The area is also famous for its artists.

Aniruddha: one of the four original expansions of the original Godhead. Aniruddha controls the mind of the living entities and is meditated upon for this purpose.

Anuvyakhyana: a Sanskrit book written in metrical form by Madhva that is a companion piece to his commentary on the *Vedanta-sutra*. It is considered his philosophical *magnum opus*. It compares Madhva's school of thought with all other Vedic schools of thought, especially various Shankarite schools. It reviews and critically comments on other Indian theories of logic, metaphysics, and epistemology from the theistic point of view. Its strength is that it considers the import of all Vedic literatures as a whole in coming up with its conclusions, whereas Shankara put undue emphasis on the *Upanishads*.

Aradhana: "worship"; the name "Radha" is derived from this word.

Arishṭanemi: the 22nd Tirthankara (ford-finder) of Jainism who was the younger cousin of Krishna and a member of the Vrishni family. He had an extraordinary body with many auspicious and spiritual marks. Krishna became his guardian and arranged for his marriage to Rajimata, the daughter of King Ugrasena. However, when he learned that animals would be killed for the wedding feast, he immediately renounced material life and became a monk with Krishna's blessings. Fifty-five days later he attained perfect spiritual enlightenment according to the Jain religion. He lived a full life and preached vigorously. He also organized a holy order of monks.

Arjuna: one of the five sons of King Pandu. Arjuna attained immortal fame because of his intimate friendship with Shri Krishna and receiving advice from Him in the *Bhagavad-gita*.

Arthashastra: a practical manual covering such subjects as economics, sociology, politics, and especially administration authored by Kautilya. It is less religiously based than previous Indian works on these subjects. It emphasizes the training and duties of a king, recruitment of competent administrators, military strategy, diplomacy, and public relations. It glorifies regal power and is a manual on how to use it.

Arupa: "formless." When referring to God in Vaiṣṇavism, "arupa" means that God has no material form limited by time and space.

Ashram: a residential school dedicated to spiritual learning and experience, usually headed by a spiritual preceptor of a particular spiritual line. Ashrams also serve as retreat centers for the laity.

Ashtakshara Mantra: the sacred chant, or mantra, of eight syllables, namely, om namo narayanaya.

Asura: a person, celestial or human, who works powerfully for self-aggrandizement by violating natural and cosmic laws; a person opposed to the devotional service of God.

Atharva Veda: the manual of psychosomatic medicine of ancient India. It was composed of various formulas and chants of a medicinal, healing, and peaceful nature, as well as formulas to afflict and counter rivals. Included in it were descriptions of healing herbs, fertility and virility formulas, and so forth.

Atman: can refer to the physical, mental, or intellectual self, but usually refers to the eternal, individual self, or soul.

Ātmārāma: "one who takes pleasure in and is satisfied by self-realization and spiritual life." The famous ātmārāma verse can be found in the *Srimad Bhagavatam* 1.7.10. Sixty-one explanations of this verse can be found in *Caitanya-caritamrta, Madhya-Lila,* Chapter 24.

Atreya: a philosopher and logician who lived in Taxila around 550 BC. He wrote the *Ayurveda,* or the "Veda of Longevity and Therapeutics." It contained eight books covering general surgery, surgery of the ear, nose, and throat, how to deal with possession by evil forces, pediatrics, treatment of poisoning cases, elixirs, aphrodisiacs, and alchemy.

Aurangzeb: the sixth of the Mughal emperors who ruled India from 1659 to 1707 and extended the empire to its most extensive boundaries. While very skilled as an administrator, Aurangzeb was a fanatical Muslim who tried to force all of India to follow his beliefs. His reign was marked by ruinous civil wars, which, in conjunction with his fanaticism, laid the seeds for the fairly rapid disintegration of the Mughal Empire after his death. He also allowed the Europeans to gain a foothold in India, and the British exploited the widespread dissension in India created by Aurangzeb to gain control over the entire subcontinent.

Avatar: "one who descends"; indicates a full or partial incarnation of God who descends from the spiritual dimension to appear on earth to fulfill a divine purpose. Vaiṣṇavism has a rich theology delineating various kinds of "avatars."

B

Badarayana-sutra: another name for the *Vedanta-sutra*. See *Vedanta-sutra*.

Bahadur Shah: the sultan of Gujarat from 1526 to 1537. He defeated Chittor in 1534, but the Mughal Emperor Humayan in turn defeated him the next year. Pressed by the Mughals, Bahadur Shah was forced to make a treaty with the Portuguese, who treacherously drowned him in 1537 during peace negotiations.

Baladeva: see Balarama.

Baladeva Vidyabhushana: the author of a Vaiṣṇava commentary on the *Vedanta-sutra* called *Govinda-bhasya*.

Balarama: on the earthly dimension, Balarama was Shri Krishna's elder half-brother 5,000 years ago. In the spiritual dimension, Balarama is the first expansion of the original Godhead and always considers Himself a servant of Shri Krishna.

Baudhayana Dharma Sutra: one of the most ancient compilations of Vedic rituals, customs, and laws written by Baudhayana and originally intended for the followers of the Taittiriya Veda. In time it became a source for the sacred law of all brahmins. Among other things, it contains the duties and customs for students, householders, the king, and religious people. Rituals for success, purification, atonement, attaining a son, and many other things are included. It advocates a broad view of life wherein reverence is held for all beings, people, sources of religiosity, and God. Unfortunately, no complete copies of it have survived to our time and we possess less of it in reliable form than any other collection of ancient Vedic law.

Banyan: an Indian fig tree known for its complexity of growth. From a central trunk, branches grow downwards to eventually sink into the ground as roots to form new trunks. The largest banyan tree has 350 large trunks and 3,000 small ones. The banyan tree is mentioned in the *Bhagavad-gita* as a good analogy for the material world. The root of the material world does come from above, or the spiritual dimension, and the material world is as complex and entangling as a banyan tree's trunks.

Bhagavad-gita: a compendium of Vedic and Vaiṣṇava psychology and philosophy expounded in the form of a discourse between Shri Krishna and Arjuna. Delineates love of God and devotional service as the ultimate means and goal of life.

Bhagavan: "He who possesses all opulences"; a name for God denoting that God is the repository of all beauty, strength, fame, wealth, knowledge, and detachment.

Bhagavata Mela: a musical dance performance with songs based on and illuminating the teachings of the *Puranas*.

Bhagavata Purana: another name for the *Srimad Bhagavatam*. See *Srimad Bhagavatam*.

Bhagavatars: brahmins who used the medium of Bharata Natyam dance to bring the message of Vaiṣṇavism to the people.

Bhagavatas: a name for practitioners of bhakti-yoga, or the devotional path of God consciousness; Vaiṣṇavas.

Bhajan: a devotional song designed to be sung by a leader and a group, usually in the vernacular.

Bhakti: unconditional love of God and the process of devotional service to God. Bhakti is considered the ultimate means and goal of life.

Bhaktiras: a mood of intense devotion to God that predominates a devotee or a literary or dramatic work.

Bhakti-rasamrta-sindhu: the Sanskrit name for the book, *The Nectar of Devotion,* by Shrila Rupa Goswami. This work is also called the complete science of bhakti-yoga and describes in detail the various loving exchanges between devotees and God. It also explains the ecstacies derived from these exchanges as well as the rules and regulations to be followed in pursuing these exchanges.

Bhaktiratnakar: the greatest history of Bengali Vaiṣṇavism from the time of Shri Chaitanya's passing to the end of the seventeenth century written by Narahari Chakravarty. The title means "the Sea of Spiritual Emotion," and it is divided into fifteen waves or chapters. It is an anthology of Vaiṣṇava lyrics and lore with 314 poems by 27 poets. One hundred and thirty-five were penned by Narahari himself. Also described are the activities of Shrinivasa Acharya and Narottama dasa Thakura, the activities of the six Goswamis of Vrindavan, a description of Navadvipa, and other topics. To many Vaiṣṇavas, it is second to only the *Caitanya-caritamrta* in importance.

Bhaktisiddhanta Sarasvati Gosvami Maharaja: the acharya who brought Gaudiya Vaiṣṇavism into the twentieth century and the spiritual teacher of His Divine Grace A.C. Bhaktivedanta Swami Prahbhupada.

Bhaktivedanta Swami Prabhupada, His Divine Grace: the foremost preacher of Vaiṣṇavism in the western world, who graced the planet from 1896 to 1977. He is best known for his prodigious literary work. His translations into English of the *Bhagavad-gita, Srimad Bhagavatam,* and *Caitanya-caritamrta,* as well as other Vaiṣṇava classics, gave the Western World its first deep insight into the soul of Vaiṣṇavism. Shrila Prabhupada also founded the International Society for Krishna Consciousness (ISKCON) and oversaw the opening of over 100 Vaiṣṇava temples around the world.

Bhakti-yoga: the process of uniting with God and realizing the self through cultivating the varieties of unconditional love.

Bharata Muni: an ancient sage who wrote the *Natya Shastra,* or the Science of Dramaturgy, which included a guide to classical Indian dance.

Bharavi: a sixth-century poet of south India who probably wrote under the patronage of the Chalukya Dynasty. His poem *Kiratarjuniya* is considered one of the five greatest Sanskrit poems. See *Kiratarjuniya*.

Bhat: a court bard in Rajasthan.

Bhaumasura: a demoniac personality who became so powerful that he began to conquer the domain of the demigods, as well as kidnapping 16,100 princesses from various kings on earth. When Indra complained to Krishna at Dwaraka about Bhaumasura's aggression, Krishna traveled to Pragjyotishapura, the demon's capital, and utterly defeated his army and slew the demon with His divine chakra weapon, thereby delivering Bhaumasura's soul.

Bhava: in cultural terms, bhava is a particular mood the artist strives to represent. In bhakti-yoga, bhava is a stage of devotional ecstasy.

Bhima: one of the five Pandava brothers known for his herculean strength and appetite.

Dharmaraja: "King of Truth"; another name for Yudhishthira. See *Yudhishthira.*

Dhatu: the essential ingredients or layers of the body and material existence.

Dhritarashtra: the father of Duryodhana who was physically and spiritually blind, allowing his family to abuse their position as regents of the Pandava brothers, culminating in the Kurukshetra War.

Dhruva Yantra: yantra generally signifies some kind of device or machine. The Dhruva Yantra was an astronomical device invented by Jai Singh II to determine the position of the pole star.

Dhyana Mantram: a mantra, or sacred chant, that invokes the inner or outer vision of a particular Deity.

Digvijayi Pandit: "one who has conquered everyone in all directions"; the title of a scholar who had earned the world championship in his field of competency by defeating all rivals in academic contests.

Diwan: a regent.

Draupadi: the pious wife of the Pandava brothers.

Duhśalā: (also spelled Duśśalā) the only daughter of King Dhritarashtra by his queen, Gandhari. She married the Raja of Sindhu, Jayadratha, who was killed in the battle of Kurukshetra.

Durga: the goddess who controls the material energy and who eliminates inimical elments in the universe through warfare and other conflicts. Durga is a feminine counterpart to Shiva.

Dwar: doorway.

E

Eklinga: (1) a village fourteen miles north of Udaipur that is an important religious shrine of Mewar founded by Bappa Rawal in honor of the Shiva deity of his guru. (2) a deity of Shiva that is worshiped at Eklinga. The deity is a *lingam,* or phallus, of Shiva and is known affectionately as *Eklingaji.*

G

Gadadhara Pandit: a highly learned devotee of Shri Chaitanya Mahaprabhu who is an incarnation of the pleasure potency of Krishna (God). He is considered one of Chaitanya's four main associates.

Gajarajan: "King of the Elephants."

Gandhara: an ancient country consisting of the land between the lower Kabul valley and the upper Indus. Gandhara was a prime melting pot of Asia, being in the path of India's invaders. At one time or another, Mongolians, Aryans, Scythians, Bactrians, Parthians, Kushans, Shakas, and Huns conquered Gandhara, whose culture reflected a synthesis of all the above mentioned groups. Greek influence was especially strong from 250 BC to AD 450, which provided the main gateway for a reciprocal influence of Greek and Vedic cultures. In spite of the numerous influences on Gandhara, Buddhism became a predominating force. Gandharian sculptors fashioned the first human images of the Buddha, which strongly influenced the Mathura School and all Indian art.

Ganesha: the eldest son of Shiva and Parvati who was accidentally beheaded by Shiva, but revived by the transplant of an elephant's head: hence, his half-human, half-elephant form. Ganesha is an extremely popular demigod in India and is especially invoked for business success and the overcoming of obstacles.

Garuda: Vishnu's human-bird carrier of extraordinary prowess.

Gatis: intricate dance steps used in the Kathak dance style.

Gaudiya: see *Gauda Desh.*

Gauda Desh: the district of Bengal where Shri Chaitanya Mahaprabhu appeared.

Gaudiya Vaiṣṇava: the school of Vaiṣṇavism founded by Shri Chaitanya Mahaprabhu and His followers. It is the most important and powerful Vaiṣṇava movement in Bengal.

Gautama Buddha: an Indian prince who renounced royal life to seek enlightenment in the fifth and sixth centuries BC. His realizations and teachings are the basis of Buddhism.

Gautama Tantra: see *Brhad-gautamiya-tantra.*

Ghat: a structure on the bank of a river or lake to facilitate bathing, sacred rituals, or the landing of a boat.

Ghee: clarified butter.

Girdhar: a name for Krishna (God) as the lifter of Govardhana Hill. When Krishna persuaded the residents of Vrindavan to stop the worship of Indra, the angry demigod, not realizing Krishna's status as the Supreme Personality of Godhead (in essence, Indra's boss), unleashed a devastating, week-long rainstorm on Vrindavan. Krishna easily lifted Govardhana Hill and used it as an umbrella to protect the residents of Vrindavan from the storm. Krishna's name of Girdhar, or Giridhari, is derived from and celebrates this pastime.

Gita Govinda: the most famous and powerful poem describing the loving exchanges between the male and female aspects of the Supreme Truth, Radha and Krishna, written by Jayadeva Goswami in the twelth century AD.

Gopa: (1) a cowherd boy; (2) the intimate male friends of Shri Krishna during the childhood years of His incarnation on earth.

Gopuras: ornate and monumental gateways characteristic of south Indian temples.

Goswami: an elevated spiritual person who has complete mastery over the urges of the senses.

Gour Hari: a nickname for Shri Chaitanya Mahaprabhu based on His golden complexion and aura.

Govinda: "He who gives pleasure to the land, cows, and senses": a name for Shri Krishna (God).

Govinda Bhasya: a commentary on the *Vedanta-sutra* written by Baladeva Vidyabhushana, which is held in the highest esteem by Gaudiya Vaiṣṇavas.

Gujarat: a state of India located in the western sector of the subcontinent. Its name only began appearing in the fifth century AD. Gujarat maintained its independence as a Vedic kingdom until AD 1297, whereon it passed into the hands of various Muslim rulers until the early eighteenth century. Then the Marathas took control until 1818, when Gujarat became part of the British Indian Empire. Its residents are famed as businesspeople, especially in textiles.

Guler: a city-state of Rajputana that evolved a highly refined and feminine school of painting in the eighteenth century. The palace women were more involved than the men in the patronage of art and inspired a cool, romantic elegance in their artists. Bright colors in textiles and flowers were contrasted to the more restrained tones of the rest of the scene. The pastimes of Krishna and Rama were the favorite themes, and the Guler style was exported to Kangra, Garhwal, and Nurpur.

Gurukula: a boarding school presided over by a spiritual preceptor for the total education of young people. The students of a gurukula follow a strict spiritual discipline, including celibacy, as well as learning secular arts and sciences according to their propensities.

Guna: a material quality: either goodness, activity, inertia, or a mixture of the three.

Gupta Dynasty: ruled most of India from the third century AD to about AD 550. A golden age of peace, prosperity, and high cultural attainment in all fields. Vaiṣṇavism was the dominant religion, and vegetarianism was the main diet.

Guru: literally means "heavy"; a spiritual teacher who is weighted down with wisdom.

Gwalior: an ancient city and princely state of Rajputana located in central India, which is now the winter capital of Madhya Pradesh. It was famous for its magnificent palaces, and its powerful fort was thought to be impregnable. Gwalior passed back and forth from Rajput to Muslim hands over the centuries. Under the patronage of Raja Man Singh's (1486-1517) consort, Mrignaina, Gwalior became the premier center of music in India, training the legendary Tansen, who is also buried there.

H

Hanuman: the perfect example of a devotee who, millenniums ago, unconditionally served the incarnation Rama in His struggle to regain His wife, Sita.

Hara: "destroyer" or "seizer"; a name for Lord Shiva as death, who destroys all material forms, from the individual body to the universe. Hara is also associated with sleep, the remover of pain.

Hare Krishna maha-mantra: the great chant for self-realization and the awakening of love of God; Hare Krishna, Hare Krishna, Krishna Krishna, Hare Hare; Hare Rama, Hare Rama, Rama Rama, Hare Hare. The maha-mantra means, "Oh God, oh energy of God, engage me in Your service."

Hari: a name for Shri Krishna (God), which means, "He who takes away everything inauspicious and attracts to the soul everything auspicious."

Hari Bol: an all-purpose Vaiṣṇava greeting, which means, "Chant the names of God."

Haridas Thakur: although born a Muslim, Haridasa Thakur became the greatest living example of chanting God's holy names among the associates of Shri Chaitanya Mahaprabhu.

Harivaṁśa (Purāna): "the geneology of Hari," a 10,000 verse appendix to the *Mahabharata* which praises Mahavishnu. In its first three sections, the creation of the world, the kings of the solar, lunar, and Yadu dynasties, and the advent of Krishna are covered. The delightful childhood pastimes and pranks of Krishna are the theme of section two. Section three recounts the incarnations of Vamana (the Dwarf incarnation) and the half-lion, half-human incarnation, Nrisinghadeva. Shiva and Vishnu are also covered. Naturally, this purana is in the mode of goodness (sattvaguna).

Hastas: rapid hand gestures used in the Kathak dance style.

Havelis: a large living compound designed to accommodate an extended Indian family.

Hastalakshana Dipika: the dance manual of the Kathakali dance style. It includes an alphabet of twenty-four gestures used to communicate the dance's meaning.

Holi: one of the four most important holidays and festivals in the Vedic religion. It occurs in spring and is especially dear to Vaiṣṇavas who commemorate Krishna's friendly dealings with His boy friends and girl friends. It is a colorful, joyous time where people spray each other with colored dyes and water. Deities are paraded about to much singing and dancing.

Hoysalas: a dynasty originating in Mysore that succeeded the Chalukyan Empire and was a dominating force in south India from 1006 to 1343. They built fortified cities that kept Muslim conquerors out of south India for several centuries. They also built the most ornate and detailed temples in India, and their sculpture work is especially appreciated.

I

Ikshvaku: one of the sons of the primordial lawgiver, Manu. Ikshvaku founded the famed Solar Dynasty at Ayodhya in the Treta Yuga, or Silver Age, hundreds of thousands of years ago. The incarnation Rama is the most famous member of the Solar Dynasty.

Indra: the presiding demigod of rain and the heavenly, or upper, planetary systems of the material universe.

Indradyumna: a great Vedic king of prehistoric India who is universally credited with building the original temple of Jagannath Puri and ordering the Jagannath Deities to be sculpted. He is said to have been of the Maga Clan and was extremely devoted to Vishnu and Vaiṣṇavism. In his dreams, Krishna revealed to him that he would come as a divine log to be made into Deities.

Indravarmin: "The Vehicle of the King of Heaven, Indra"; a replica of which was built by Jai Singh II to tour his new city, Jaipur.

Īśa Upaniṣad, or Śrī Īśopaniṣad: in this short Upanishad of eighteen verses and an invocation is a compendium of Vedic wisdom regarding the nature of

philosophy was refined and continued by Chaitanya. Because of Nimbarka's personal skill in refuting Shankarite philosophy and his brilliant presentations of how God's pastimes (lilas) were the spontaneous sport and creation of the ever-perfect and ever-blissful Supreme Being, his teachings contained the potency to maintain the individuality of the Kumara line in spite of its similarity to other Vaiṣṇava schools.

Kummi: a gentle, feminine form of Kathakali dance. While the conventions of Kathakali are followed, this style strikes a balance between swift and graceful movements at a lilting pace with soft gestures. The themes of Kummi are mostly based on the pastimes of Krishna and Shiva.

Kurus: see *Kauravas.*

Kuruvanji: a series of dance ballets performed in the Bharata Natyam style that are popular in Tamil Nadu. There are about thirty of these ballets current, and each recounts the tale of a heroine's love for her hero. A fortuneteller, or Kuruvanji, is pivotal to each tale by telling the heroine whether or not her love will prosper.

Kusa grass: a variety of grass that is considered spiritually auspicious. It is used by meditators to sit on and by priests in the performance of Vedic rituals.

Kushana: the name of Mongolian tribes who migrated from Central Asia to form an empire that at one time stretched from the borders of Persia to northern India and Afganisthan. They exerted their influence from 165 BC to AD 200. The Indian branch established a capital at Mathura. They were assimilated into Indian culture and took Vedic names. They tolerated all religions, but favored and spread Mahayana Buddhism over much of Asia. The Kushans were the link between Roman and Chinese civilizations, and their empire served as an East-West melting pot.

Kutiyattam: "acting together"; a Sanskrit drama form of Kerala that greatly influenced Kathakali. Kutiyattam is the earliest of theatrical arts in Kerala and can only be performed on special stages built in a temple compound. The actors (including a clown who translates the Sanskrit dialogue into Malayalam) have the right to jokingly insult anyone in the audience, including dignitaries. Several actors are on stage at once, and performances last from six to twenty days. Because this art form has not adapted itself to modern times like Kathakali, it is only performed today in a few larger temples.

L

Lakshmana: the half-brother of Lord Ramachandra by their common father, Dasharatha, and his wife, Sumitra. Lakshmana is also considered an incarnation of God and loyally accompanied and served Rama throughout His exile and struggle to regain His kidnapped wife, Sita.

Lalita-madhava: a drama in ten parts describing the pastimes of Krishna in Dwaraka, written by Shrila Rupa Goswami.

Lila: a pastime. In Vaiṣṇavism, "lila" usually refers to a pastime or activity of God in the material universe.

Lota: a metallic vessel for carrying water.

M

Madana-gopāla: "Herdsman of love"; a name for Krishna as the loving cowherd boy, who attracts all beings by His love and delightful pastimes.

Madana-mohana: "Krishna, the all-attractive lover who attracts even Cupid"; the first Deity of God to be worshipped in Vrindavan, who slackens the devotee's attraction to material enjoyments and helps to reestablish the soul's personal relationship to God.

Madar: the son of the Muslim general Ghazni Miyan. His father became a religious mendicant, retiring from material life for spiritual pursuits. Madar enlisted with the Pathans and became a fierce warrior against the Hindus. He became a symbol of war-like prowess, and his name was often used as a battle cry. Surprised by a hostile force at his wedding, he fought until his death defending his nuptial party. Evidently, the exploits of father and son are confusingly celebrated together to this day, especially in Rajasthan.

Madhurya Bhava: the ecstasy experienced by a devotee in a conjugal relationship with God. See *madhurya-rasa.*

Madhurya-rasa: the highest stage of unconditional love between the devotee and God, characterized by an exchange of the intimate feelings and experiences of conjugal lovers.

Madhva: the great Vaiṣṇava teacher who revived a theistic understanding of the Vedic scriptures. Madhva (AD 1238-1317) founded the Brahma-Madhva School of Vaiṣṇavism, which survives to this day.

Mahabharata: the epic poem compiled by Vyasa describing the conflict between the Kurus and the Pandavas. The *Bhagavad-gita* is a section of the *Mahabharata.*

Mahalakshmi: "The Great Goddess of Fortune"; a name for the female side of God, who is the source of all energies and embodies the three modes of material energy (the gunas).

Maha-mantra: the great chant for the deliverance of the mind: Hare Krishna, Hare Krishna, Krishna Krishna, Hare Hare/Hare Rama, Hare Rama, Rama Rama, Hare Hare. In this mantra the chanter requests God's personified energy (Hare) and God's Supreme Personhood (Krishna and Rama) to engage the soul in divine service. Almost all schools of Vedic thought consider this mantra to be the "maha-mantra," or the "great mantra," and recommend its chanting.

Maharaja: a king.

Maharana: a title for king adopted by the monarchs of Mewar.

Maharani: when a queen survives her husband, the new king's wife becomes the rani, or queen, and the royal widow becomes the maharani, or great queen or royal matriarch.

Maha-rasa: the great dance of unconditional love between Radha and Krishna, the Supreme Male and Female Personalities of Godhead.

Mahatma Gandhi: the modern father of Indian Independence, who lived from 1869-1948. From 1893 to 1914, Gandhi worked as a lawyer in South Africa, while also successfully fighting for the civil and human rights of Indians there. For the rest of his life he fought for the independence of India, using the tools of non-violent, civil disobedience and *satyagraha,* or soul force. He was intensely devoted to the *Bhagavad-gita,* reading it daily for inspiration. Towards the end of his life, he worked against Hindu-Muslim conflict and was assassinated by a Hindu fanatic. He is considered to be one of the greatest positive forces of the twentieth century, whose campaigns against British rule drew worldwide attention and sympathy.

Mahavira: "Great Hero"; the name of the twenty-fourth tirthankara (ford-finder) of the Jain religion. While often credited as being the founder of the Jain religion, within the tradition itself, Mahavira (?599-467? BC) is only the Jina, or Conqueror, of this age, one in a long line of Jinas. Undoubtedly, Mahavira, who at the age of 30 renounced all worldly ties and became an extreme ascetic, did reform and revitalize the religion, especially by his excellent skills as a preacher and organizer of a large body of male and female monks. The five great vows taken by Mahavira and required of all monks are: to be non-violent to all living beings, including observance of a vegetarian diet; not to take anything not given; to be truthful; to practice strict celibacy in thought, word, and deed; and, to own no possessions. See *Jain.*

Mahavishnu: an expansion of the original Godhead who creates the material universes. He lies down in the Causal Ocean and manifests all of the universes from His nostrils. As a direct expansion of the Godhead, Mahavishnu is as worshipable as the Godhead in Vaiṣṇavism.

Mahayana Buddhism: The School of the Great Vehicle for Salvation; also called the Northern School of Buddhism, because it became popular in Tibet, Mongolia, China, Korea, and Japan. Mahayana Buddhism appeals more to the heart and intuition rather than the intellect, and therefore it is a more devotional form of Buddhism. This school holds that Transcendental Reality is revealed in the things of nature and discourages asceticism. The goal of Theravada, or Pali, Buddhism is personal salvation. Mahayana Buddhism encourages its devotees to aspire to Bodhisattva-hood, wherein the Bodhisattva renounces passing on to nirvana, or salvation, so he or she can stay in the world to help other souls become enlightened.

Mahmud Khalji: usurped the throne of Malwa in 1436 and ruled there until his death in 1469. He spent most of his time in conquest, but was checked by Maharana Kumbha of Mewar.

Malwa: the territory of the ancient Malava clan who wounded Alexander the Great during his conquest of India. It is a sacred Vedic city and a traditional center of learning, which passed into the hands of many dynasties, including the Guptas, Huns, Chalukyas, Mughals, and Marathas, as well as being independent at times.

Manas: "the mind" in the widest application of this term, including intellect, intelligence, perception, will power, and so forth. Manas is the internal organ of perception and cognition. It is also translated as "mindstuff."

Mandala: a cosmic pattern designed to elicit a psychic or spiritual response from the viewer.

Mandalas: a series of set postures used in the Kathak dance style.

Maṇḍapas: canopies.

Mandara: a coral tree which grows in the heavenly dimension of the material universe. Krishna took the mandara tree (one of five celestial varieties) from Indra's pleasure garden and brought it to Vrindavan on earth.

Maṇḍūkya Upanishad: in twelve verses this work describes four states of consciousness: waking; dreaming; dreamless sleep; and, the ultimate state of consciousness that is eternal and superconscious.

Manipuri: the classical Indian dance style indigenous to the Indian state of Manipur. While based on ancient, classical tradition, Manipuri has developed its own distinctive style and is considered the most free, spontaneous, easy, and flowing of the classical Indian dance forms. Manipur became overwhelmingly Vaiṣṇava in the eighteenth century, and many authorities consider that Manipuri dance expresses the pastimes of Radha and Krishna in an unexcelled and fascinating manner.

Mantra: "mind deliverance"; a spiritual sound vibration (usually a name for God) that purifies consciousness and awakens the soul's natural love of God.

Mantra-yoga: the process of awakening God consciousness through the chanting of spiritual sound vibrations (mantras).

Manu: the author of the Codes or Institutes of Manu, the most ancient record of the religious and secular laws, customs, relationships, and duties of people in ancient Vedic civilization.

Marathas: the last major Indian Empire to exist before the British conquest of India. Founded by Shivaji, one of India's greatest patriots and freedom fighters, who in the 17th century defied and defeated the might of the Mughal Empire and Aurangzeb to carve out an independent Maratha state. At its height, the Maratha Empire controlled much of western and central India. Internal disputes and conflicts weakened the Marathas, and by 1819 the British had inflicted total military defeat on them.

Maurya: a great Empire that drove the Greeks out of India and united the nation for a sustained period of prosperity and cultural attainment. Lasted from 322 to 185 BC. Most notable monarchs were its founder, Chandragupta Maurya, and Ashoka.

Maya: that aspect of the material energy that allows living beings to be physically, mentally, and spiritually illusioned. In Vaiṣṇavism, maya usually refers to the individual soul's forgetfulness of its eternal relationship with God.

Mayavadi: a follower of the various schools of Indian philosophy which hold that God is ultimately impersonal or void and that all individuality is inherently illusory. This point of view was popularized by Shankara and is fond of calling all manifestations of the universe "maya," or illusion; therefore the name "mayavadi," or "those who speak of maya (illusion)."

Merta: the foremost of the clans of the Rajputana kingdom of Marwar. Mirabai was born into this family. The valley of Merta is one of the most fertile farming areas in India.

Mewar: see Chapter 13.

Mohini Atam: an important dance sytle of Kerala which uses both the vigorous and gentle modes of Kathakali. Mohini Atam is usually designed for solo performances. The dancing is accompanied by the chanting of a sacred story and

Pali Buddhism: (also known as the Hinayana, or Theravada, School of Buddhism) the prevalent form of Buddhism practiced in southeast Asia and Sri Lanka. It is a moral, ethical way of life founded on Gautama Buddha's Four Noble Truths and Noble Eightfold Path. It denies the existence of an immortal soul and God, although the karma of an individual continues to reincarnate into the world until nirvana, or final extinction, is realized. Buddha is a man who showed the way to nirvana, which each individual must pursue for him or herself. Its scriptures are written in the Pali language.

Pallava: the name of a dominant empire of south India from the third to the ninth centuries AD. The Pallavas excelled in architecture, foreign trade, and art. They built Mahabalipuram, which holds the greatest surviving treasures of their art.

Pandavas: King Pandu's five sons: Yudhishthira, Arjuna, Bhima, Nakula, and Sahadeva.

Pancha: "five."

Pandit: a title given to a learned person.

Pandyas: an ancient dynasty that ruled the southern tip of India with varying fortunes from at least 300 BC. Malik Kafir captured the Pandya territory in the early fourteenth century, but the dynasty was revived by the Nayyaka family from 1420 to 1736. The Pandyas are largely responsible for the distinctive features of south Indian architecture and temple design. The Nayyakas refurbished the Shri Rangam temple complex.

Panini: the author of the earliest standard Sanskrit grammar; its 4000 aphorisms, or sutras, are considered to be the most original and subtlest work of grammar in world history. Little is known of Panini's life, but his magnificent work in grammar was considered to be divinely inspired like the *Vedas* themselves.

Paramatma: "Supersoul"; a partial representation of the Godhead who lives in the heart of every living being and in the nucleus of every atom. In the living being, the Paramatma witnesses all activities and is the agency of the law of karma (cause and effect). The Paramatma fulfills the desires of the living being through the forces of nature. By seeking the counsel of the Paramatma, the human being is guided onto the path of spiritual life.

Parampara: a line of spiritual teachers who faithfully transmit the full body of their school's spiritual insights from generation to generation.

Parans: the 120 basic dance arrangements of the Bharata Natyam dance style.

Pārśvanātha: the 23rd Tirthankara of Jainism who was born as the son of the mighty Iksvaku King, Asvamena, and Queen Vamadevi, who both ruled in Varanasi. After a charmed youth and royal marriage he renounced the world at the age of thirty along with 300 other princes. After remaining equiposed in the midst of adoration and atttack, Pārśvanātha preached Jainism on the banks of the Ganges and Yamuna Rivers, making many converts, including his father. He emphasized charity, virtue, asceticism, and character. After many years of preaching and being an auspicious influence wherever he went, Pārśvanātha retired to Sammeta mountain, attained complete spiritual perfection, and attained nirvana, final release.

Parvati: the beautiful daughter of the Himalayas who married Shiva and is his female counterpart.

Pashupatra Weapon: an arrow of Shiva used with the Pinaka bow. The missile is as bright as the sun and burns all that it touches. By performing austerities, Arjuna gained this weapon from Shiva.

Patita-pāvanī: a name for Ganges water, meaning "the deliverer of all sinful living beings."

Pradyumna: one of the four original expansions of the Godhead in Vaiṣṇavism who controls intelligence.

Prahlada Maharaja: a great Vaiṣṇava saint of ancient times who was the son of the demoniac, atheistic ruler of the universe, Hiranyakashipu. In spite of the severest persecutions, Prahlada maintained and even preached God consciousness in his father's kingdom and was saved from certain death by the incarnation of God, Nrisinghadeva.

Prakara: walls enclosing a temple.

Prapatti: when the soul completely surrenders to and relies on God.

Prasadam: food which has been cooked and offered to God in love and devotion. Prasadam is said to nourish body and soul. Vaiṣṇavas prefer to only "honor" prasadam in their diet.

Praśna Upanishad: in this Upanishad, six sincere seekers of truth approach the sage Pippalada for enlightenment. After a one year interval of continued spiritual disciplines by the seekers, the sage answers each of their questions in turn. He teaches them to perceive Brahman, Spirit, as the foundation and animating principle of all things from the body, mind, and senses to the sun, moon, and other natural phenomena. By abiding in this awareness of spirit, the seekers can return to the eternal, spiritual abode after death to enjoy perfect peace and happiness in association with the Supreme Brahman (Spirit).

Prithviraj: the brave king of Sambhar, Ajmer, and Delhi. He accepted the burden of resisting the Muslim invasion of India, and in the First Battle of Tarain in 1191, he won. But in the Second Battle of Tarain, 10,000 Muslim calvarymen armed with bows outmaneuvered his slower army, and he was defeated and killed. His valour and love were legendary.

Pur: city.

Purana: eighteen ancient Vedic scriptures which record prominent cosmic events in the history of the earth and the universe. The *Bhagavata Purana,* or *Srimad Bhagavatam,* contains the history of Shri Krishna's incarnation and is the most important *Purana* for Vaiṣṇavas.

Purappad: "going forth"; the opening sequences of a Kathakali dance performance that depicts the world in its various moods and phases.

Purnam: "perfect, complete, and whole"; refers to the intrinsic, true nature of all souls and God as being perfect and complete.

R

Radha: the most intimate and beloved name in Vaiṣṇavism for the Supreme Female Personality of Godhead. Radha is the eternal consort and pleasure energy of Krishna (God).

Radha-Gopinatha: the female incarnation of God (Radha) and Gopinatha, a name for Krishna meaning, "He who gives pleasure to the gopis (the feminine side of God)."

Radharamana: "the lover of Radha"; a name for Krishna (God).

Rādhārānī: see *Radha*.

Ragamala: a style of Rajput painting that puts the sentiment of a *raga* (a selection of musical notes) into pictorial representation. In other words, it is a visual commentary on a particular mode of Indian music and the sentiment it invokes. The loving exchanges of Radha and Krishna are most popular in this style, although other Deities are also featured.

Raja Man Singh: ruled Amber (later known as Jaipur) from AD 1590 to 1614. Although a devout Vaiṣṇava, Raja Man Singh was also the commander-in-chief of the imperial army of the Mughal Emperor, Akbar the Great. He also served as Governor of districts like Kabul, Bengal, Bihar, and the Deccan. He constructed the Amber Palace as well as patronizing the construction of the Govinda temple in Vrindavan. His reign was one of the highpoints of Rajput-Mughal cooperation and interchange.

Rajputana: "Abode of Kings"; the name for the state of Rajasthan before Indian Independence.

Rama: (1) a name for God as the source of all pleasure; (2) the incarnation of Godhead as Lord Ramachandra, the ideal monarch.

Ramanuja, or Ramanujacharya: one of the greatest acharyas or teachers in Vaiṣṇava history. Ramanuja (AD 1017-1137) was the greatest exponent of the Shri School of Vaiṣṇavism and oversaw the Shri Rangam temple.

Rama-rajya: "the rule of Rama"; an ideal form of God-conscious government as epitomized by the executive leadership of Lord Ramachandra.

Ramayana: (1) the epic Sanskrit poem written by Valmiki, based on the pastimes of the incarnation Ramachandra; (2) any work written in the vernacular language that retells Rama's story.

Rana: king.

Ranchhorji: a name for Shri Krishna, meaning "one who has left the battlefield." After Krishna had dispatched his own uncle, Kamsa, who had imprisoned his own father and usurped the throne of Mathura, an ally of Kamsa, King Jarasandha, unsuccessfully besieged Mathura seventeen times. On the eighteenth try, Krishna fled the battlefield, because He had received a confidential letter from His soon-to-be first wife, Rukmini, requesting His immediate presence so she wouldn't have to marry someone else. Although Krishna had defeated Jarasandha seventeen times and could do it again, He exhibited the divine quality of renunciation and left the battlefield to rescue Rukmini. All of Krishna's pastimes are worshipable in Vaiṣṇavism, therefore, Krishna is also worshiped in Deity-form as "Ranchhorji."

Rani: queen.

Rasa: a particular relationship between the soul and God, as well as the sweet tastes or experiences that come from that relationship.

Rasa-lila: the eternal dance of unconditional love between Krishna (God) and the female energies of God, the gopis.

Raslila: a musical-dance reenactment of the eternal exchange of love between Radha, Krishna, and the gopis, as well as a second act portraying one of the other pastimes of Krishna's life.

Rasudharis: highly advanced Vaiṣṇavas who glorify Krishna through spiritual music and dance.

Ratha: a chariot.

Ratha-yatra: "the Festival of the Chariots"; one of the oldest ongoing religious observances in the world, originally held every year in Jagannath Puri to commemorate the return of Krishna to Vrindavan. The highlight of the festival is the procession of the Deity of Lord Jagannatha in a giant chariot.

Ravana: the ten-headed demon king of Sri Lanka who kidnapped Rama's wife, Sita, and was ultimately defeated by Rama.

Rig Veda: the oldest book of the original four *Vedas* which contains methods of communing with the higher forces of the universe to promote personal and social well-being on the earthly plane.

Rishi: a sage.

Romaharshana, or Romaharsana: the highly intelligent sage who is also known as Suta. He was entrusted by Vyasa with perpetuating the *Puranas*. Through his six main disciples, Romaharshana succeeded in this task.

Rudra School: one of the four great schools of Vaiṣṇavism founded by Visnuswami. See *Visnuswami*.

Rukmini: the only daughter of Maharaja Bhismaka, the King of Vidarbha. She is an incarnation of the female aspect of the Godhead. Her oldest brother, Rukmi, negotiated her marriage to an enemy of Krishna, Shishupala. However, Rukmini's heart was set on marrying Krishna, and she invited Him to intervene. Krishna kidnapped her, and Rukmini became Krishna's first and most beloved wife.

S

Sac-cid-ananda: "eternity, awareness, and bliss"; which are the three major qualities of the soul and God.

Sadhana: a regulated program or discipline for spiritual advancement.

Sadhana-bhakti: a regulated program of do's and don'ts for the awakening of the soul's natural love of Godhead.

Sadhu: a holy person.

Sahadeva: the youngest of the Pandava brothers, born of the union of Pandu's second wife, Madri, and one of the demigod Asvini-kumaras. Sahadeva was an accomplished astrologer and manager of cows, as well as the twin brother of Nakula.

Sakhya-bhakti-rasa: a continuous state of ecstasy which results from a devotee fully realizing that he or she is of the same essence as God and exchanges friendship with God in a reciprocal manner. See *sakhya-rasa*.

Sakhya-rasa: the third primary love relationship between the devotee and God, characterized by feelings of equality and friendship.

learned and self-realized brahmin. Sudama's wife was pained to see the poverty-stricken condition of her materially detached husband and urged him to visit his rich friend, Krishna. Krishna warmly received Sudama at Dwaraka, but Sudama was so overwhelmed by unconditional love of Krishna that he neglected to ask Krishna for anything. Upon returning home, Sudama discovered a gorgeous palace on the site of his hut and thought that he had lost everything. To his amazement, Sudama was told that his wife was the mistress of the palace, his new home provided for him by Krishna. This incident shows that God already knows the needs of His pure devotees and will provide for their needs without even being asked to do so.

Sumantu Muni Aṅgirā: a pupil of Vyasa who, under his guidance, collected the hymns of the Atharva Veda, which Vyasa then arranged into their present form. Sumantu was also entrusted by Vyasa to pass on the Atharva Veda to posterity.

Sunga: an Indian dynasty which took over the Mauryan Empire. They ruled much of present-day India from 185 to 73 BC, during which time India enjoyed a strong Sanskrit revival.

Surya: the demigod of the sun, who is a powerful manifestation of divine energy.

Sutra: a highly elegant and concise expression of knowledge written in a philosophical code.

Śvetāśvatara Upanishad: see *Shvetashvatara Upanishad.*

Swami: a person who is in control of the mind and senses and is a member of the renounced order of spiritual life.

T

Taittrīya Upanishad: begins with proclaiming that "the knower of Brahman attains the Supreme." Then the five sheaths that enclose and hide the Absolute are described, as well as the techniques of piercing these sheaths of relativity. In this Upanishad, Brahman is defined as, "That from which all these beings are born, by which, after being born, they live, and into which they merge when they cease to be."

Tamala: a tree with dark bark, white blossoms, and fragrant leaves that thrives near rivers. The tamala tree is especially associated with Krishna's conjugal expressions of divine love.

Tansen: one of the most famous and gifted singers and musicians in India's history, who graced the court of Akbar.

Taxila: an ancient city located in Gandhara, which housed the most famous educational complex of its time, being mentioned in both the *Mahabharata* and the *Ramayana*. Taxila's schools were open to students of all castes and creeds, who were educated for nominal fees. Medicine, law, and mystical sciences could be studied, but Taxila's schools are mostly famous for Buddhistic studies, painting, and sculpture. Many great Indian personalities like Panini, Patanjali, Atreya, and Kautilya either came from or were educated in Taxila.

Tilak: an ornamental mark worn on the forehead of a devotee, usually made of clay and water from a holy place. The design of the mark indicates the spiritual school that the devotee adheres to. For a picture of Ramanuja, or Shri Vaiṣṇava, tilak, see page 410. Vaiṣṇava tilak always has two vertical lines indicating that God and souls are one, yet unique in identity.

Tirtha: a holy place where pilgrims go to benefit from a spiritual atmosphere and association.

Tol: a school.

Trimurti: "having three forms"; usually refers to Brahma, Vishnu, and Shiva, the Lords of Creation, Preservation, and Destruction, respectively, but also refers to any three-headed statue.

Tuladan: the custom of a newly crowned monarch to give away in charity precious gems equal to his body weight.

Tulasi: A basil plant who is a great devotee and very loved by Krishna. The leaves, buds, and the entire tulasi plant itself are used in the Vaiṣṇava worship of God.

U

Udaipur: see Chapter 13.

Uddhava: an intimate, eternal friend of Krishna, who appeared on earth to help in Krishna's pastimes. Uddhava is considered the best of Krishna's friends and is always ready to serve the Divine.

Upanishads: the philosophical section of the Vedic literature, which posits various philosophical methods of approaching the Absolute Truth. There are 108 Upanishads.

Upasana-kanda: the section of the *Vedas* describing the spiritual path of unconditional love and service to the Godhead.

Uttara-mimamsa: another name for the *Vedanta-sutra.* See *Vedanta-sutra.*

V

Vaikuntha: "without anxiety"; a name for the spiritual planets that comprise the spiritual universe where all existence is eternal, full of knowledge, and blissful. All beings in the Vaikuntha planets are fully devoted to the service of God.

Vaishampayana: an ancient sage who was entrusted by Vyasa to teach the *Yajur Veda*. Vaishampayana also recited the *Mahabharata* to King Janamejaya.

Vaiṣṇava: "Vishnu-worshiper"; a person who aspires to unconditionally love and serve God as the Supreme Personality, or Vishnu, or Krishna.

Vallabhacharya: an extremely learned and precocious scholar of Vedic religion, who was born into a family of Vaiṣṇava brahmins and lived from 1481 to 1533. He propounded the philosophy of shuddhadvaita, or "purified nondualism," which corrected what Vallabhacharya saw as a major defect in Shankaracharya's philosophy, namely, that the universe was separate from God. Vallabha said that the universe and individual souls are limited manifestations of God. Vallabha promoted intense devotion to Radha and Krishna as the personal Godhead. Salvation was from grace and surrendering oneself totally to God, whom the soul could associate with for eternity in the spiritual world. Vallabha's movement is extremely influential, especially in northern India, and is characterized by joyous and ecstatic worship as personified by Vallabha's life.

Vana: forest.

Vanayatra: a month-long pilgrimage held annually by walking through all the holy places of Vrindavan associated with Krishna's pastimes.

Varaha: the boar incarnation of God, who saved the earth planet from a cosmic disaster in the primeval past.

Varaha Purana: narrates the story of the third incarnation of Vishnu, Lord Varaha, a boar incarnation who saved the earth after it had fallen out of orbit. The importance of holy places and mantras is stressed. It is in the mode of goodness (sattva-guna) and contains 14,000 verses.

Vāsudeva: (1) the father of Krishna in His earthly pastimes; (2) a transcendental awareness of pure goodness from which arises God consciousness.

Vasudeva: a name for Krishna (God) meaning "the all-pervading one," "the proprietor of everything material and spiritual," and "the son of Vasudeva".

Vatsalya-rasa: the transcendental love relationship between God and the devotee in which the devotee wants to care for God as a parent cares for a child.

Vayu Purana: a *purana* revealed by the demigod of air, Vayu. It is considered tamasic (of the mode of ignorance) in quality and is mostly devoted to a glorification of Shiva and his attributes.

Veda: knowledge.

Vedanta: "the conclusion of knowledge"; in Vaiṣṇavism, the unconditional love and service of God.

Vedanta-darsana: another name for *Vedanta-sutra*. See *Vedanta-sutra*.

Vedanta-sutra: the essence of all Vedic knowledge written in terse code form by Vyasa.

Vedic: anything pertaining to the ancient civilization of India based on the *Vedas*.

Venu Krishna: a name for Krishna as the player of the transcendental bamboo flute which attracts all devotees and living beings by its beauty.

Vidyapati: a famous poet of Mithila who received the patronage of King Shivasimha. His beautiful songs in Maithili (which strongly resembles Bengali) about Radha and Krishna were especially inspirational to Shri Chaitanya, and they became even more popular with Bengali Vaiṣṇavas than in Vidyapati's homeland. His style of poetry vitally influenced all Bengali poetry, even up to Tagore in the twentieth century.

Vijaya Stambh: the "Victory Tower" built by Maharana Kumbha in Chittor, illustrating Vedic and other religions.

Vijaynagar: an empire that succeeded the Hoysalas in the Deccan that had been founded "for the protection of gods, cows, and brahmins." Vijaynagar was fabulously wealthy and enjoyed a brisk foreign trade from Lisbon to Peking. They were great patrons of architecture and all the arts. Unfortunately, religion became very external in Vijaynagar, and many abuses of the people and the Vedic religion were tolerated. The Golden Age of Vijaynagar was from 1336 to 1565. The rulers unjustly antagonized their Muslim neighbors, who united to crush a Vijaynagar army numbering over 700,000 in 1565. For five months, the capital city, Vijaynagar, and its environs were ruthlessly demolished. Vijaynagar survived this defeat in diminished form until 1646.

Vimana: a superimposition on the roof of a temple or other buildings that gives the impression of many roofs over one structure. The crowning piece of the vimana reinforces this impression.

Vishishtadvaita: the philosophy of Ramanuja that posits three distinct categories of existence: unconscious nature, or matter; the conscious living beings (plant, animal, and human); and God, who is the repository of all good qualities. God is one and is the animating principle of all existence. Salvation is achieved by realizing that the soul is distinct from matter and consists of divine attributes. The self-realized soul must then dedicate all of its life to the service of God, that service itself being salvation and the highest good.

Vishnu: (1) the incarnation of Godhead who creates and maintains the material universe; (2) the all-pervading Personality of Godhead.

Vishnu Purana: a classical and long (7,000 stanzas) *Purana* in the form of a dialogue between Parashara and Maitreya. It explains how Vishnu (God) is the creator and sustainer of the world, which is a marvelously harmonious system. It is in the mode of goodness and is considered one of the best *Puranas*.

Vishnu-sahasra-nama: "the thousand names of Vishnu (God)"; one of the most famous and popular prayers in all of India. It is reverently recited by people of all castes and creeds, especially during religious feast days. It was first recited at the end of the Mahabharata War by the dying Bhishma to King Yudhishthira while Krishna looked on. The *Vishnu-sahasra-nama* is found in Chapter 149 of the Anushasanika Parva of the *Mahabharata*. One hundred-and-seven slokas, or verses, of this chapter contain the 1000 names. This prayer glorifies the nature and qualities of God, the Ultimate Reality, also showing the incredible variety of ways that are available to do this. Vyasa gathered all the names of God used by ancient sages into this prayer and put them in a logical progression revealing God's nature. It is called the "essence of the essence of the Vedas" and the "heart and quintessence of the *Mahabharata*." In fact, the *Mahabharata* has been called a commentary on the *Vishnu-sahasra-nama*. Its recitation is considered a "mahamantra" (great mantra), and Bhishma called it a supreme religious exercise. Many people call it the greatest theistic prayer of India. It is recited for mental cleansing and to cure diseases not affected by medical treatment.

Vishnuswami: the founder of the Rudra School, one of the four great schools of modern Vaiṣṇavism. Little is definitely known of Vishnuswami's life and teachings, since none of his writings have survived. He is thought to have lived in the thirteenth century and taught that all living beings have emanated out of

Notes and Asides

Publisher, date, and place of publication are given only with the first citation of each book.

PREFACE

page vi

Guruvayur, Guruvayur, Trichur District, Kerala, India: Guruvayur Devaswom Publi Publication, 1977, p. 68.

page viii

Dominique Lapierre, *The City Of Joy,* Garden City, New York; Doubleday, 1985.

page viii

Ashoka's achievements are documented in, Pitirim A. Sorokin, *The Ways And Power Of Love,* Boston, The Beacon Press, 1954, pp. 66-69.

page ix

Alvin Toffler, *The Eco-Spasm Report,* New York, Bantam Books, 1975, p. 68.

page x

Pitirim A. Sorokin, *The Crisis Of Our Age,* New York, E. P. Dutton & Co., Inc., 1941, p. 67.

page x

Ibid., p. 65.

INTRODUCTION

page 1

Will Durant, *The Case for India,* New York, Simon and Schuster, 1930, p. 4.

page 1

Ernest Wood, *An Englishman Defends Mother India,* Madras, Ganesh & Co., 1929, p. 15.

page 2

Dr. Radhakrishnan, *The Hindu View of Life,* New York, Macmillan, 1954 (originally published in 1927), pp. 12-13.

page 2

A Handbook Of Hindu Religion, Tirupati, India, Tirumalai-Tirupati Devasthanams, 1977, p. 1.

page 3

E. E. Cummings, "A Poet's Advice to Students," *E. E. Cummings, A Miscellany Revised,* Edited by George Firmage, New York, October House, Inc., 1965, p. 335. Originally appeared in the Ottawa Hills *Spectator,* October 26, 1955.

page 5

Erich Fromm, *Man For Himself,* New York, Holt, Rinehart, and Winston, 1947, p. 237.

page 6

Arthur Koestler, *The Roots of Coincidence,* London, Hutchinson and Co. (Publishers) Ltd., 1972, p. 140.

page 6

Joe Kamiya et al., *Biofeedback and Self-Control,* Chicago, Aldine & Atherton, Inc., 1971, p. xi.

page 6

Richard F. Nyrop et al., *Area Handbook for India,* Washington, D.C., Superintendent of Documents, U.S. Government Printing Office, 1975, p. 161.

page 7

His Divine Grace A.C. Bhaktivedanta Swami Prabhupada, *Srimad Bhagavatam, First Canto, Part 1,* New York, The Bhaktivedanta Book Trust, 1972, p. 248.

page 7

Leo Tolstoy, *War And Peace,* New York, Simon and Schuster, 1942, p. 1314.

page 8

Carl Jung, *Modern Man In Search Of A Soul,* New York, Harcourt, Brace & World, Inc., 1933, p. 217.

page 8

Ibid.

page 8

A. H. Maslow, *The Farther Reaches Of Human Nature,* New York, The Viking Press, 1971, p. 31.

page 8

Ibid., p. 44.

page 8

Ibid.

page 9

Phillimore as quoted in Ernest Wood, *An Englishman Defends Mother India, p. 15.*

page 9

Ernest Wood, ibid., pp. 15-16.

page 10

E. F. Schumacher, *Small Is Beautiful: Economics as if People Mattered,* New York, Harper & Row, 1973, p. 38.

page 10-11

F. Max Muller, *India: What Can It Teach Us?,* New York, Funk & Wagnalls, 1883, p. 24.

page 11

Ralph Waldo Emerson, *Essays & Lectures,* "The American Scholar," (An Oration delivered before the Phi Beta Kappa Society at Cambridge, August 31, 1837), New York, The Library Of America, 1983, p. 68.

page 11

His Divine Grace A.C. Bhaktivedanta Swami Prabhupada, *Bhagavad-gita As It Is,* Los Angeles, The Bhaktivedanta Book Trust, 1983, pp. 449-450. Verse 2 of Chapter 9. Originally published by Macmillan, 1972. The Bhaktivedanta Book Trust edition was revised after consulting the author's original manuscript. The page numbering of the later edition does not exactly correspond to the page numbering of the Macmillan edition.

CHAPTER 1: HIMALAYAS

page 10
His Divine Grace A.C. Bhaktivedanta Swami Prabhupada, *Bhagavad-gita As It Is,* p. 537. Verse 25 of Chapter 10.
page 14
His Divine Grace A.C. Bhaktivedanta Swami Prabhupada, *Srimad Bhagavatam, Fifth Canto, Part Two,* New York, Bhaktivedanta Book Trust, 1975, p. 121.
page 17
Ibid.
page 17
Ibid., p. 122.
page 17
Annales de L'Institut Pasteur (Journal de Microbologie), Paris, Tome Dixieme, 1896, p. 522, as quoted and translated in Ernest Wood, *An Englishman Defends Mother India,* p. 277.
page 19
Ibid., in original *Journal,* p. 515; in quoted source, p. 276.
page 19
Ibid., in original *Journal,* p. 514; in quoted source, p. 276.
page 19
Eric Newby, *Slowly Down the Ganges,* New York, Charles Scribner's Sons, 1966, p. 16.

CHAPTER 2: KURUKSHETRA

page 42
His Divine Grace A. C. Bhaktivedanta Swami Prabhupada, *Bhagavad-gita As It Is,* pp. 56-58. Verses 28 to 30 of Chapter 1.
page 42
Ibid., p. 71. Verse 46 of Chapter 1.
page 42
Aldous Huxley, Introduction to *The Song of God: Bhagavad-Gita,* translated by Swami Prabhavananda and Christopher Isherwood, New York, Mentor, 1972, p. 13.
page 44
Robert S. De Ropp, *Science and Salvation,* New York, St. Martin's Press, 1962, p. 80.
page 44
A.L. Basham, *The Wonder That Was India,* New York, The Macmillan Company, 1954, p. 253.
page 44
Ibid., p. 342.
page 45
His Divine Grace A.C. Bhaktivedanta Swami Prabhupada, *Bhagavad-gita As It Is,* pp. 215-218.
page 45
Dr. J. Bruce Long, The Death That Ends Death, an essay in *Death: The Final Stage of Growth,* edited by Elisabeth Kubler-Ross, Englewood Cliffs, Prentice Hall, 1975, p. 57.
page 45
Ibid.
page 45
His Divine Grace A.C. Bhaktivedanta Swami Prabhupada, *Bhagavad-gita As It Is,* pp. 88. Verse 12 of Chapter 2.
page 45
Ibid, p. 89.
page 47
Macropaedia, Volume 15, Chicago, Encyclopaedia Britannica, 1977, p. 152.
page 47
Karen Horney, "Finding The Real Self," *The American Journal Of Psychoanalysis,* Volume IX, Number 1, 1949, p. 6.
page 48
His Divine Grace A.C. Bhaktivedanta Swami Prabhupada, *Srimad Bhagavatam, Third Canto, Part Four,* New York, Bhaktivedanta Book Trust, 1974, p. 370. Part of Verse 20 of Chapter 31.
page 49
Dr. Kenneth Pelletier, *Mind as Healer, Mind as Slayer,* New York, Delta, 1977.
page 49
His Divine Grace A.C. Bhaktivedanta Swami Prabhupada, *Bhagavad-gita As It Is,* pp. 312-313. Verses 5-6 of Chapter 6.
page 49
Ibid., p. 335. Verse 26.
page 50
Roberto Assagioli, M.D., *The Act of Will,* Baltimore, Penguin Books, 1973, p. 211.
page 50
Ibid., p. 212.
page 52
Ibid.
page 52
Ibid.
page 52
His Divine Grace A.C. Bhaktivedanta Swami Prabhupada, *Bhagavad-gita As It Is,* pages 96, 101, 106-108. Verses 17, 20, 23-25 of Chapter 2.
page 54
Roberto Assagioli, M.D., *The Act of Will,* p. 214.
page 54
Encyclopedia of World Religions, London, Octopus Books Limited, 1975, p. 122.
page 54
Roberto Assagioli, M.D., *The Act of Will,* pp. 214-215.
page 54
Ibid., p. 216.

New York, Bhaktivedanta Book Trust, 1975, p. 130.

page 139

Ernest Wood, *An Englishman Defends Mother India,* p. 132.

page 139

Thomas Troward, *The Edinburgh Lectures On Mental Science,* New York, Dodd, Mead & Company, 1909, p. 19.

page 142

Theodore Roszak, *Where The Wasteland Ends,* p. 105.

page 142

Dr. Donald Campbell, "Scientific Reasons For Not Trusting Psychology When It Conflicts With Religious Tradition," a Lenten Meditation given on March 28, 1971, at the First Baptist Church, Evanston, Illinois, and obtained from personal correspondence with Dr. Campbell, p. 2.

page 144

Time, "Morals Make a Comeback," September 15, 1975, p. 94.

page 144

Psychology Today, Alice Travis, "The Experimenting Society: To Find Programs That Work, Government Must Measure Its Failures," September, 1975, pp. 47-56.

page 144

Ibid., p. 56.

page 145

His Divine Grace A.C. Bhaktivedanta Swami Prabhupada, *Sri Caitanya-caritamrta, Madhya-Lila, Volume 5,* New York, The Bhaktivedanta Book Trust, 1975, p. 42. Verse 85 of Chapter 12.

page 146

Ibid., p. 51. Part of Verse 105 of Chapter 12.

page 146

Ibid., p. 63. Verse 133 of Chapter 12.

page 146

His Divine Grace A.C. Bhaktivedanta Swami Prabhupada, *Bhagavad-gita As It Is,* pp. 279-280. Part of Verse 6 and all of Verse 7 of Chapter 5.

page 148

Pitirim A. Sorokin, *The Ways and Power of Love; Types, Factors, and Techniques of Moral Transformation,* Boston, Beacon Press, 1954, p. 3.

page 148

Ibid., p. 312.

page 149

Ibid.

page 151

Ibid., p. 3.

page 154

Ibid., p. 313.

page 155

His Divine Grace A.C. Bhaktivedanta Swami Prabhupada, *Sri Caitanya-caritamrta, Madhya-Lila, Volume 2,* New York, The Bhaktivedanta Book Trust, 1975, p. 181. Verse 144 of Chapter 5.

page 159

Sri Rupa Siddhanti Goswami et al., *Vedanta-sutra,* p. 45.

page 160

Manly P. Hall, *The Inner Lives of Minerals, Plants, and Animals,* Los Angeles, The Philosophical Research Society, Inc., 1973, p. 41.

page 162

The findings of Dr. Bose are summarized in Manly P. Hall's, *The Inner Lives of Minerals, Plants, and Animals,* pp. 14-15.

page 162

Ibid., p. 15.

page 162

Sir Jagadis Chandra Bose, as quoted in Manly P. Hall, *The Inner Lives of Minerals, Plants, and Animals,* p. 15.

page 162

William Wordsworth, "The Prelude," *The Complete Poetical Works of Wordsworth,* Boston, Houghton Mifflin Company, 1932, p. 140.

page 162

Franklin Loehr, *The Power of Prayer on Plants,* Garden City, Doubleday, 1959.

page 163

Royal Dixon, *The Human Side of Plants,* New York, Frederick A. Stokes Company, 1914, p. 198.

page 163

Manly P. Hall, *The Inner Lives of Minerals, Plants, and Animals,* p. 6.

page 163

His Divine Grace A.C. Bhaktivedanta Swami Prabhupada, *Bhagavad-gita As It Is,* p. 98. From Verse 20 of Chapter 2.

page 165

Royal Dixon, *The Human Side of Plants,* p. 201.

page 165

As quoted in Manly P. Hall, *The Inner Lives of Minerals, Plants, and Animals,* p. 4.

page 166

His Divine Grace A.C. Bhaktivedanta Swami Prabhupada, *Sri Caitanya-caritamrta, Madhya-Lila, Volume 7,* New York, The Bhaktivedanta Book Trust, 1975, pp. 110-113. Verses 194 to 202 of Chapter 17.

page 167

His Divine Grace A.C. Bhaktivedanta Swami Prabhupada, *Srimad Bhagavatam, Fifth Canto, Part One,* New York, The Bhaktivedanta Book Trust, 1975, p. 336.

page 167

Healthy People, The Surgeon General's Report on Health Promotion And Disease Prevention 1979, p. 130.

page 168

His Divine Grace A.C. Bhaktivedanta Swami Prabhupada, *Bhagavad-gita As It Is,* p. 727.

page 168

Gerald and Patricia Mische, *Toward a Human World Order,* New York, Paulist Press, 1977, p. 341.

page 169

Theodore Roszak, *Where The Wasteland Ends,* p. 108.

page 169

Ibid., p. 109.

CHAPTER 5: DWARAKA

page 173

J. H. Dave, *Immortal India,* Volume 1, Bombay, Bharatiya Vidya Bhavan, 1970, p. 53.

page 174

Ibid.

page 174

His Divine Grace A.C. Bhaktivedanta Swami Prabhupada, *KRSNA: The Supreme Personality of Godhead, Volume 2,* New York, The Bhaktivedanta Book Trust, 1982, p. 333.

page 175

Ibid.

page 175

His Divine Grace A.C. Bhaktivedanta Swami Prabhupada, *Srimad Bhagavatam, First Canto, Part Two,*

New York, The Bhaktivedanta Book Trust, 1972, p. 181. Text 27 of Chapter 10.
page 175
Ibid., p. 222. Text 22 of Chapter 11.
page 177
Ibid., p. 202. Text 7 of Chapter 11.
page 177
His Divine Grace A.C. Bhaktivedanta Swami Prabhupada, *KRSNA, Volume 2,* p. 333.
page 177
Ibid., p. 100.
page 179
His Divine Grace A.C. Bhaktivedanta Swami Prabhupada, *Srimad Bhagavatam, First Canto, Part Two,* p. 232. Verse 30 of Chapter 11.
page 180
Ibid., p. 186.
page 181
His Divine Grace A.C. Bhaktivedanta Swami Prabhupada, *KRSNA, Volume 2,* p. 106.
page 181
Ibid., p. 105.
page 184
His Divine Grace A.C. Bhaktivedanta Swami Prabhupada, *Srimad Bhagavatam, First Canto, Part Two,* p. 232.
page 186
His Divine Grace A.C. Bhaktivedanta Swami Prabhupada, *KRSNA, Volume 2,* p. 353.
page 187
His Divine Grace A.C. Bhaktivedanta Swami Prabhupada, *Srimad Bhagavatam, First Canto, Part Two,* p. 246. Part of Verse 38 of Chapter 11.
page 187
Ibid., The remainder of Verse 38 of Chapter 11.

page 189
His Divine Grace A.C. Bhaktivedanta Swami Prabhupada, *The Nectar of Devotion (a summary study of Srila Rupa Goswami's Bhaktirasamrta-sindhu),* New York, The Bhaktivedanta Book Trust, 1975, p. 152.
page 189
Ibid.
page 190
Ibid.
page 190
Ibid., p. 297.
page 190
Ibid., p. 298.
page 190
His Divine Grace A.C. Bhaktivedanta Swami Prabhupada, *The Nectar of Devotion,* p. 298.
page 191
His Divine Grace A.C. Bhaktivedanta Swami Prabhupada, *Sri Caitanya-caritamrta, Madhya-Lila, Volume 3,* p. 127.
page 191
Ibid., p. 126. This is the 43rd Verse of the *Stotraratna.*
page 191
A.L. Basham, *The Wonder That Was India,* p. 330.
page 191
Ibid.
page 192
His Divine Grace A.C. Bhaktivedanta Swami Prabhupada, *Bhagavad-gita As It Is,* pp. 582, 588-590. Parts of Verses 37, 43, and 44 of Chapter 11.
page 192
Ibid., pp. 586-587. Part of Verses 41 and 42, Chapter 11.
page 193
As quoted in His Divine Grace A.C. Bhaktivedanta Swami Prabhupada, *The Nectar of Devotion,* p. 302.
page 196
His Divine Grace A.C. Bhaktivedanta Swami Prabhupada, *KRSNA, Volume 2,* pp. 101-102.
page 197
Varaha Purana, as quoted in J.H. Dave, *Immortal India, Volume I,* p. 55.

CHAPTER 6: VRINDAVAN
page 201
Norvin Hein, *The Miracle Plays of Mathura,* New Haven and London, Yale University Press, 1972, p. 8. A delightful book on the cultural life of Vrindavan. Dr. Hein obviously loved his stay there and goes far beyond a merely academic presentation to give the reader deep insight into the soul of Vaiṣṇavism.
page 204
Ibid.
page 204
Ibid. Both short quotes are from the same page.
page 205
Skanda Purana as quoted in Miles Davis, Ph.D., *Touring The Land Of Krishna,* El Cerrito, California, International Institute of Indology, 1984, p. 15. Dr. Davis' highly recommended book is impossible to get at bookstores, but is easily obtainable from:

International Institute of Indology
2441 Clare Street
San Pablo, California 94806

Send $11.95 and $1.00 for postage and handling.
page 205
Norvin Hein, *The Miracle Plays of Mathura,* p. 1.
page 205
George L. Hart III, *A Rapid Sanskrit Method,* Madison, University of Wisconsin, Department of Indian Studies, 1972, p. iv.
page 207
His Divine Grace A.C. Bhaktivedanta Swami Prabhupada, *Srimad Bhagavatam, First Canto, Part One,* p. 95. Verse 6 of Chapter 2.
page 208
Encyclopedia of World Religions, p. 118.
page 208
His Divine Grace A.C. Bhaktivedanta Swami Prabhupada, *KRSNA, Volume 1,* New York, The Bhaktivedanta Book Trust, 1970, p. 142.
page 211
Edmond Szekely, *Cosmos, Man and Society,* Ashingdon, England, The C.W. Daniel Company LTD, 1936, p. 243. In his section on longevity Professor Szekely produced this handy table of the ages of the Old Testament Patriarchs.
page 214
Good News Bible, p. 2.
page 214
The Holy Bible, King James Version, New York, New American Library, 1974, p. 15.
page 217
Gautami Tantra as quoted in Miles Davis, Ph.D., *Touring The Land Of Krishna,* p. 15.
page 218
Richard F. Nyrop et al., *Area Handbook for India,* p. 166.
page 218
Bhagavan Das, *The Science of Social Organization,* Benares, Theosophical Publishing Society, 1910,

ume 5, p. 260. Part of Verse 74 of Chapter 14.
page 267
Ibid., pp. 260-261. Part of Verse 75 and Verses 76-78.
page 267
Ibid., p. 263. Verse 82.
page 267
Ibid., p. 332. Verse 227. In the *Brahma-samhita* itself, it is Verse 56 of Chapter 5.
page 267
His Divine Grace A.C. Bhaktivedanta Swami Prabhupada, *Sri Caitanya-caritamrta, Adi-Lila, Volume 2,* p. 184.
page 269
Srinivasa Acarya, as quoted in His Divine Grace A.C. Bhaktivedanta Swami Prabhupada, *Sri Caitanya-caritamrta, Madhya-Lila, Volume 9,* p. 62.
page 269
His Divine Grace A.C. Bhaktivedanta Swami Prabhupada, *Sri Caitanya-caritamrta, Madhya-Lila, Volume 9,* p. 62. Verse 104 of Chapter 23.
page 269
Ibid. Verse 104 of Chapter 23.
page 269
His Divine Grace A.C. Bhaktivedanta Swami Prabhupada, *Sri Caitanya-caritamrta, Madhya-Lila, Volume 7,* p. 311-312. Verses 127-130 of Chapter 19.
page 270
Miles Davis, *Touring The Land Of Krishna,* p. 36.
page 271
His Divine Grace A.C. Bhaktivedanta Swami Prabhupada, *Sri Caitanya-caritamrta, Adi-Lila, Volume 2,* p. 201. Verse 62 of Chapter 8.
page 271
Ibid.
page 271
The story of Ramacandra's visit to Jagannath Puri can be found in His Divine Grace A.C. Bhaktivedanta Swami Prabhupada, *Sri Caitanya-caritamrta, Antya-Lila, Volume 3,* New York, The Bhaktivedanta Book Trust, 1975, pp. 83-130, Chapter 8.
page 272
His Divine Grace A.C. Bhaktivedanta Swami Prabhupada, *Sri Caitanya-caritamrta, Adi-Lila, Volume 2,* p. 202. Part of Verse 65 of Chapter 8.
page 272
Ibid., p. 206. Part of Verse 73.
page 272
Ibid., pp. 207-208. Verses 75-77.
page 272
His Divine Grace A.C. Bhaktivedanta Swami Prabhupada, *Sri Caitanya-caritamrta, Madhya-Lila, Volume 1,* New York, Bhaktivedanta Book Trust, 1975, p. 234. Verse 90 of Chapter 2.
page 272
Pitirim A. Sorokin, "Reply to Professor Weisskopf," in Abraham A. Maslow, Editor, *New Knowledge In Human Values,* p. 227.
page 272
Ibid.
page 272
His Divine Grace A.C. Bhaktivedanta Swami Prabhupada, *Sri Caitanya-caritamrta, Adi-Lila, Volume 2,* pp. 209-210. Verses 79-80 of Chapter 8.
page 273
Ibid., p. 349. Part of Verse 158 of Chapter 10.
page 273
Ibid.
page 273
Ibid.
page 275
Miles Davis, *Touring The Land Of Krishna,* p. 67.
page 275
Ibid., p. 68.
page 277
Acharya Vishwambhar Goswami, a personal letter to the authors dated March 5, 1986. The entire text of the letter relevant to the appearance of the Deity is as follows:

> You have asked me about the manifestation of Radha Raman. You might be aware about the manifestation of Nrisinghadeva from the pillar. It is mentioned in the *Bhagavatam.* Gods do not take birth like human beings. There is something supernatural in their manifestation. So it was actually the love, devotion, and ardent desire of Gopal Bhatta which compelled Shaligram Shila to take this deity form, which was named Radha Raman.
>
> There are certain other causes. First, Shaligram Shila is generally found in round form without any physical signs. The Shila cannot be decorated with ornaments and clothes. Some devotees offered clothes and ornaments to Gopal Bhatta to be offered to the Shaligram. But Gopal Bhatta refused, as his Shila had no physical form. How can he decorate Him? This gave him great mental sufferings.
>
> Second, Mahaprabhu (Shri Chaitanya) came to Vrindaban, and having seen Braj, He went back to Puri. When Gopal Bhatta came to Vrindaban, he came to know that Mahaprabhu went back to Puri. He was very much upset, and he felt himself very unfortunate for not seeing Mahaprabhu in Vrindaban.
>
> These circumstances made him more emotional for Deity in physical form, and Mahaprabhu. On the Appearance Day of Nrisinghadeva (Narshima Caturdasi), Gopal Bhatta was observing total fast and reading the chapter on Prahlad Maharaj in the Bhagavatam. This made him thousandfold emotional and he became unconscious, and remained in the same position throughout the night. In the early morning when Gopal Bhatta regained consciousness, he saw that Shila had been transformed into the very beautiful and charming Deity, which was named as Radha Raman. The sign of Shaligram are still on the shoulder and the waist.
>
> God is supposed to be all-powerful. He can take any form he likes. He can do or undo anything. He is cause of all causes. But the main cause of His taking form was an unalloyed love and devotion from Gopal Bhatta, which closely resembled Prahlad's devotion to Nrisinghadeva.

page 277
His Divine Grace A.C. Bhaktivedanta Swami Prabhupada, *Sri Caitanya-caritamrta, Adi-Lila, Volume 2,* p. 313. Part of Verse 93 of Chapter 10.
page 277
Ibid., pp. 316-317. Verses 99, 100, part of 101, and 102.
page 278
Miles Davis, *Touring The Land Of Krishna,* p. 152.
page 278
Ibid., p. 63.
page 279
Pitirim A. Sorokin, "The Power of Creative, Unselfish Love," an article in Abraham H. Maslow, Editor, *New Knowledge in Human Values,* p. 11.
page 279
Ibid.
page 279
His Divine Grace A.C. Bhaktivedanta Swami Prabhupada, *Sri Caitanya-caritamrta, Madhya-Lila, Volume 8,* p. 423. Verse 159 of Chapter 22.

CHAPTER 7: PASTIMES OF KRISHNA IN INDIAN ART
page 283
Ananda K. Cooramaswamy, *The Dance Of Siva,* New York, Dover Publications, Inc., 1985, p. 18. Originally published in 1924.

page 283
Laura Shapiro, "5,000 Years of Splendor," *Newsweek,* September 16, 1985, p. 78.
page 283
Ibid., p. 77.
page 283
Pramod Chandra, *The Sculpture of India: 3000 B.C.–1300 A.D.,* Washington, D.C., National Gallery of Art, 1985, pp. 16-17.
page 284
Ibid., p. 16.
page 284
Ibid., pp. 17-18.
page 284
Ibid., p. 7.
page 284
Richard F. Nyrop et al., *Area Handbook for India,* p. 264.
page 284
A.L. Basham, *The Wonder That Was India,* p. 346.
page 284
Richard F. Nyrop et al., *Area Handbook for India,* p. 264.
page 284
Ibid.
page 284
A.L. Basham, *The Wonder That Was India,* p. 346.
page 287
Ananda K. Cooramaswamy, *The Dance Of Siva,* p. 7.
page 287
A.L. Basham, *The Wonder That Was India,* p. 347.
page 287
Ibid., p. 346.
page 287
Romain Rolland in his Foreward to Ananda K. Cooramaswamy, *The Dance Of Siva,* p. xiii.
page 287
Rabindranath Tagore as quoted in Ananda K. Cooramaswamy, *The Dance Of Siva,* p. 28.
page 288
Stephen A. Tyler, *India: An Anthropological Perspective,* Pacific Palisades, California: Goodyear Publishing Company, 1973, p. 130.
page 288
Roberto Assagioli, M.D., *Psychosynthesis, A Manual of Principles and Techniques,* New York, Penguin Books, 1965, p. 283.
page 288
Ibid.
page 288
Ibid.
page 290
Pitirim A. Sorokin, *The Ways and Power of Love, Types, Factors, and Techniques of Moral Transformation,* p. 318.
page 290
Ibid.
page 290
Rev. J.F. Kearns, "Silpa Sastra," in, *Indian Antiquary, A Journal Of Oriental Research,* Bombay, Education Society's Press, 1876, p. 230.
page 290
Ibid., p. 236.
page 290
Ibid.
page 293
Ananda K. Cooramaswamy, *The Dance Of Siva,* p. 39.
page 293
Sukracharya, as quoted in ibid., p. 21.
page 293
Ananda K. Cooramaswamy, *The Dance Of Siva,* p. 22.
page 293
Ramayana, as quoted in ibid., p. 23.
page 294
Michelangelo, as quoted in Romain Rolland, *Michelangelo,* Albert & Charles Boni, Inc., 1935, p. 152.
page 294
Leonardo Da Vinci, *The Notebooks Of Leonardo Da Vinci,* Edited by Edward MacCurdy, New York, Garden City Publishing Co., Inc., 1941-42, p. 854.
page 294
Ananda K. Cooramaswamy, *The Dance Of Siva,* p. 42.
page 294
Ibid., p. 24.
page 294
Ibid.
page 295
Ibid., p. 27.
page 295
Benedetto Croce as quoted in ibid., p. 33.
page 295
Ananda K. Cooramaswamy, *The Dance Of Siva,* p. 25.
page 297
P. Banerjee, *The Life Of Krishna In Indian Art,* New Delhi, National Museum, 1978, p. 1.
page 297
His Divine Grace A.C. Bhaktivedanta Swami Prabhupada, *Sri Caitanya-caritamrta, Madhya-Lila, Volume 7,* p. 73. Verse 135 of Chapter 17.
page 299
His Divine Grace A.C. Bhaktivedanta Swami Prabhupada, *Sri Caitanya-caritamrta, Madhya-Lila, Volume 9,* p. 448. Part of Verse 278 of Chapter 25.
page 299
Ibid.
page 299
His Divine Grace A.C. Bhaktivedanta Swami Prabhupada, *Sri Caitanya-caritamrta, Madhya-Lila, Volume 7,* p. 300. Part of Verse 106 of Chapter 19. This quote originally is Verse 82 of the *Padyavali.*
page 299
His Divine Grace A.C. Bhaktivedanta Swami Prabhupada, *Krsna Book, Volume 1,* pp. 147-148.
page 301
Rabindranath Tagore, *Art & Aesthetics,* New Delhi, Inter-National Cultural Center, 1961, p. 33.
page 301
Pramod Chandra, *The Sculpture of India: 3000 B.C.–1300 A.D.,* p. 7.
page 302
His Divine Grace A.C. Bhaktivedanta Swami Prabhupada, *Sri Caitanya-caritamrta, Madhya-Lila, Volume 7,* p. 146. Verse 34 of Chapter 18. Originally appears in *Srimad Bhagavatam* (10.21.18).
page 302
Pramod Chandra, *The Sculpture of India: 3000 B.C.–1300 A.D.,* p. 180.
page 302
A.L. Basham, *The Wonder That Was India,* p. 375.
page 302
Ibid.
page 305
Ibid., p. 376.
page 305
Ibid.
page 306
Ibid., p. 309.
page 306
Ibid., p. 372.
page 306
A.C. Jain, *Tourist's Hand Book Of India,* Delhi, Jainco Publishers, undated, p. 39.

page 371
Ibid., p. 326. Verses 127-128.
page 373
Ibid., p. 329. Verses 133-134.
page 373
Maulawi Sher 'Ali, *The Holy Qur'an,* The Oriental and Religious Publishing Corporation Ltd., Rabwah Pakistan, 1979 edition, p. 20. Most of Verse 115 of Chapter 2.
page 374
Ibid., p. 19.
page 374
His Divine Grace A.C. Bhaktivedanta Swami Prabhupada, *Sri Caitanya-caritamrta, Adi-Lila, Volume 3,* pp. 370-371. Verses 217-218 of Chapter 17.
page 374
Ibid., p. 372. Verse 220.
page 374
Ibid., Part of Verse 221.
page 374
Ibid., Verse 222.
page 374
Ibid., pp. 372-373.
page 376
Shrila Thakur Bhaktivinode, *Shri Caitanya Mahaprabhu,* p. 16.
page 376
His Divine Grace A.C. Bhaktivedanta Swami Prabhupada, *Sri Caitanya-caritamrta, Adi-Lila, Volume 3,* p. 266.
page 376
Ibid.
page 377
Shrila Thakur Bhaktivinode, *Shri Caitanya Mahaprabhu,* p. 19.
page 379
A.H. Maslow, *The Farther Reaches Of Human Nature,* p. 177.
page 379
Ibid.
page 379
Ibid.
page 381
His Divine Grace A.C. Bhaktivedanta Swami Prabhupada, *Srimad Bhagavatam, Second Canto, Part One,* The Bhaktivedanta Book Trust, New York, 1972, p. 22.
page 381
Pitirim A. Sorokin, *The Ways and Power of Love, Types, Factors, and Techniques of Moral Transformation,* p. 319.
page 382
His Divine Grace A.C. Bhaktivedanta Swami Prabhupada, *Srimad Bhagavatam, Third Canto Part Four,* p. 108.
page 382
Vedanta Sutra as quoted in ibid.
page 382
His Divine Grace A.C. Bhaktivedanta Swami Prabhupada, *Srimad Bhagavatam, Third Canto, Part Four,* p. 108.
page 382
Padma Purana as quoted in, His Divine Grace A.C. Bhaktivedanta Swami Prabhupada, *Sri Caitanya-caritamrta, Madhya-Lila, Volume 7,* p. 71. Text 133 of Chapter 17.
page 382
His Divine Grace A.C. Bhaktivedanta Swami Prabhupada, *Sri Caitanya-caritamrta, Adi-Lila, Volume 3,* p. 269. Verse 22 of Chapter 17.
page 383
Dr. Robert E. Ornstein, *Psychology Of Consciousness,* New York, Penguin Books, 1975, p. 130.
page 383
Ibid., p. 185.
page 383
His Divine Grace A.C. Bhaktivedanta Swami Prabhupada, *Srimad Bhagavatam, Sixth Canto, Part One,* p. 110. Verse 19 of Chapter 2.
page 383
His Divine Grace A.C. Bhaktivedanta Swami Prabhupada, *Sri Caitanya-caritamrta, Adi-Lila, Volume 2,* p. 67. Text 83 of Chapter 7.
page 383
Ibid., p. 76. Text 96.
page 385
Satyanarayana dasa, "From the Editor's Desk," *Sri Mayapur Magazine,* Number Two, undated, Bhaktivedanta Book Trust, p. 4.
page 386
Ibid., p. 26.
page 387
O.B.L. Kapoor, *The Philosophy and Religion of Sri Caitanya,* p. ix.

CHAPTER 10: SHRI RANGAM

page 391
J.H. Dave, *Immortal India,* Volume I, p. 124.
page 391
R.K. Das, *Temples Of Tamilnad,* Bombay, Bharatiya Vidya Bhavan, 1964, p. 108.
page 392
Ibid., p. 117.
page 392
Jeannine Auboyer, *Sri Ranganathaswami,* Paris, Unesco, 1969, p. 21.
page 392
Ibid.
page 392
Ibid.
page 395
Ibid., p. 26.
page 395
Ibid., p. 8.
page 395
A.L. Basham, *The Wonder That Was India,* p. 358.
page 395
Jeannine Auboyer, *Sri Ranganathaswami,* p. 121.
page 396
R.K. Das, *Temples Of Tamilnad,* p. 109.
page 396
Jeannine Auboyer, *Sri Ranganathaswami,* p. 14.
page 396
R.K. Das, *Temples of Tamilnad,* p. 110.
page 396
Ibid.
page 398
Jeannine Auboyer, *Sri Ranganathaswami,* p. 13.
page 401
Ibid.
page 402
J.H. Dave, *Immortal India,* Volume 1, p. 126.
page 402
M. Yamunacharya, *Ramanuja's Teachings In His Own Words,* Bombay, Bharatiya Vidya Bhavan, 1970, p. 1.
page 402
J.H. Dave, *Immortal India, Volume 1,* p. 126.
page 402
Ibid.
page 402
M. Yamunacharya, *Ramanuja's Teachings In His Own Words,* p. 1.

page 402
J.H. Dave, *Immortal India, Volume 1,* p. 126.
page 402
M. Yamunacharya, *Ramanuja's Teachings In His Own Words,* p. 1.
page 402
Ibid.
page 403
P. Banerjee, *The Life Of Krishna In Indian Art,* p. 120.
page 403
J.H. Dave, *Immortal India, Volume I,* p. 131.
page 405
M.N. Venkata Ramanappa, *Outlines of South Indian History,* Delhi, Vikas Publishing House PVT LTD, 1975, p. 121.
page 405
M. Yamunacharya, *Ramanuja's Teachings In His Own Words,* p. 3.
page 405
Ibid.
page 405
Ibid., p. 5.
page 405
Ibid., pp. 5-6.
page 407
Ibid., p. 9.
page 407
Ibid., p. 10.
page 408
Dr. S. Krishnaswami Aiyangar, "Life And Times," in *Three Great Acharyas,* Madras, G A Natesan & Co., undated, p. 105.
page 411
M. Yamunacharya, *Ramanuja's Teachings In His Own Words,* p. 19.
page 411
Ibid.
page 411
Ibid.
page 411
Ibid.
page 411
Ibid., p. 20
page 412
Ibid.
page 412
Ibid.
page 412
Ibid., p. 19.
page 412
Ibid., p. 6.
page 414
M.N. Venkata Ramanappa, *Outlines of South Indian History,* p. 123.
page 414
M. Yamunacharya, *Ramanuja's Teachings In His Own Words,* p. 36.
page 414
Ibid., p. 21.
page 415
Professor Rangacarya, "Ramanuja And Vaishnavism," in *Three Great Acharyas,* p. 172.
page 415
Lucille Schulberg, *Historic India,* p. 122.
page 415
Professor Rangacarya, "Ramanuja And Vaishnavism," in *Three Great Acharyas,* p. 174.
page 417
A.L. Basham, *The Wonder That Was India,* p. 332.
page 417
Ibid.
page 417
M.N. Venkata Ramanappa, *Outlines of South Indian History,* pp. 124-125.
page 417
P.N. Srinivasachari, *"The Visistadvaita of Ramanuja,"* in *The Cultural Heritage of India, Vol. I* Calcutta, The Ramakrishna Mission, Institute of Culture, 1937, pp. 570-571.
page 419
Ibid., p. 571.
page 419
A.L. Basham, *The Wonder That Was India,* p. 332.
page 419
Valmiki, *Ramayana,* as quoted in His Divine Grace A.C. Bhaktivedanta Swami Prabhupada, *Sri Caitanya-caritamrta, Madhya-Lila, Volume 8,* p. 343.
page 419
His Divine Grace A.C. Bhaktivedanta Swami Prabhupada, *Sri Caitanya-caritamrta, Madhya-Lila, Volume 8,* p. 342. Verse 33 of Chapter 22.
page 420
Erich Fromm, *Escape from Freedom,* New York, Rinehart & Company, Inc., 1941, p. 261.
page 423
M. Yamunacharya, *Ramanuja's Teachings In His Own Words,* p. 23.
page 423
Jeannine Auboyer, *Sri Ranganathaswami,* p. 29.
page 423
Ibid., p. 31.
page 423
Ibid.
page 425
M.N. Ramanappa, *Outlines of South Indian History,* p. 104.
page 425
Jeannine Auboyer, *Sri Ranganathaswami,* p. 16.
page 425
Ibid., p. 17.
page 426
Kulashekhara, *Mukundamala-stotram,* as translated by His Divine Grace A.C. Bhaktivedanta Swami Prabhupada, *The Prayers of King Kulashekhara,* unpublished manuscript, p. 21. Verse 26.
page 426
Marco Polo, *The Travels of Marco Polo (the Venetian),* revised from Marsden's translation and edited by Manuel Komroff, Livright Publications, 1953, p. 201.
page 429
His Divine Grace A.C. Bhaktivedanta Swami Prabhupada, *Sri Caitanya-caritamrta, Madhya-Lila, Volume 3,* p. 340. Verse 87 of Chapter 9.
page 429
Ibid., p. 354. Verse 115.
page 429
Ibid., p. 376. Verse 155.
page 430
Ibid., pp. 346-347. Verses 99-101.
page 433
Ibid., p. 348. Verse 102.
page 433
Ibid., p. 349. Verse 104.
page 433
Ramanuja, *Gadya-traya,* as quoted in J.H. Dave, *Immortal India, Volume 1,* p. 132.

CHAPTER 11: MAHABALIPURAM
page 437
India, New York, Greystone Press, 1965, p. 119.

page 514
Satish Davar, "A filigree city spun out of nothingness," ibid., p. 53.
page 517
Ibid., p. 52.
page 517
Ibid.
page 517
Ibid., p. 51.
page 517
Mulk Raj Anand, "Homage to Jaipur," *Homage to Jaipur,* p. 4.
page 518
A.L. Basham, *The Wonder That Was India,* p. 9.
page 518
Stephen A. Tyler, *India: An Anthropological Perspective,* p. 2.
page 518
Ibid., p. 130.
page 518
Satish Davar, "A filigree city spun out of nothingness," *Homage to Jaipur,* p. 53.
page 518
Daulat Singh, *Jaipur,* p. 15.
page 519
Gayatri Devi of Jaipur and Santha Rama Rau, *A Princess Remembers,* p. 155.
page 519
Ibid., p. 156.
page 520
Mulk Raj Anand, "An Epistle Dedicatory To The Master Builder Sawai Jai Singh," *Homage to Jaipur,* p. 20.
page 520
The relevant verses are: "Even if one commits the most abominable actions, if he is engaged in devotional service, he is considered saintly because he is properly situated. He quickly becomes righteous and attains lasting peace. O son of Kunti, declare it boldly that My devotee never perishes." His Divine Grace A.C. Bhaktivedanta Swami Prabhupada, *Bhagavad-gita As It Is,* pp. 483 and 485. Verses 30-31 of Chapter 9. For commentary on these Verses, see ibid., pp. 484-486.
page 522
V.S. Bhatnagar, "Chronology of Jaipur Incorporating Culture Chart," *Homage to Jaipur,* unnumbered page at book's end.
page 525
G.R. Kaye, *The Astronomical Observatories Of Jai Singh,* p. 1.
page 525
Lieut.-Col. James Tod, *Annals And Antiquities Of Rajasthan, Volume III,* London, Oxford University Press, 1920 (originally published in 1829), p. 1346.
page 525
Sawai Jai Singh's Observatory, Jaipur, India: Reference Book Co. of India, undated, p. 3.
page 526
G.R. Kaye, *The Astronomical Observatories Of Jai Singh,* p. 17.
page 526
Ibid., pp. 82-83.
page 526
Ibid., p. 40.
page 527
J. Bernoulli, *Des Pater Joseph Tieffenthalers historisch-geographische Beschreibung von Hindustan, Volume I,* 1785, p. 244 f., French edition, p. 316 f.
page 528
John Lord, *The Maharajahs,* p. 211.
page 528
Fodor's India, Nepal and Sri Lanka 1986, p. 172.
page 528
G.R. Kaye, *The Astronomical Observatories Of Jai Singh,* p. 37.
page 528
Daulat Singh, *Jaipur,* p. 30.
page 531
George O. Abell, *Realm Of The Universe,* Philadelphia, Saunders College/Holt, Rhinehart and Winston, 1980, p. 19.
page 531
Ibid., p. 21.
page 532
Tracy Ladd, in his pamphlet, *The Vedic Astrologer,* Los Angeles, p. 2.
page 532
Ibid.
page 535
B.L. Dhama, *A Guide To The Jaipur Astronomical Observatory,* Jaipur, Undated, p. 10.
page 535
Jai Singh, as quoted in W. Hunter, "Some Accounts of the astronomical labours of Jayasingha, Rajah of Ambhere or Jayanagar," *Asiatic Researches or Transaction of the Society instituted in Bengal, Vol. V,* 1799, p. 177 f. and p. 424. Also quoted in G.R. Kaye, *The Astronomical Observatories Of Jai Singh,* p. 10.
page 535
Richard R. Nyrop et al., *Area Handbook for India,* p. 274.
page 536
Will Durant, *Our Oriental Heritage,* New York, Simon and Schuster, 1954, pp. 529-530.
page 536
P.N. Oak, *World Vedic Heritage,* p. 153.
page 536
Ibid.
page 536
Dr. A.W. Joshi, "Technological Development in Ancient India," published in the *annual research journal, 1981,* of the Institute for Rewriting Indian History, New Delhi, as cited in ibid., p. 189.
page 536
P.N. Oak, *World Vedic Heritage,* p. 151.
page 537
Carl Sagan, *Cosmos,* New York, Random House, 1980, p. 258.
page 537
Richard F. Nyrop et al., *Area Handbook for India,* p. 256.
page 537
Dr. M. Winternitz, *A History Of Indian Literature Volume I,* Calcutta, University of Calcutta, 1927, p. 8.
page 537
Mulk Raj Anand, "An Epistle Dedicatory To the Master Builder Sawai Jai Singh," *Homage to Jaipur,* p. 9.
page 539
Ibid., p. 24.
page 539
Satish Davar, "A filigree city spun out of nothingness," *Homage to Jaipur,* p. 56.
page 539
Jamila Brijbhushan, "Enamels and Jewellery," *Homage to Jaipur,* p. 101.
page 539
Ibid.
page 540
Ibid.
page 540
Ibid.

page 540
Ibid.
page 540
Ibid., p. 102.
page 540
Beverly Beyer and Ed Rabey, "Brilliant Taste, Color of Raj India," *Los Angeles Times,* January 15, 1984, Part IV, p. 19.
page 540
Daulat Singh, *Jaipur,* p. 30.
page 540
Kanwarjit Kang, "Album of Wall Paintings," *Homage to Jaipur,* p. 69.
page 542
Daulat Singh, *Jaipur,* p. 31.
page 542
Asok Kumar Das, "Miniatures," *Homage to Jaipur,* p. 83.
page 542
Gayatri Devi of Jaipur and Santha Rama Rau, *A Princess Remembers,* p. 249.
page 542
Daulat Singh, *Jaipur,* p. 18.
page 542
Gayatri Devi of Jaipur and Santha Rama Rau, *A Princess Remembers,* p. 250.
page 544
Ibid.
page 544
Ibid.
page 544
Ibid.
page 547
Abraham H. Maslow, in, International Study Project, Inc., compiled with the assistance of Bertha G. Maslow, *Abraham H. Maslow: A Memorial Volume,* Monterey, California, Brooks/Cole Publishing, 1972, p. 53.
page 548
V.S. Bhatnagar, "Chronology of Jaipur Incorporating Culture Chart," *Homage to Jaipur,* unnumbered pages at book's end.
page 548
John Lord, *The Maharajahs,* p. 211.
page 548
Satish Davar, "A filigree city spun out of nothingness," *Homage to Jaipur,* p. 57.
page 548
Fodor's India, Nepal and Sri Lanka 1986, p. 172.
page 549
John Lord, *The Maharajahs,* p. 210.
page 549
Ibid.
page 549
Rosita Forbes, quoted in Gayatri Devi of Jaipur and Santha Rama Rau, *A Princess Remembers,* p. 91.
page 551
Ibid.
page 551
Ibid, p. 170.
page 551
Mulk Raj Anand, "Homage To Jaipur," *Homage to Jaipur,* p. 4.
page 551
Gayatri Devi of Jaipur and Santha Rama Rau, *A Princess Remembers,* p. 170.
page 551
Ibid., p. 172.
page 552
Sir Mirza Ismail, as cited in ibid., p. 199.
page 552
Gayatri Devi of Jaipur and Santha Rama Rau, *A Princess Remembers,* p. 199.
page 555
Ibid., p. 205.
page 555
Nani A. Palkhivala, "White Papers on Indian States," as quoted in ibid., p. 320.
page 556
The Times (London), as cited in John Lord, *The Maharajahs,* p. 214.
page 556
Anonymous source quoted in Gayatri Devi of Jaipur and Santha Rama Rau, *A Princess Remembers,* p. 314.
page 557
Ibid., p. 315.
page 557
Ibid.
page 557
Prince Philip, as cited in ibid., p. 316.
page 557
Gayatri Devi of Jaipur and Santha Rama Rau, *A Princess Remembers,* p. 196.
page 558
Ibid., p. 267.
page 560
Ibid., p. 260.
page 560
Ibid., p. 267.
page 563
Ibid. p. 269.
page 563
Ibid.
page 563
Ibid., p. 267.
page 563
Ibid., p. 274.
page 563
Ibid.
page 565
John F. Kennedy, as quoted in ibid., p. 285.
page 566
Gayatri Devi of Jaipur and Santha Rama Rau, *A Princess Remembers,* p. 275.
page 566
Jack Lord, *The Maharajahs,* p. 214.
page 566
Gayatri of Jaipur and Santha Rama Rau, *A Princess Remembers,* p. 275.
page 571
Abraham A. Maslow, "Psychological Data and Value Theory," Abraham A. Maslow, Editor, *New Knowledge In Human Values,* p. 121.
page 571
Abraham A. Maslow, *Motivation And Personality,* New York, Harper & Row, 1970 (Second Edition), p. 283.

CHAPTER 13: UDAIPUR

page 575
Lord Curzon, as cited in Ashok Singhal, *Udaipur,* Goyal Brothers, undated, Seventh Edition, p. 53.
page 575
Rudyard Kipling, as cited in ibid., p. 54.
page 575
Hugh Davenport, *The Trials & Triumphs Of The Mewar Kingdom,* Udaipur, Maharana of Mewar Charitable Foundation, undated, p. 37.
page 576
Balwant Sinha Mehta and Jodh Singh Mehta, *Pratap*

page 639
Hemchandra Raychaudhuri, *Materials for the Study of the Early History of the Vaisnava Sect,* New Delhi, Oriental Books Reprint Corporation, 1975 (originally published in 1920), p. 76.
page 640
P. Georgi, *Alphabetum Tibetanum,* as quoted in ibid., p. 77.
page 640
Albrecht Weber, *Uber die Krishnajanmashtami,* as quoted in ibid., p. 86.
page 641
Hemchandra Raychaudhuri, *Materials for the Study of the Early History of the Vaisnava Sect,* p. 92.
page 641
Ibid.
page 641
Sir William Jones, *The Works Of Sir William Jones, Volume III,* "On The Gods Of Greece, Italy, And India," (originally written in 1784), London, 1807, p. 375.
page 641
For Megasthenes description of India see, J.W. McCrindle, *Ancient India as Described by Magasthenes and Arrian,* Bombay, Thacker & Co., 1877. Also noteworthy is, Allen Dahlquist, *Megasthenes and Indian Religion,* Delhi, Motilal Banarsidass, 1962.
page 641
Norvin Hein, *The Miracle Plays Of Mathura,* p. 4.
page 642
Richard Garbe's contribution to this subject is found in his book, *Indien und das Christentum,* Tubingen, J.C.B.Mohr (P. Siebeck), 1914.
page 642
Allan Dahlquist, *Megasthenes and Indian Religion,* p. 18.
page 642
Hemchandra Raychaudhuri, *Materials for the Study of the Early History of the Vaisnava Sect,* p. 22.
page 642
Ibid. p. 18.
page 642
R.P. Kangle, *The Kautiliya Arthasastra, Part II,* Bombay, University of Bombay, 1963, pp. 13-14.
page 642
Georg Buhler, "Baudhayana Dharma Sutra," in F. Max Muller, *The Sacred Books Of The East,* Volume XIV, Oxford, Clarendon Press, 1882, p. 254.
page 642
Hemchandra Raychaudhuri, *Materials for the Study of the Early History of the Vaisnava Sect,* p. 39.
page 642
Ibid.
page 642
The Cambridge History of India, Volume 1, Edited by E.J. Rapson, New York, The Macmillan Company, 1922, pp. 167, 275, 276, 408, 409, 419, 422, 526, and 558.
page 644
Journal of the Royal Asiatic Society, J.H. Marshall, "Notes On Archaeological Exploration In India, 1908-9," London, Royal Asiatic Society, October, 1909, p. 1054.
page 644
Hemchandra Raychaudhuri, *Materials for the Study of the Early History of the Vaisnava Sect,* p. 59.
page 644
Hemchandra Raychaudhuri, "The *Mahabharata* and the Besnagar Inscription of Heliodorus," *Journal & Proceedings Of The Asiatic Society Of Bengal,* New Series, Volume XVIII, Calcutta, Asiatic Society Of Bengal, 1922, p. 270.
page 644
Ibid., p. 271. See also Benjamin Preciado-Solis, *The Krishna Cycle in the Puranas,* Delhi, Motilal Banarsidass, 1984, p. 34.
page 644
Hemchandra Raychaudhuri, *Materials for the Study of the Early History of the Vaisnava Sect,* p. 59.
page 644
Kunja Govinda Goswami, *A Study Of Vaisnavism From The Advent Of The Stungas To The Fall Of The Guptas In The Light Of Epigraphic, Numismatic And Other Archaeological Materials,* Calcutta, Calcutta Oriental Book Agency, 1956, p. 6.
page 644
Hemchandra Raychaudhuri, "The *Mahabharata* and the Besnagar Inscription of Heliodorus," *Journal & Proceedings of the Asiatic Society Of Bengal,* New Series, Volume XVIII, 270.
page 645
Ahmad H. Dani, *Alberuni's India,* Lexhore, India, University of Islamabad, 1973, p. 37.
page 645
Thomas J. Hopkins, "Interview With Thomas J. Hopkins," in Steven J. Gelberg, Editor, *Hare Krishna, Hare Krishna,* New York, Grove Press, Inc., 1983, p. 117.
page 645
Hemchandra Raychaudhuri, *Materials for the Study of the Early History of the Vaisnava Sect,* p. 61.
page 645
His Divine Grace A.C. Bhaktivedanta Swami Prabhupada, *Srimad Bhagavatam, First Canto, Part One,* p. 81. Verse 20 of Chapter 1.
page 645
Ibid., p. 168.
page 646
Archaeological Survey of India, Annual Report, Volume XX, 1885, p. 49.
page 646
The identity of "the five heroes of the Vrishni Clan" is revealed in the *Vayu Purana,* verses 1-4 of Chapter 97. See also J.N. Banerjea, *Pauranic and Tantric Religion,* Calcutta, Calcutta University Press, 1966, pp. 29-31.
page 646
Kavi Rāj Shyamal Das *The Journal of the Asiatic Society Of Bengal, Volume LVI,* Part 1, "Antiquities at Nagarī," Calcutta, Asiatic Society Of Bengal, 1887, p. 77 ff., No. 1 and Pl. V.
page 646
K.P. Jayaswal, *Epigraphia Indica, Volume XVI,* "The Ghosundi Stone Inscription," Calcutta, Government of India Press, 1921-22, p. 27.
page 646
Ibid., p. 26.
page 648
Hemchandra Raychaudhuri, *Materials for the Study of the Early History of the Vaisnava Sect,* pp. 69-70.
page 648
A.K. Narain, "Two Hindu Divinities on the Coins of Agathocles from Ai-Khanum," *The Journal of the Numismatic Society of India, Volume XXXV,* 1973, pp. 73-77.

CHAPTER 15: VAIṢṆAVA LITERATURE
page 653
Will Durant, *Our Oriental Heritage,* p. 407.
page 653
His Divine Grace A.C. Bhaktivedanta Swami Prabhu-

pada, *Sri Isopanisad,* New York, The Bhaktivedanta Book Trust, 1972, p. xiii.
page 654
Ibid.
page 654
Will Durant, *Our Oriental Heritage,* p. 406.
page 654
Ibid.
page 654
Ibid., p. 407.
page 654
His Divine Grace A.C. Bhaktivedanta Swami Prabhupada, *Srimad Bhagavatam, First Canto, Part One,* Verse 40, p. 217. Verses 16-18 of Chapter 4.
page 655
His Divine Grace A.C. Bhaktivedanta Swami Prabhupada, *Sri Isopanisad,* p. xiii.
page 655
His Divine Grace A.C. Bhaktivedanta Swami Prabhupada, *Srimad Bhagavatam, First Canto, Part One,* pp. 222-223. Verses 21 and 22 of Chapter 4.
page 655
Will Durant, *Our Oriental Heritage,* p. 407.
page 655
Richard F. Nyrop et al., *Area Handbook for India,* p. 165.
page 655
Will Durant, *Our Oriental Heritage,* p. 408.
page 656
Billy Graham, *Angels: God's Secret Agents,* New York, Simon & Schuster, Inc., 1977.
page 656
Satsvarupa dasa Goswami, *Readings in Vedic Literature,* New York, The Bhaktivedanta Book Trust, 1977, p. 41.
page 657
Ainslee T. Embree, *The Hindu Tradition,* New York, Vintage, 1972, p. 5.
page 657
His Divine Grace A.C. Bhaktivedanta Swami Prabhupada, *Bhagavad-gita As It Is,* p. 133-134.
page 658
Satsvarupa dasa Goswami, *Readings in Vedic Literature,* p. 42.
page 658
Sayana Acarya, trans., *Rg Veda,* Mathura, India: Vedanurgi Acarya Gopala Prasada, 1868, p. 32.
page 658
Atharva-veda, as quoted in His Divine Grace A.C. Bhaktivedanta Swami Prabhupada, *Bhagavad-gita As It Is,* p. 516.
page 658
His Divine Grace A.C. Bhaktivedanta Swami Prabhupada, *Srimad Bhagavatam, Sixth Canto, Part One,* p. 56. Most of Srimad Bhagavatam, First Canto, Part One, Verse 40 of Chapter 1.
Madhva, as quoted in ibid., p. 57.
page 659
His Divine Grace A.C. Bhaktivedanta Swami Prabhupada, *Bhagavad-gita As It Is,* p. 129. Verses 42-43 of Chapter 2.
page 659
Ibid., p. 481. Verse 20 of Chapter 9.
page 659
Ibid.
page 659
His Divine Grace A.C. Bhaktivedanta Swami Prabhupada, *Bhagavad-gita As It Is,* p. 482. Verse 21 of Chapter 9.
page 659
Abinash Chandra Bose, *Hymns from the Vedas,* Bombay, Asia Publishing House, 1966, p. 48.
page 659
Journal of the Royal Asiatic Society Of Bengal, Vol. VII, No. 1, P.C. Sengupta, "The Solar Eclipse in the Ṛgveda and the Date of Atri," Calcutta, Royal Asiatic Society Of Bengal, August, 1941.
page 659
Will Durant, *Our Oriental Heritage,* p. 408.
page 661
Schopenhauer as quoted in Max Muller, *India: What Can It Teach Us?,* p. 254.
page 661
Will Durant, *Our Oriental Heritage,* p. 410.
page 661
Ibid.
page 661
Richard F. Nyrop et al., *Area Handbook for India,* p. 257.
page 662
His Divine Grace A.C. Bhaktivedanta Swami Prabhupada, *Bhagavad-gita As It Is,* p. 132.
page 662
Will Durant, *Our Oriental Heritage,* p. 412.
page 662
Sarvepalli Radhakrishnan, *Indian Philosophy, Volume 1,* London, George Allen & Unwin LTD, 1923. This quote is pieced together from the following three citings, pp. 177, 176-177, 177.
page 662
Ibid., p. 145.
page 663
Satsvarupa dasa Goswami, *Readings in Vedic Literature,* p. 43.
page 663
Ibid.
page 663
Will Durant, *Our Oriental Heritage,* p. 413.
page 663
His Divine Grace A.C. Bhaktivedanta Swami Prabhupada, *Sri Caitanya-caritamrta, Madhya-Lila, Volume 2,* p. 270. Verse 141 of Chapter 6.
page 663
Ibid., pp. 270-271.
page 664
Katha Upanishad as quoted in His Divine Grace A.C. Bhaktivedanta Swami Prabhupada, *Sri Caitanya-caritamrta, Adi-Lila, Part 2,* p. 99.
page 664
His Divine Grace A.C. Bhaktivedanta Swami Prabhupada, *Sri Isopanisad,* p. 91.
page 664
His Divine Grace A.C. Bhaktivedanta Swami Prabhupada, *Sri Caitanya-Caritamrta, Adi-Lila Part 2,* p. 92.
page 665
Will Durant, *Our Oriental Heritage,* p. 51.
page 665
Ibid., p. 513.
page 665
Satsvarupa dasa Goswami, *Readings in Vedic Literature,* p. 46.
page 665
Will Durant, *Our Oriental Heritage,* p. 511.
page 665
Satsvarupa dasa Goswami, *Readings in Vedic Literature,* p. 47.
page 665
His Divine Grace A.C. Bhaktivedanta Swami Prabhupada, *Srimad Bhagavatam, First Canto, Part One,* p. 93.

Index

A

C

D

E

F

G

H

I

J

L

M

N

S

V

W

Y

Z

Guide to Sanskrit Pronunciation

Throughout the centuries, the Sanskrit language has been written in a variety of alphabets. The mode of writing most widely used throughout India, however, is called *devanāgarī*, which literally means "the city writing of the *devas*, or gods." The *devanāgarī* alphabet consists of forty-eight characters, including thirteen vowels and thirty-five consonants. The ancient Sanskrit grammarians arranged the alphabet according to concise linguistic principles, and this arrangement has been accepted by all Western scholars. The system of transliteration used in this book conforms to a system that scholars in the last fifty years have almost universally accepted to indicate the pronunciation of each Sanskrit sound.

The short vowel **a** is pronounced like **u** in but; long **ā** like the **a** in f**a**r; and short **i** like **i** in p**i**n. Long **ī** is pronounced as in p**i**que, short **u** as in p**u**ll, and long **ū** as in r**u**le. The vowel **ṛ** is pronounced like the **ri** in **ri**m. The vowel **e** is pronounced as in th**ey**; **ai** as in **ai**sle; **o** as in g**o**; and **au** as in h**ow**. The *anusvara* (**ṁ**), which is a pure nasal, is pronounced like the **n** in the French word *bo***n**, and *visarga* (**ḥ**), which is a strong aspirate, is pronounced as a final **h** sound. Thus **aḥ** is pronounced **aha**, and **iḥ** like **ihi**.

The guttural consonants—**k**, **kh**, **g**, **gh**, and **ṅ**—are pronounced from the throat in much the same manner as in English. **K** is pronounced as in **k**ite, **kh** as in Ec**kh**art, **g** as in **g**ive, **gh** as in di**g h**ard, and **n** as in si**ng**. The palatal consonants—**c**, **ch**, **j**, **jh**, and **ñ**—are pronounced from the palate with the middle of the tongue. **C** is pronounced as in **ch**air, **ch** as in staun**ch h**eart, **j** as in **j**oy, **jh** as in he**dgeh**og, and **ñ** as in ca**ny**on. The cerebral consonants—**ṭ**, **ṭh**, **ḍ**, **ḍh**, and **ṅ**—are pronounced with the tip of tongue turned up and drawn back against the dome of the palate. **Ṭ** is pronounced as in **t**ub, **ṭh** as in ligh**t h**eart, **ḍ** as in **d**ove, **ḍh** as in re**d-h**ot, and **ṇ** as in **n**ut. The dental consonants—**t**, **th**, **d**, **dh**, and **n**—are pronounced in the same manner as the cerebrals but with the forepart of the tongue against the teeth. The labial consonants—**p**, **ph**, **b**, **bh**, and **m**—are pronounced with the lips. **P** is pronounced as in **p**ine, **ph** as in u**ph**ill, **b** as in **b**ird, **bh** as in ru**b h**ard, and **m** as in **m**other. The semivowels—**y**, **r**, **l**, and **v**—are pronounced as in **y**es, **r**un, **l**ight, and **v**ine respectively. The sibilants—**ś**, **ṣ**, and **s**—are pronounced, respectively, as in the German word *s***prechen** and the English words **sh**ine and **s**un. The letter **h** is pronounced as in **h**ome.

Photo Credits

Geary J.C. Sheridan
Forward 0,
6, 9, 11, 12, 15, 16, 21, 22, 27, 28, 34, 36, 38, 43, 203, 213, 216, 227, 243, 248, 251, 258, 357, 364, 366, 369, 370, 390, 393, 394, 404, 406, 409, 410, 415, 418, 421, 424, 428, 431, 432, 436, 440, 468, 470, 481, 487, 494, 501, 503, 504, 509, 510, 512, 521, 524, 529, 530.

Elaine Naish Sheridan 759.

Smithsonian Institute 304.

Thierry Bernard
230, 478, 516, 562, 564, 567, 568, 570, 628.

David Osborn
538, 541, 543, 545, 553.

Jack B. Hebner, Jr.
Dust Jacket front and back pictures,
0, 2, 5, 25, 31, 32, 66, 68, 71, 72, 77, 78, 82, 84, 89, 90, 92, 95, 98, 100, 105, 170, 172, 176, 178, 183, 185, 188, 194, 263, 280, 282, 285, 286, 289, 291, 292, 296, 298, 300, 303, 307, 309, 312, 315, 316, 336, 388, 397, 399, 400, 422, 434, 449, 443, 445, 446, 450, 452, 455, 456, 458, 461, 464, 467, 474, 476, 484, 489, 492, 497, 498, 515, 523, 533, 534, 546, 550, 554, 559, 561, 572, 574, 577, 580, 583, 585, 586, 591, 592, 596, 598, 601, 604, 607, 608, 612, 616, 619, 622, 625, 631, 634, 636, 638, 643, 647, 650, 652, 660, 672.

The Bhaktivedanta Book Trust
18, 46, 51, 55, 58, 62, 64, 108, 110, 113, 116, 119, 123, 126, 129, 132, 134, 137, 140, 143, 147, 150, 153, 158, 161, 164, 198, 200, 206, 209, 219, 222, 224, 233, 237, 240, 254, 266, 268, 274, 320, 322, 325, 326, 329, 331, 334, 339, 342, 344, 348, 350, 353, 354, 359, 360, 372, 375, 378, 380, 384, 413, 676.

Author

GEARY J.C. SHERIDAN

Born in Santa Monica, California, 1955, Geary J.C. Sheridan follows a distinguished line of Statesmen, entrepreneurs and philanthropists.

His European ancestry may be traced back as far as Major General Patrick Sarsfield, a favorite hero of the Irish national tradition, Lord High Chancellor of Ireland and Earl of Lucan (1691) under James II — last Roman Catholic King of Great Britain. In American lore, his Great Grandfather, General Phillip Sheridan, played a leading role for the Union in ending the American Civil War.

More recently, his grandparents on both sides of the family have distinguished themselves in contemporary American society. J. Carroll Naish, one of the great Hollywood character actors is honored with a star on the Hollywood Boulevard Walk of Fame; and Beverly and John Stauffer (Stauffer Chemical Company) founded the Stauffer Foundation, which has made major contributions to Stanford University, University of Southern California, Whittier College, and Pepperdine University, as well as supporting worthy organizations like the Boy's Club and Children's Village.

The departed Elaine Naish Sheridan, a compassionate mother, had always given her best to her two sons, three daughters and husband. She had instilled great values of benevolence and hard work, to name a few, into her son, Geary Sheridan, the author, which have guided him in all his undertakings.

Following family tradition, Geary Sheridan, a practicing Vaiṣṇava since 1978, founded the Vedic Heritage Foundation in 1985, serving as President since its inception. The specific purpose of the Vedic Heritage Foundation is to perpetuate, promulgate and disseminate the ancient Vedic Literature.

Geary J.C. Sheridan has made extensive travels throughout the Indian sub-continent in the 1980's, from which he obtained a great insight into its magnificent ancient culture. Mr. Sheridan has expertly fused the philosophical and sociological thought of both East and West into an enchanting amalgam of great inspirational and educational worth — embodied in *Vaiṣṇava India.*

Geary J.C. Sheridan
Author of Vaiṣṇava India